POSITIVE DISCIPLINE
FOR PRESCHOOLERS

REVISED 4TH EDITION

ALSO IN THE POSITIVE DISCIPLINE SERIES

POSITIVE DISCIPLINE
FOR PRESCHOOLERS

REVISED 4TH EDITION

FOR THEIR EARLY YEARS—
RAISING CHILDREN WHO ARE RESPONSIBLE,
RESPECTFUL, AND RESOURCEFUL

Jane Nelsen, EdD, Cheryl Erwin, MA,
and Roslyn Ann Duffy

HARMONY
BOOKS · NEW YORK

Copyright © 1994, 1998, 2007, 2019 by Jane Nelsen, Cheryl Erwin, and Roslyn Duffy

All rights reserved.
Published in the United States by Harmony Books, an imprint of Random House,
a division of Penguin Random House LLC, New York.
harmonybooks.com

Harmony Books is a registered trademark, and the Circle colophon is a trademark of
Penguin Random House LLC.

Earlier editions were published by Prima Publishing, Roseville, California, in 1994 and 1998.
A revised edition was published in paperback by Three Rivers Press, an imprint of the Crown
Publishing Group, a division of Penguin Random House LLC, New York, in 2007.

Library of Congress Cataloging-in-Publication Data is available upon request.

ISBN 978-0-525-57641-9
Ebook ISBN 978-0-525-57642-6

Printed in the United States of America

Book design by Elina Nudelman
Illustrations by Paula Gray
Cover design by Sarah Horgan
Cover photograph by Getty Images/Ariel Skelley

10 9 8 7 6 5 4 3 2 1

Fourth Edition

To my seven children, my twenty-two grandchildren, my fifteen great-grandchildren (and still counting), and my ever supportive husband.

—Jane

To all the children—this world's best hope; to all the parents and teachers who are passionately committed to supporting and encouraging them; and to Philip, Amanda, Evie, and Drew, who continue to teach me the joys of being a mom and a nanna. And, of course, to David for his enduring encouragement and support.

—Cheryl

To our children Blue, Manus, Rose, and Bridget and their partners; to our wonderful grandchildren; and to all the children, parents and staff of the Learning Tree Montessori, who have become family too. And to Vinnie, who makes it all possible.

—Roslyn

CONTENTS

CONTENTS

PREFACE (BY THE CHILDREN)

"*My name is Emma and I am three and a half years old. I talk a lot now. I get frustrated when people won't read me the same book over and over again, or when they try to leave out a part. My favorite question is 'Why?' I like to dress up and try on all kinds of different characters. I like to have stories told to me all the time. I like to have someone to play with me all the time too. And I don't like to have my playtime interrupted.*"

"*I am Jeffrey F. Fraser. The 'F' stands for Frank, like my grandpa. I like talking. Yesterday I turned five years old. We can be friends and I will invite you to my birthday party. When I pick what I want to do, I pay attention really good. I have a little brother. He's okay as a playmate if there's nobody better. I think this tooth is getting loose. Do you want to hear me count? I can sing a song for you. Do you want to play with me? Okay, you be the bad guy and I'll be the good guy. . . .*"

"*I'm four years old. I'm Cyndi. I have sparkly shoes. Do you know what kind of underwear I have on? They have the days on them. See how sparkly my shoes are when I twirl? I'm too big to be taking naps. If you read me a story, I'll be happier. I am really not tired. Do you want to see my shoes?*

I am going to marry Chad. Do you know Chad? He has a Batman cape. Can you read me a story now?"

"I'm Maria. My hair is long. I never wear dresses 'cuz I'm going to be a fireman. I am four and three-quarters years old. Callie is my bestest friend. Sometimes Callie won't play with me. She is four and a half. I can play with Gina too. I like to eat lunch with Callie and Gina. I want to sit next to them—not across the table from them. I like it when the teachers teach me things."

This is a book about us—the children. Each one of us is different. Not all three-year-olds or five-year-olds will be like us, but you will probably find a little bit of us in the children you know. This book will help you get to know us and find out what the world is like for us. It will give you lots of ideas about how to help us grow and how to encourage and teach us. We are alike and we are different. We want to be loved; this book is for the people who love us.

We are delighted to have this opportunity to update and revise one of the most popular books in the *Positive Discipline* series. This new edition includes suggestions for dealing with the ever-expanding role of technology in our lives, new information on building secure attachments and dealing with trauma, and a deeper exploration of teaching preschoolers the social, emotional, and life skills they need. We know you are busy, so we have added a "Questions to Ponder" section at the end of each chapter to provide easy ways to use the tools presented and to better understand Positive Discipline concepts. And yet, as they say, the more things change, the more they stay the same.

The centuries-old parenting debate continues: to punish or not to punish. Many parents and teachers who still believe that punishment works have given up the idea of spanking but believe that the best way to motivate children to change their behavior is by subjecting them to punitive time-outs, grounding, the taking away of privileges, and humiliating lectures. They often try to disguise the fact that these are punishments by calling them "logical consequences." They are convinced that the only alternative to punishment is permissiveness and a world full of spoiled, entitled children.

Other parents, who are strongly against punishment, have gone to the other extreme. They don't consciously choose permissiveness, but that is what they end up with when they don't know what else to do when they give up punishment. In the name of love they are raising children who feel entitled to receive whatever they want the moment they want it. These parents believe they are creating a strong relationship with their children and that they are helping their children feel a sense of belonging and significance. Their goal is an admirable one, but they need more understanding of how to help their children feel significant and capable through contribution—an emphasis we make clear in our discussion of the long-term results of being both kind and firm at the same time.

Many parents are drawn to Positive Discipline because they know punishment is not effective in the long term and they like the idea of being kind and firm at the same time. They just don't fully understand what it means to be kind and firm at the same time—which is much easier to say than it is to do. In this revision we hope to help parents and teachers understand the importance of being kind and firm at the same time, what it means (how it relates to belonging and significance), and what it looks like.

Being kind and firm at the same time is essential to meet the primary need of all children—to feel a sense of belonging and significance. However, it has become clear that we have not done a good enough job of explaining how children develop a sense of significance. Many parents and teachers think that belonging and significance are the same. They are not. *Belonging comes from a sense of connection and unconditional love. Significance comes from a sense of feeling capable, being responsible, and making a contribution.*

When parents and teachers are kind but not firm, they actually rob children of opportunities to develop the sense of their own capability and the innate desire to contribute to others. Yes, the desire to contribute is innate, but it has to be nurtured to develop fully. Let us explain.

In Chapter 5, we discuss the research of Michael Tomasello and Felix Warneken. They demonstrated that children as young as eighteen months have an inborn desire to contribute. However, this ability requires frequent practice to develop fully. When children aren't provided with opportunities to feel capable and to contribute to their family or classroom, this ability may atrophy. At the same time, when they are "spoiled," their ability to demand undue service (entitlement) strengthens. Parents who believe their children have plenty of time to learn contribution later in life do not understand how difficult it is to revive atrophied *responsibility muscles* when *entitlement muscles* have grown so strong.

Rudolf Dreikurs, a colleague of Alfred Adler, had another way of explaining the importance of being both kind and firm at the same time. He said, "One does not win the friendship and regard of a child by humiliating him or giving in to his whims."

So, exactly what does kind *and* firm look like? One example is to use the word "and" with children: "I know you don't want to do your chores right now *and* I really appreciate your help. What was our agreement about when they would be done?" Or "I know you don't want to go to bed *and* it's bedtime. Is it your turn to choose a book, or mine?" Or even "I can understand why you would rather watch TV than pick up your toys *and* what does it say on the bedtime routine chart we created?" And this one, which is one of our favorites: "I love you *and* the answer is no."

Being kind and firm at the same time does not always require using the word "and." Sometimes a loving look that conveys "Nice try" can work wonders on a child's behavior because it shows kindness and firmness with a little humor thrown in. It can be kind and firm to suggest you both take a positive time-out to calm down before continuing a discussion, or to invite the child to put the "problem" on the family or class meeting agenda so you can brainstorm for solutions. In fact, every Positive Discipline tool we suggest for parents and teachers requires kindness and firmness at the same time to be effective. It is the second of the five criteria for Positive Discipline.

FIVE CRITERIA FOR POSITIVE DISCIPLINE

1. Does it help children feel a sense of belonging and significance?
2. Is it respectful (kind and firm at the same time)?
3. Is it effective in the long term?
4. Does it teach valuable social and life skills for good character?
5. Does it invite children to discover how capable they are, and how to use their power constructively?

Last but not least is the importance of *modeling* what you hope to teach your children. It is so interesting to hear parents and teachers complain about children who do not control their own behavior when the parent or teacher does not control his or her own behavior. In Chapter 2 we invite you to consider the characteristics and life skills you want your children to develop—a sort of GPS for your parenting journey. We also encourage you to consider what *you* need to model in order to help your child develop these characteristics and skills. When parents and teachers brainstorm the list of what they need to model, it looks very similar to the characteristics and life skills they hope their children will develop:

- Self-regulation (control my own behavior)
- Focus on solutions
- Problem-solving skills
- Respect for self and others
- Listening skills
- Empathy
- Compassion
- Mistakes as opportunities to learn
- Faith in my child
- Honesty
- Sense of humor
- Flexibility
- Resilience

- Belief in personal capability
- Responsibility

Being the kind of person you want your child to be is not always an easy assignment, but the Positive Discipline skills and concepts in this newly revised edition can help you find your way to becoming a confident parent with the skills for raising a capable, contributing, happy child.

PART ONE

The Foundation

CHAPTER 1

Why Positive Discipline?

Parenting classes, preschool websites, and chat groups often echo with similar questions: "Why does my three-year-old bite?" or "How do I get my five-year-old to stay in bed at night?" Child development experts, preschool directors, and therapists' offices overflow with parents whose offspring have reached the ages of three, four, or five and who are wondering what on earth has happened. Listen for a moment to these parents:

"Our little boy was such a delight. We expected trouble when he turned two—after all, everyone had warned us about the 'terrible twos'—but nothing happened. Until he turned three, that is. Now we don't know what to do with him. If we say 'black,' he says 'white.' If we say it's bedtime, he's not tired. And trying to brush his teeth turns into a battle. We must be doing something wrong!"

"Sometimes I wonder if any sound comes out when I open my mouth. My five-year-old doesn't seem to hear anything I say to her. She won't listen to me at all. Is she always going to act like this?"

"We couldn't wait for our son to begin talking, but now we can't get him to stop. He has figured out that he can prolong any conversation by saying, 'Guess what?' He is our delight and despair, in almost equal measure."

"I thought it was cute when my three-year-old could use her little fingers to find all kinds of things on my cellphone. Now that she is five, she wants to play with the phone all the time and has terrible tantrums when I take it away from her. What can we do?"

As you will discover in the pages that follow (or as you may already realize), ages three to six are busy, hectic years for young children—and for their parents and caregivers. Researchers tell us that human beings have more physical energy at the age of three than at any other time in their life span—certainly more than their weary parents. An inborn drive for emotional, cognitive, and physical development is urging them to explore the world around them; they're acquiring and practicing social skills and entering the world outside the protected haven of the family. And preschoolers have ideas—lots of them—about how that world should operate. Their ideas, along with their urges to experiment and explore, often do not mesh with their parents' and caregivers' expectations.

What you will discover in the chapters ahead may be a bit different from what you grew up with. It may help to know that Positive Discipline is evidence-based, fits with what we know about children's growth and development and the latest brain research, and is designed to provide practical, effective tools for understanding and nurturing your child.

Adler and Dreikurs: Pioneers in Parenting

Positive Discipline is based on the work of Alfred Adler and his colleague Rudolf Dreikurs. Adler was a Viennese psychiatrist and a contemporary of Sigmund Freud—but he and Freud disagreed about almost everything. Adler believed that human behavior is motivated by a desire for belonging, significance, connection, and worth, which are influenced by our early decisions about ourselves, others, and the world around us. Recent research validates Adler's theories and tells us that children are hardwired from birth to seek connection with others, and that children who feel a sense of connection to their families, schools, and communities are less likely to misbehave (other than the age-appropriate power struggles as children seek to discover who they are separate from their parents and caregivers). Adler believed that everyone has equal rights to dignity and respect (including children), ideas that found a warm reception in America, a land he adopted as his own after immigrating here.

Rudolf Dreikurs, a Viennese psychiatrist and student of Adler's who came to the United States in 1937, was a passionate advocate of the need for dignity and mutual respect in *all* relationships—including the family. He wrote books about teaching and parenting that are still widely read, including the classic *Children: The Challenge*.

As you will learn, what many people mislabel as "misbehavior" in preschoolers has more to do with emotional, physical, and cognitive development and age-appropriate behavior. Through Positive Discipline, parents and caregivers can respond to this misbehavior with loving guidance that helps children develop the characteristics and life skills that will serve them well throughout their lives.

What Is Positive Discipline?

Positive Discipline is effective with preschoolers because it is different from conventional discipline. It has nothing to do with punishment (which many people think is synonymous with discipline) and everything to do with teaching—which begins with modeling the skills and values you hope your children will develop. This raises a question: "Is Positive Discipline for me or for my children?" The answer is both—but you first.

To be effective, you must model what you want to teach. It does not make sense to expect a child to be respectful if you are not respectful. Punishment is not respectful. You cannot expect a child to control his

11

or her behavior when you don't control your own. Does this mean you have to be perfect? No. A foundational principle of Positive Discipline, as Dreikurs taught over and over, is to have the courage to be imperfect and to see mistakes as opportunities to learn. It's a gift to your children (and to yourself) when you can say, "You made a mistake. Fantastic. Let's explore what you can learn from this and how you can find solutions to fix the mistake."

As your child matures and becomes more skilled, you will be able to involve him in the process of finding solutions and setting limits. He can practice critical-thinking skills, feel more capable, and learn to use his power and autonomy in useful ways—to say nothing of feeling more motivated to follow solutions and limits he has helped create. The principles of Positive Discipline will help you build a relationship of love and respect with your child and will help you live and solve problems together for many years to come.

The building blocks of Positive Discipline include:

- **Mutual respect.** Parents and caregivers model firmness by respecting themselves and the needs of the situation; they model kindness by respecting the needs and humanity of the child.

- **Understanding the belief *behind* behavior.** All human behavior has a purpose. You will be far more effective at changing your child's behavior when you understand why it is happening. (Children start creating the beliefs that form their personality from the day they are born.) Dealing with the belief is as important (if not more so) than dealing with the behavior.

- **Effective communication.** Parents and children (even young ones) can learn to listen well and use respectful words to ask for what they need. Parents will learn that children "hear" better when they are invited to think and participate instead of being told what to think and do. And parents will learn how to model the listening they expect from their children.

- **Understanding a child's world.** Children go through different stages of development. By learning about the developmental tasks your child faces and taking into account other variables such as birth order, temperament, and the presence (or absence) of social and emotional skills, your child's behavior becomes easier to understand. When you understand your child's world, you can choose better responses to her behavior.

- **Discipline that teaches rather than punishes.** Effective discipline teaches valuable social and life skills, and is neither permissive nor punitive.

- **Focusing on solutions instead of punishment.** Blame never solves problems. At first you, as the parent, will decide how to approach challenges and problems. But as your child grows and develops, you will learn to work together to find respectful, helpful solutions to the challenges you face, from spilled juice to bedtime woes.

- **Encouragement.** Encouragement celebrates effort and improvement, not just success, and helps children develop confidence in their own abilities. Encouragement is also the foundation for creating a sense of belonging—the primary need of all children (and adults).

- **Children *do* better when they *feel* better.** Where did parents get the crazy idea that in order to "make" children do better, parents should make them feel shame, humiliation, or even pain? Children are more motivated to cooperate, learn new skills, and offer affection and respect when they feel encouraged, connected, and loved.

- **Connection before correction.** It is always the relationship that matters most. When your child feels a sense of belonging and significance and your connection to each other is strong, it becomes much easier to understand feelings and behavior, and to find solutions together.

- **Contribution.** If a child *only* feels connection without a sense of contribution, that child may develop an entitled or "Me first!" attitude. Your child is more likely to learn the skills and character qualities you desire when you find ways for her to help you and others, and to contribute to her home, classroom, and community.

More About "Discipline"

Do these parents' words sound familiar?

"I have tried everything when it comes to discipline, but I am getting absolutely nowhere! My three-year-old daughter is very demanding, selfish, and stubborn. What should I do?"

"What can I do when nothing works? I have tried time-out with my four-year-old, taking away a toy or television, and spanking him— and none of it is helping. He is rude, disrespectful, and completely out of control. What should I try next?"

"I have a class of 15 four-year-olds. Two of them fight all the time, but I can't get them to play with anyone else. I put them in time-out, I threaten to take away recess if they play together, and this morning I started yelling when one of them tore up the other's drawing. I don't know where to turn—they won't listen to anything I say. How should I discipline them?"

When people talk about "discipline," they usually mean "punishment," because they believe the two are one and the same. Parents and teachers sometimes yell and lecture, spank and slap hands, take away toys and privileges, and plop children in a punitive time-out to "think about what you did." Unfortunately, no matter how effective punishment may seem at the moment, years of research have shown that it does not create the long-term learning or social and life skills adults truly want for their children. Punishment only makes a challenging situation worse, inviting both adults and children to plunge headfirst into power struggles.

Positive Discipline is based on a different premise: that children (and adults) do better when they feel better. Positive Discipline is about teaching (the meaning of the word "discipline" is "to teach"), understanding, encouraging, and communicating—not about punishing.

Most of us absorbed our ideas about discipline from our own parents, our society, and years of tradition and assumptions. Parents often believe that children must suffer (at least a little) or they won't learn anything. But in the past few decades, society and culture have changed rapidly. Our understanding of how children grow and learn has also changed, and how we teach children to be capable, responsible, confident people must change as well.

What Children Really Need

There is a difference between wants and needs, and your child's needs are simpler than you might think. All genuine needs should be met. But when you give in to all of your child's wants, you can create huge problems for your child and for yourself.

For example, your preschooler needs food, shelter, and belonging. She needs warmth, trust, and security. She does not need a smartphone or tablet, a television in her bedroom, or the new toy her friend has—but she may certainly *want* these things. She may love staring at the television screen, but experts tell us that any kind of screen time at this age may hamper optimal brain development. (More about this later.) You get the idea.

From his earliest moments in your family, your young child has four basic needs:

1. A sense of belonging and significance (connection)
2. A sense of personal power and autonomy (capability)
3. Social and life skills (contribution)
4. Kind and firm discipline that *teaches* (with dignity and respect)

If you can provide your child with these needs, he will be well on his way to becoming a competent, resourceful, happy human being.

THE IMPORTANCE OF BELONGING AND SIGNIFICANCE

"Well, of course," you may be thinking. "Everyone knows a child needs to belong." Most parents believe that what a child really needs is quite simple: he needs love. But love alone does not always create a sense of belonging or worth. In fact, love sometimes leads parents to pamper their children, to punish their children, or to make decisions that are not in their child's long-term best interest.

Everyone—adults and children alike—needs to belong somewhere. For young children, the need to belong is even more crucial. After all, they're still learning about the world around them and their place in it. They need to know they are loved and wanted even when they have a tantrum, spill their cereal, break Dad's favorite mug, or make yet another mess in the kitchen.

Children who don't believe they belong become discouraged, and discouraged children often misbehave. Notice the word "believe." You may know your child belongs and is significant. But if he doesn't believe it (sometimes for the darnedest reasons, such as the birth of another baby) he may try to find his sense of belonging and significance in mistaken ways. *In fact, most young children's misbehavior is a sort of "code" designed to let you know that they don't feel a sense of belonging and need your attention, connection, time, and teaching.*

When you can create a sense of belonging and significance for every member of your family, your home becomes a place of peace, respect, and safety.

PERSONAL POWER AND AUTONOMY (CAPABILITY)

Your preschooler will never learn to make decisions, acquire new skills, or develop confidence if you don't make room for him to practice—mistakes and all. *Parenting in the preschool years involves a great deal of letting go of the need for perfection.*

Words alone are not powerful enough to build a sense of competence and confidence in children. Children feel capable when they experience capability and self-sufficiency by doing, imperfectly, as they learn and develop new skills.

Developing autonomy and initiative are among the earliest developmental tasks your child will face. And while parents may not exactly like it, even the youngest child has personal power—and quickly learns how to use it. If you doubt this, think about the last time you saw a four-year-old jut out his jaw, fold his arms, and say boldly, "No! I don't *want* to!"

Part of your job as a parent will be to help your child learn to channel his considerable power in positive directions—to help solve problems, to learn life skills, to develop a sense of responsibility, and to respect and cooperate with others.

SOCIAL AND LIFE SKILLS

Teaching your child skills—how to get along with other children and adults, how to feed and dress herself, how to be responsible—will occupy most of your parenting hours during the preschool years. But the need for social and practical life skills never goes away. In fact, true self-worth does not come from being loved, praised, or showered with goodies—it comes from having *skills*.

Research has shown clearly that academic success—the ability to thrive and learn in school—depends on the development of self-regulation, emotional awareness, and the ability to get along and work with others. No child is born with these complex skills, but teaching them is part of the Positive Discipline process.

When children are young, they love to imitate parents. Your child will want to hammer nails with you, squirt the bottle of bathroom cleaner, and cook breakfast (with lots of supervision). As he grows more capable, you can use these everyday moments to teach him how to become a competent, capable person. Working together to learn skills can occasionally be messy, but it's also an enjoyable and valuable part of raising your child.

KIND AND FIRM DISCIPLINE THAT TEACHES

Punishment may appear to work in the short term. After all, children generally stop what they were doing when you yell, threaten, shame, or spank. But what you don't see is what your child is thinking, feeling, and deciding to do as a result of this experience.

Preschoolers have *so* much to learn. Respectful, firm teaching not only strengthens the bond between parent and child but is more effective over time in changing behavior. Still, parents may struggle with the idea that punishment doesn't "work" the way they think it should.

Why Some Parents Don't Accept Non-punitive Methods

Because all children (and all parents) are unique individuals, there are usually several non-punitive solutions to any problem. Parents may not immediately understand or accept these solutions; indeed, Positive Discipline requires a paradigm shift—a radically different way of thinking about discipline. Parents often ask the wrong questions. They usually want to know:

- How do I make my child mind?
- How do I make my child understand "no"?
- How do I get my child to listen to me?
- How do I make this problem go away?

Most frazzled parents want answers to these questions, but these questions are based on short-term thinking. Parents will be eager for non-punitive alternatives when they ask the right questions—and see the results this change in approach creates for them and their children. Here's a good start:

- How do I help my child feel capable?
- How do I help my child feel belonging and significance?
- How do I help my child learn respect, responsibility, and problem-solving skills?

- How do I get into my child's world and understand his developmental process?
- How can I use problems as opportunities for learning—for my child and for me?

These questions address the big picture and are based on long-term thinking. When parents find answers to the long-term questions, the short-term questions take care of themselves. Children will "mind" and cooperate (at least most of the time) when they feel belonging and significance, they will understand "no" when they are developmentally ready and are involved in finding solutions to problems, and they'll listen when parents listen to *them* and talk in ways that invite listening. Problems are solved more easily when children are involved in the process.

We have included Positive Discipline tips in every chapter of this book, along with "Questions to Ponder" sections to invite you to explore on your own, and we will present suggestions for non-punitive methods that will help your child develop into a capable and loving person.

Discipline Methods to Avoid

Most parents have done it at one time or another. But please:
- If you are spanking, stop.
- If you are screaming, yelling, or lecturing, stop.
- If you are using threats or warnings, stop.

All of these methods are disrespectful and encourage doubt, shame, guilt, and/or rebellion—now and in the future.

"Wait just one minute," you may be thinking. "These methods worked for my parents. You're taking away every tool I have to manage my child's behavior. What am I supposed to do, let my child do anything she wants?" Of course not. Permissiveness is disrespectful and does not teach responsibility and important life skills. You can never really control anyone's behavior but your own, and your attempts to control your child will usually create more problems and more power struggles. Now let's look at several methods that invite cooperation (when applied with a kind and firm attitude) while encouraging your preschooler to develop character and valuable life skills.

Life with an active, challenging preschooler becomes much easier when you accept that positive learning does not take place in a threatening atmosphere. Children don't listen when they are feeling scared, hurt, or angry. Punishment derails the learning process.

Methods That Invite Cooperation

If punishment doesn't work, what does? Here are some suggestions. Remember, your child's individual development is critical in these years; remember too that nothing works all the time for all children. As your unique child grows and changes, you'll have to return to the drawing board many times, but these ideas will form the foundation for years of effective parenting.

THREE TIPS FOR BEGINNING POSITIVE DISCIPLINE

1. Get children involved:
   a. In the creation of routines
   b. Through the use of limited choices
   c. By providing opportunities to help
2. Teach respect by being respectful.
3. Use your sense of humor.

GET CHILDREN INVOLVED

"Education" comes from the Latin root *educare*, which means to "draw forth." This may explain why children so often tune you out when you instead try to "stuff in" through constant demands and lectures.

Instead of telling children what to do, find ways to involve them in decisions and to ask them what they think and perceive. Curiosity questions (which often begin with "what" or "how") are one way to do this. Ask, "What do you think will happen if you push your tricycle over the curb?" or "What do you need to do to get ready for preschool?"

Children who are involved in decision-making experience a healthy sense of personal power and autonomy. For children who are not yet able to talk, say, "Next we ____," while kindly and firmly showing them what to do.

There are several particularly effective ways of getting preschoolers involved in cooperation and problem-solving. Here are three suggestions:

Create routines together. Please note the word "together." Too many parents and caregivers create routine charts instead of involving their children. Young children learn best by repetition and consistency, so you can ease the transitions of family life by *involving* them in creating reliable routines. Routines can be created for every event that happens over and over: getting up, bedtime, dinner, shopping, and so on. Here are some suggestions for creating a routine chart.

- Sit down *with* your child and invite her to help you make a routine chart.
- Ask her to tell you the tasks involved in the routine (such as bedtime); you can add whatever she forgets.
- Let her help you decide on the order those tasks should be done in.
- Take pictures of her doing each task that can be pasted next to each item.
- Provide art materials for her to illustrate the chart.
- Hang the chart where she can see it.
- Let the routine chart become the boss.

When your child gets distracted, you can ask, "What's next on your routine chart?" (Routine charts are like maps that help children remember the steps to a task. They are not sticker or reward charts, which take away from your child's inner sense of capability and responsibility by shifting focus to the reward.)

Offer limited choices. Having choices gives children a sense of power: they have the power to choose one possibility or another. Choices also invite a child to use his thinking skills as he contemplates what to do. And, of course, young children often love it when choices include an opportunity to help.

- "What is the first thing you will do when we get home—help me put the groceries away, or read a story? You decide."
- "Would you like to carry the blanket or the cracker box as we walk to the car? You decide."

Adding "You decide" increases your child's sense of power. Be sure the choices are developmentally appropriate and that all of the choices are options you are comfortable with. When your child wants to do something else, you can say: "That isn't one of the choices. You can decide between this and this."

Provide opportunities for your child to help you. Young children often resist a command to get in the car but respond cheerfully to a request like "I need your help. Will you carry the keys to the car for me?" Activities that might easily have become power struggles can become opportunities for laughter and closeness if you use your instincts and your creativity. Allowing your child to contribute (even when it's messy or inconvenient) also sets the stage for cooperation later on.

TEACH RESPECT BY BEING RESPECTFUL

Parents usually believe children should *show* respect, not have it shown *to* them. But children learn respect by experiencing it. Be respectful when you make requests. Don't expect a child to do something "right now" when you are interrupting something she is thoroughly engaged in. Give her some warning: "We need to leave in a minute. Do you want to swing once more or slide again?" Carry a small timer around with you. Teach her to set it to one or two minutes. Then let her put the timer in her pocket so she can be ready to go when the timer goes off.

Remember too that shame and humiliation—such as a child might feel if she were spanked in the middle of the park (or anywhere else, for that matter)—are disrespectful, and research clearly shows that a child who is treated with disrespect is likely to return the favor. Kindness and firmness show respect for your child's dignity, your own dignity, and the needs of the situation.

USE YOUR SENSE OF HUMOR

No one ever said parenting had to be boring or unpleasant. Learn to laugh together and to create games to get unpleasant jobs done quickly. Humor is often the best way to approach a situation.

Three-year-old Nathan had an unfortunate tendency to whine and Beth was at her wits' end. She had tried talking, explaining, and ignoring, but nothing seemed to have any effect. One day Beth tried something that was probably more desperation than inspiration. As Nathan whined that he wanted some juice, Beth turned to him with a funny look on her face. "Nathan," she said, "something is wrong with Mommy's ears. When you whine, I can't hear you at all!"

Again Nathan whined for juice, but this time Beth only shook her head and tapped her ear, looking around as if a mosquito were buzzing near her head. Nathan tried again, but again Beth shook her head. Then Beth heard something different. The little boy took a deep breath and said in a low, serious voice, "Mommy, can I have some juice?" When Beth turned to look at him, he added "Please?" for good measure.

Beth laughed and scooped Nathan up for a hug before heading to the kitchen. "I can hear you perfectly when you ask so nicely," she said. From that time on, all Beth had to do when Nathan began to whine was tap her ear and shake her head. Nathan would draw an exasperated breath—and begin again in a nicer tone of voice.

Not everything can be treated lightly, of course. But rules become less difficult to follow when laughter lightens the mood.

Let the Message of Love Get Through

Even the most effective non-punitive parenting tools must be used in an atmosphere of caring and unconditional acceptance. Be sure you take time for hugs and cuddles, for smiles and loving touch. Your child will do better when she feels better, and she will feel better when she lives in a world of respect and belonging.

QUESTIONS TO PONDER

1. Choose a behavior that you and your child frequently struggle with. Consider which parts of this behavior may represent skills your child needs help to develop. Once you have identified problem areas, what can be modified to make this task easier or what skills need to be practiced?

2. Think of a behavior of your own that you want to stop doing. List three things you can do in the moment when you notice that you are about to behave in the old way (for instance, yelling or losing your temper).

3. Take a moment to consider some of the Positive Discipline concepts you have just learned about. What is your response to the idea that discipline is not the same as punishment? Do you believe that parents can be kind *and* firm at the same time? How do these ideas compare with your own upbringing?

CHAPTER 2

Enter the World of Your Preschooler

Preschoolers are such engaging little people. They can share ideas, show curiosity, exercise a budding sense of humor, build relationships of their own, and offer open arms of affection and playfulness to those around them. They can also be stubborn, defiant, confusing, and downright defeating.

Most parents worry about the world their children will inherit; they wonder how best to raise their children so that they can live successful, happy lives. And they watch the occasionally frustrating behavior of those same children and wonder what lies ahead—and what to do about it.

"Where Has My Baby Gone?"

Carlota watched three-year-old Manuel's progress across the playground—he was no longer toddling. She felt a jolt of surprise as Manuel climbed to the very top of the domed bars with sure-footed skill. "Where has my baby gone?" she wondered. "Who is this new little person?"

Dana automatically reached down to take her daughter's hand when the light at their corner turned green. Five-year-old Marta looked at her mother and made a face. Marta was willing to walk beside her mom, but holding hands was for babies. Dana felt a bit silly. She realized Marta was careful and capable enough to cross the street without having her hand held, but at that moment Dana's own hand suddenly felt very empty.

Learning to Let Go

At times it may seem to you that parenting is all about learning to let go. When your child is weaned from the breast or the bottle, you must let go of the special closeness nursing brings. When you leave your child in someone else's care, even for as little as half an hour, you must let go in still another way.

Letting go is a process that begins the moment a baby separates from his mother's body, and it is essential to the healthy growth and development of each human being. Hanging on—which usually is done in the name of love—often becomes overprotection and smothering, and prevents healthy growth. It often seems to watching parents that each step a child takes carries her further from their arms. The challenge of parenting lies in finding the balance between nurturing, protecting, and guiding, on one hand, and allowing your child to explore, experiment, and become a capable, confident person, on the other.

The truth is that your child will always need your guidance, encouragement, and love, but parenting does take a different shape as he grows and changes. At fourteen, he will need both love and limits, but he must make many life decisions on his own. In the same way, children at four years of age are far from self-sufficient, but they need some independence with which to learn and practice new skills. Providing a balance between guidance and independence requires you to adapt as he grows.

The World Out There

During these years, parents often find themselves scrambling to keep up as preschoolers discover the many other people who share their world. As a child's horizons expand, she may no longer view Mom, Dad, or her immediate family members as the most important people in that world.

Your child will discover the world of friends. He will notice skin colors, body shapes, and lifestyles that differ from his own. He will begin to make decisions about the world and how it works, and what he must do to find love and belonging. Every experience matters to your child as he develops his own unique approach to life.

During these years, your child will learn her first lessons about empathy, cooperation, and kindness. Learning to build and maintain healthy relationships will take up most of her energy. Teaching social and emotional skills (and helping smooth over the crises that are often part of the learning process) will keep her parents and caregivers busy indeed.

Raising an active preschooler is a big task and can feel overwhelming. No wonder parents find that they can hardly watch television or pick up a magazine without being offered the latest advice on discipline and development. Bookstore shelves, blogs, and Internet sites overflow with information covering every aspect of parenting. In fact, most parents find that the problem isn't having enough information; it's knowing where to start and whom to trust. Positive Discipline is based on principles of dignity and respect that help parents with differing views (and even the most loving parents occasionally disagree) find discipline methods that work for them, and on the growing body of research detailing how young children learn and grow.

All Kinds of Parents, All Kinds of Families

Parents come in many shapes and types, and busy preschoolers have a gift for bringing out differences in parenting styles and opinions. Rarely is there one "right" way to raise children. Consider your differences as opportunities to learn and grow (for everyone involved), as well as the means to model valuable life skills such as cooperation, respect, and compromise.

Preschoolers may be raised in households with two parents, a single parent, adoptive parents, grandparents, or stepparents. Their parents may be of different genders or of the same gender. There may be several siblings or no other children nearby. We believe that children can grow up with a healthy sense of belonging and significance in any sort of family. The decisions adults make about which values will be taught and reflected in their daily lives are what will shape a child's early life. A foundation of love, respect, and dignity is what matters most.

All families face pressure and stress. But with so many kinds of parents and families, can there really be one discipline philosophy that fits for all of them? Well, yes. For families that need additional support and information, check out *Positive Discipline for Single Parents*,[1] *Positive Discipline for Your Stepfamily*,[2] and *Positive Discipline for Parenting in Recovery*.[3]

What Do You Want for Your Child?

Positive Discipline (both the philosophy and the skills that go with it) offers effective, loving ways to guide your youngster through these challenging years. Whether you are a parent, a teacher, or a childcare provider, you will find ideas and practical tools in these pages that will help you give the children in your care the best start in life.

Children need all the confidence, wisdom, and problem-solving skills we can give them. They also need to believe in their own worth and dignity, to possess a healthy sense of self-esteem, and to know how to live, work, and play with those around them. It is the rare parent who doesn't occasionally feel overwhelmed and confused, who doesn't worry that his or her best just won't be good enough. The stakes are so high, and you love your child so much. Where should you begin?

Actually, the end is a good place to begin. It is important to have a destination in mind so you can focus on parenting skills that help you achieve what you want for your child in the long term, instead of focusing on short-term fixes that may not teach the life skills and character qualities you want your child to have.

The Importance of Long-Term Parenting

It is easy in the rush of daily life with a preschooler to focus on the crisis at hand. There's the morning to get through, with lunches to pack and jackets to grab and children who may or may not be willing to get dressed or put on their shoes. Parents must get to work, and children must go off to childcare or preschool or be supervised at home. Later on, dinner and household duties demand time and attention, and then there's bedtime at the end of the day. Just getting everyone fed, bathed, and to sleep can take your last remaining ounce of energy.

There's more that parents must do, however. You must think and dream and plan. You must decide what matters most to you in life and what you ultimately want to impart to your child. These last, most important tasks are often the ones parents never have time to do. But think for a moment: Wouldn't it be helpful, as you embark on the parenting journey, to know your final destination? How will you get there if you don't have a picture of where you want to go?

Perhaps one of the wisest things you can do right now is to take a moment to ask yourself, "What do I want for my child?" When your child has grown to be an adult, what qualities and characteristics do you want her to have? You may decide that you want your child to be confident, compassionate, and respectful. You may want her to be responsible, hardworking, and trustworthy. Most parents want their children to be happy, to have rewarding work and healthy relationships. Whatever you want for your child, how will you bring it to pass? How will your child learn to have a contented, successful life? The good news is that the discipline methods you will learn in this book are designed to help your children develop the social and life skills that will help them achieve these goals.

WHAT DO YOU WANT FOR YOUR CHILDREN?

Here is a typical list from parents and caregivers:

Self-discipline	Self-reliance
Decision-making skills	Problem-solving skills
Self-motivation	Self-confidence
Cooperation/collaboration skills	Social skills
Creativity	Ability to see positives
Values	Resilience
Leadership skills	Foresight
Endurance	Accountability
Responsibility	Respect for self and others
Empathy/caring	Tolerance
Sense of humor	Determination
Thinking skills/judgment skills	Public-spiritedness/social interest
Honesty	Lifelong learning skills
Adaptability	Communication skills

Kind and Firm

As we noted in the introduction, there is one Positive Discipline tool that supports all the rest: the ability to be both kind and firm at the same time. This is no small challenge. Any of us can be tempted to punish a child when a favorite crystal bowl is lying shattered on the kitchen floor. It is equally tempting to buy that candy bar at the checkstand if it will avoid a public tantrum.

Being kind and firm in the face of these daily disasters gets easier (and the disasters fewer) when you realize that prevention is often possible:

Why was that tempting bowl left to sparkle on the table your preschooler uses? Was taking a tired and hungry child to the store setting both of you up for frustration? Prevention can eliminate a lot of mischief—yours and theirs.

But even the sweetest preschooler will misbehave or make mistakes from time to time. In these moments, kind and firm parenting is called for. Kindness shows respect for the humanity of the child and emphasizes the teaching of valuable skills. Firmness backs up your words with necessary action, helping children learn that you mean what you say and are trustworthy. It is helpful when you can be mindful of what you say—no small challenge for the overwhelmed parent of a busy preschooler.

It is possible to offer empathy, support, and love while still following through with a limit, or doing what you have said you would do. Kindness with firmness can be summed in one simple phrase: "I love you and the answer is no."

Kindness in the face of that broken bowl would include commiserating with a child's dismay at what happened, then helping him find a way to make amends of some sort. This could mean holding the dustpan while the broken pieces are swept into it or coming up with a list of small jobs to earn money toward its replacement. These choices should be based on a child's age and abilities. Kindness means not lecturing, shaming, or humiliating a child; firmness means being sure that the agreed-upon tasks are done.

At the other parenting extreme is excessive control, which often invites resistance, defiance, or passivity. Children are always making decisions about themselves, you, and the world around them. Learning to act with kindness and firmness at the same time will not make your problems vanish overnight, but you may be surprised at the difference it makes in your home.

Get into Your Child's World

Understanding your preschooler's developmental needs and limitations is critical to parenting during these important years. Be empathetic when your child becomes upset or has a temper tantrum out of frustration with her lack of abilities. Empathy does not mean rescuing. It means understanding. Validating feelings is one of the most powerful tools you can use to create a connection and to help your children feel a sense of belonging, which creates a foundation for feeling capable. Give your child a hug and say, "You're really disappointed right now. I know you want to stay longer." Then hold your child and let her experience her feelings before you gently guide her to leave. Your child has the opportunity to learn that she can survive disappointment.

Getting into your child's world also means seeing the world from her perspective and recognizing her abilities—and her limitations. Occasionally, ask yourself how you might be feeling (and acting) if you were your child. For example, you may expect your four-year-old to run errands with you without whining because that is "good behavior," while your child may feel deserving of a special treat for his cooperation. It can be illuminating to view the world through a smaller person's eyes.

Accept and Appreciate Your Child's Uniqueness

Children develop differently and have different strengths. Expecting from a child what he cannot give will only frustrate both of you. Your sister's children may be able to sit quietly in a restaurant for hours, while yours get twitchy after just a few minutes, no matter how diligently you prepare (refer to Chapters 3 and 6 for more on this subject). If you simply accept that, you can save yourself and your children a lot of grief by waiting to have that fancy meal when you can enjoy it in adult company—or when your children have matured enough for all of you to enjoy it together.

It may help to think of yourself as a coach, helping your child to succeed and learn how to do things. You're also an observer, learning about the unique human being who is your child. Watch carefully as you introduce new opportunities and activities; discover what your child is interested in, what your child can do by himself, and what he needs help learning from you.

Say What You Mean, Then Follow Through with Kindness and Firmness

Children usually sense when you mean what you say—and when you don't. It's usually best not to say anything unless you mean it and can say it respectfully—and can then follow through with dignity and respect. The fewer words you say, the better!

> Three-year-old Liam crawled into his dad's bed every night, even though Sean had told him that he needed to stay in his own bed. Sean decided that instead of getting into his own bed after tucking Liam in, he would sit on the sofa and read.
>
> So the next time Liam came out of his room and didn't find Dad in bed, he came into the living room. He began to dance to try to get Sean's attention, but Sean continued to read as if nothing was happening. It didn't take long for Liam to tire of his game. It wasn't fun when he got no response. Eventually Liam went back to his own bed.

Sometimes "following through" means doing nothing and having faith that your child will follow the expectations that have been laid out. It also might mean wordlessly removing a child from the slide when it is time to go, rather than getting into an argument or a battle of wills. When this is done kindly, firmly, and without anger, it will be both respectful and effective.

Act, Don't Talk—and Supervise Carefully

Minimize your words and maximize your actions. As Rudolf Dreikurs once said, "Shut your mouth and act."

Arianna had a different way of handling the bedtime challenge. She told her four-year-old son, Ben, that every time he got out of bed after their routine of reading a story and giving hugs and kisses, she would kindly and firmly take him back to his bed, kiss him on the cheek, and leave. These words did not keep Ben in his bed, but Arianna's actions did. Every time Ben got out of bed, she kindly and firmly led him back to his bed, gave him a kiss, and left. The first night she led Ben back to his bed five times (without saying a word). The second night it took three times. The third night Ben just had to give it one more try, but once did it. After that they both enjoyed their story time, hugs, and kisses, and the bedtime hassles ended.

Acting without talking can be surprisingly effective.

Be Patient

Understand that you may need to teach your child many things over and over before she is developmentally ready to understand. For example, you can encourage your child to share, but don't expect her to understand the concept and do it on her own when she doesn't feel like it. (More on social skills in Chapter 7.) Don't take your child's behavior personally. Act like the adult (sometimes that's easier said than done) and do what is necessary without guilt or shame.

In the Name of Love

It is wise to remember that sometimes love is not enough to raise a healthy, happy child. It is knowledge and skills that give legs to the love you feel. No one is born knowing how to raise an active preschooler. Parents learn from their own parents and experiences; most do the best they can, and all will make mistakes. Society has never questioned the need for training in occupational fields, but somewhere along the line the notion got planted that raising children should come "naturally" and that needing help was an admission of inadequacy.

The truth is that good parents take parenting classes, read books, and ask lots of questions. We encourage you to get involved with a parenting group in your community or to consider starting one yourself. Support groups exist for adoptive parents, grandparents who are raising their grandchildren, and just about every other imaginable form of family. It is not weakness to ask for help—it is wisdom.

Trust Your Heart

There is so much in our crowded lives that must be juggled and balanced, and no one can challenge and stretch a parent or teacher like a young child (or a classroom full of them!). For now, remember that it is always *relationships* that matter most. It is often the quiet, everyday moments—the cuddle before bed, the tears after a quarrel, working and laughing side by side—where the best sort of parenting (and teaching) takes place.

QUESTIONS TO PONDER

1. What's in your toolbox? List the parenting tools you use most often. Which do you believe help you accomplish your parenting

goals? Are there any that might be creating problems for you and your child?

2. What do you want for your child? Choose one thing from the list on page 30, or focus on a life skill or quality that matters to you. Describe the ways you may unintentionally discourage the development of this trait. Then list ways that you can actively encourage this trait.

3. If you share the task of parenting with a partner, other relatives (especially if you live with extended family members), or even a roommate or two, you will most likely disagree from time to time about how best to respond to your child's behavior. Unless the disagreement is over fundamental issues such as whether or not to spank, there are probably many ways to find compromises. Think of one thing that you and your partner (or another person involved in your child's care) disagree about that you might be willing to compromise over.

CHAPTER 3

Understanding Developmental Appropriateness

Each human being is a work of art. Look at the variety in appearance alone: skin color, hair color and texture, shape of the nose, color of the eyes, height and weight—each person is unique. And physical characteristics are only the beginning of our uniqueness.

Temperament is as individual as a fingerprint. So is the rate at which we develop and grow. Understanding developmental appropriateness means taking into account things all children are generally able to do, think, and accomplish at different ages—as well as individual variations of each child's development within the broader context of her family, culture, and life circumstances. That is a lot to consider.

Age-Appropriateness: How to Teach and Empower

Around the age of one to two, children enter the "me do it" stage. This is when they develop a sense of autonomy versus doubt and shame.[1] (To learn more, see *Positive Discipline: The First Three Years*.)[2] The ages of two through six herald the development of a sense of initiative versus guilt, meaning that it is a child's developmental job to explore and experiment. Can you imagine how confusing it is to a child to be punished for what she is developmentally programmed to do? She is faced with a real dilemma (at a subconscious level): "Do I ignore my developmental instincts and develop a deep sense of guilt, or do I follow my biological drive to develop initiative by exploring and experimenting in my world?" Punishment—a typical adult reaction to new and challenging behavior—leads to a sense of guilt and shame.

These stages of development do not mean children should be allowed to do anything they want. They do explain why Positive Discipline tools (such as curiosity questions, involving children in focusing on solutions, providing reasonable choices, and setting reasonable limits with loving kindness and firmness) encourage initiative.

Your child's brain is forming connections that will influence her personality and approach to life. Remember the list of characteristics and life skills you created in Chapter 2? You most likely want your child to decide, "I am capable. I can try, make mistakes, and learn. I am loved. I am a good person." If you are tempted to try to teach your child by using guilt, shame, or punishment, you will be creating discouraging beliefs that are difficult to reverse in adulthood.

One way to use developmentally appropriate parenting tools is to build on a child's strengths—those things she can already do—and challenge her to learn a bit more with a small nudge in a new direction. The child who can count to three can begin counting out three spoons to use at breakfast, select three crayons for coloring, or stir the pancake batter three times. A child masters these new skills with an adult's

help, then with an adult counting aloud nearby, and finally on her own. You will use this process over and over for many kinds of learning throughout these years, as your child grows from the helpless baby you cradled in your arms to the wonderful and capable child you will soon accompany to her first elementary school classroom.

Age and Windows of Opportunity

Children are, in many ways, similar. Johnny and Mary, for instance, both learned to walk in the first thirteen months of life. Children are different too. Mary doggedly pulled herself along the furniture and took her first steps at ten months of age, while Johnny was still contentedly crawling at eleven months.

Picture a window in your mind. Although the window is framed on all sides, there is a great deal of space in the middle. There are age-windows for physical, intellectual, and emotional development, but each child has his or her own individual schedule within those windows, neither exactly like nor completely unlike anyone else's.

Let's take a look at some of the factors that influence a child's perceptions and behavior.

Process Versus Product

The way children see the world changes a lot between the ages of three and six. It isn't until around age four or five that children begin to do things with a specific goal in mind. Until that time they are far more interested in the doing itself (the process) than the end result of what they do (the product).

Imagine that it's a busy Friday evening, and you're off on a quick trip to the grocery store with your preschooler. You have a definite goal in mind—to grab the necessary ingredients for dinner in time to get home, prepare and eat the meal, and still be on time for your older son's soccer game. For your young child, however, the product just isn't the point. A trip to the store is all about the process—the smells, the colors, the feelings, and the experience. Being sandwiched into a busy schedule just doesn't allow time to enjoy the process!

Children may not share our goal-oriented expectations. But it isn't always possible to go along with a child's relaxed approach either—sometimes we really do need to run in, grab the chicken, and run home again. Being aware of your child's tendency to focus on process rather than product can help you provide a balance. There may be times when you can take a leisurely browse through the store, enjoying the smell of flowers, the colors of fruit, and the textures of vegetables. When you must hurry, take time to explain to your child why. You can explain that you want him to hold your hand and that you will have to walk past the toys and other interesting things. You can offer to let him help you find the chicken and carry it to the checkout stand. Then you will walk back to the car and drive home. Helping a young child understand what is expected and what will happen makes it easier for him to cooperate with you.

Patsy arrived at the childcare center one afternoon just in time to see Laura and her son leaving with a huge, colorful painting. Patsy looked around eagerly to see what her son Paul had painted, but none of the pictures had his name on them. Baffled, Patsy cornered the teacher and asked why Paul hadn't had a chance to paint that day. "Paul was very interested in the paint," the teacher said, "but not in putting it on the paper. He stirred the colors and experimented with the feeling of the paint on his fingers, then decided he'd really rather build with blocks."

Paul's mom will feel reassured when she understands this process-oriented aspect of Paul's development—even when she feels disappointed at not having a painting to display on the refrigerator at home.

Point of View

What does the world look like when you are less than three feet tall? How might your choices, needs, and behavior be influenced by this particular point of view? Well, get down on your knees and take a look around.

What does the painting six feet up the wall look like from this angle? How inviting is a conversation with adult knees? What kind of challenge does hand-washing present when the sink begins a foot above where you end? Understanding a young child's physical perspective and limitations can help parents and teachers fit the environment to a child's abilities. Whenever you take the time to think about such factors and make appropriate adjustments, you will increase your child's feeling of competence and decrease his frustration—which may make both misbehavior and the need for discipline less likely.

"For Real?": Fantasy and Reality

Children often have difficulty understanding what they see, hear, and experience. At three, children have little understanding of the difference between what is real and fantasy.

Three-year-old Philip's mom was excited to take him to see the Disney classic *Beauty and the Beast*. She explained that the movie was fun but did have some scary parts. "It isn't real," Karen told her small son. "You don't need to be afraid." Philip grinned and bounced up and down, too excited about seeing the movie to pay much attention to his mother's warning.

Everything went well until the scene where the enraged beast emerges. Suddenly, with a shriek like a teakettle boiling over, Philip leaped from his own seat into his mother's lap, where he huddled shaking for the rest of the movie.

"Hey, kiddo, didn't we tell you the movie wasn't real?" Karen asked her small son on the way out to the car.

Philip looked up at his mom in amazement. "But Mom," he said slowly, "it *was* real. I *saw* it!"

Philip's mom learned that the best lectures in the world don't change the fact that a child's definition of reality is far different from an adult's.

By age five, the difference between fantasy and reality becomes clearer, but a child's interpretation of what he perceives is still limited by his development. Young children do make sense of the world but not in the same way adults do. Images on a screen are very real to a child. They have not developed a filter that separates the snarling cartoon cat from a real potential threat or differentiates repeated images of violence or destruction on the news from newly occurring events. Parents sometimes reprimand children for what is actually typical development, or interpret a child's words as "lying." If you can accept your child's feelings with empathy and encouragement, your child will feel safe sharing his world with you.

"Tell Me the Truth!": Young Children and Lying

Q. *How do I deal with my four-year-old's lies? She lies about even little things. I can't let her get away with such behavior. Please offer some advice on how I should handle this delicate situation.*

A. Children can "lie" for all sorts of reasons. Sometimes they are confused about what is real and what is not. They may lie because they are anxious for approval and don't want to admit doing something they shouldn't have done. Sometimes they want to avoid the consequences of their actions, or they want people to like them. (Adults may lie for exactly the same reasons.)

Your statement about letting her "get away with it" gives a clue about your attitude. At four, most children can understand that their behavior has consequences, but they don't have maturity and judgment. They still need far more teaching than they do "discipline." *If your daughter suspects that wrong choices and mistakes will earn her punishments or lectures, she will not want to tell you the truth.*

Children are not born understanding the difference between truth and lies, and they will not automatically value honesty. Parents should plan to do some teaching on why trust and telling the truth are important, but don't expect young children to understand until they are more mature. It is also true that children are more likely to value honesty when they see the adults around them practicing it. (In other words, your children will not learn to be truthful if they hear you calling in sick to work because you would rather sleep in.)

Most children (and most adults) lie from time to time. Remember that mistakes are inevitable—especially when you're four—and if they're viewed as opportunities to learn rather than sins or failures, they're not as scary. If you want your child to be truthful, you must be willing to listen, refrain from shaming or punishing, and work with her to develop her skills and understanding as problems arise. When a child does not tell the truth and is spanked, sent to time-out, or shamed, she learns unintended lessons. Punishment only *appears* to work; usually it produces children who are fearful or who may try to wriggle out of taking responsibility for their actions.

Listen to one father's experience with his son's "lying":

Colin is not thrilled to find the broken egg on the kitchen floor. "Hey," he calls, with exasperation in his voice, "who broke this egg?" Four-year-old Sammy replies calmly, "An alligator did it."

Colin knows there aren't any alligators in Kansas. He wants to find a way to handle the situation that both solves the egg problem and teaches Sammy the importance of telling the truth. "An alligator!" he exclaims. "Was it orange? I think I just saw it in the driveway." Sam grins and agrees that it was an orange alligator.

Colin smiles too, and then says, "You know, I'm just pretending that there was an alligator. I know we don't have alligators around here." He then suggests that they clean up the broken egg together, knowing there will be opportunities to talk as they work.

"Sam, were you afraid I would yell at you about the egg?" Sam drops his eyes and nods slowly. Colin makes his voice warm and gentle as he says, "I know it's tempting to blame things on an alligator or to make up something that didn't really happen. But it's important for you to know that you can tell me the truth, even when you feel scared. Do you know why it's important to tell the truth?" Sam shakes his head. Colin ruffles his son's hair. "I want to be able to trust what you tell me, buddy. I love you very much, and I want to know that when you tell me something, it's what really happened."

Sam looks up and says slowly, "I love you too, Daddy. I was just pretending."

Colin says, "Yes, I know we were pretending. And it's fun to pretend sometimes. It's important to know that we can tell the truth, though. We're pretending when we make up a story together. We're lying when we use a story to avoid admitting we've made a mistake."

Sam will probably have to learn this lesson more than once. After all, few adults can claim to be completely truthful all of the time either. Colin could also simply have asked Sam if he felt scared. Or he could have asked the original question in a less threatening way, saying, "Sam, this broken egg made a mess. How can we solve this problem? Can you clean it up by yourself, or would you like me to help?"

Removing the sense of fear and getting the message of love through to our children (or even participating in a bit of nonsense with them) can help them learn to tell the truth.

WAYS TO RESPOND TO LYING

Here are some suggestions to consider using when your child tells a "lie."

- Join in, pretending with the child by exaggerating the story and making it funny and absurd.
- Focus on solutions rather than on blame. Instead of asking who made the mess, ask if the child needs help cleaning it up, or if the child has ideas about how to solve the problem.
- When you suspect a lie, state it: "That sounds like a story to me. I wonder what the truth is?"
- Empathize with a child. Ask if he feels scared to admit to making a mess. Assure him we all feel scared at times.

- Explain the need to accept responsibility for his actions: "We all make mistakes, but blaming others, even imaginary people, does not take away responsibility for what we did."
- Talk about the meaning of trust. Help a child see the connection between telling the truth and having others trust what he says.

Children and Stealing

Ownership is another example of a child's differing thought processes. Young children don't make the same assumptions about property rights that adults do. (In fact, the development of morals and ethics continues well into adolescence.) Because children learn by watching adults, they sometimes make surprising decisions about what they've seen.

Jason goes into the supermarket with his mom. He watches Mom pick up a copy of the free local paper and place it in her purse. Further down the aisle a woman is offering samples of cookies. Mom takes one for her and offers one to Jason, who munches on it happily as they complete their shopping.

When they arrive at the car, Mom lifts Jason into his car seat and discovers a bulge in her son's pocket. Further examination reveals a candy bar.

"You stole this," Mom exclaims, shocked.

Jason doesn't know how to answer—he has no idea what stealing is.

It's not really surprising that Jason is confused: What difference is there between the paper, the cookies, and the candy bar? If Mom is paying attention, she may realize that the problem is not one of stealing or dishonesty but of differing perceptions. Now her task is to help her little boy understand why he can take some things out of the supermarket but not others, and why the candy bar must be returned.

If Mom lectures Jason, shames him, and makes him feel guilty and afraid, he may be more likely to believe that right and wrong are a matter of getting caught. He may also be less able to apply what he has learned to a future situation. Discipline is meant to teach, and mistakes are opportunities to learn. We can't say it often enough!

"Who Am I?"

How children define themselves in relation to the rest of the world changes so much in the preschool years.

> Alice walks into the preschool shaking her head. She prides herself on being a no-frills sort of person: she wears no makeup, pulls her hair back simply, and usually dresses in jeans and T-shirts. Right behind mom is her daughter, Sally—and four-year-old Sally is a sight to behold. She is wearing a lacy pink princess dress, a sparkly tiara in her hair, her best shiny shoes, and a jangly assortment of bracelets on her arms. Sally, it seems, is as fond of ruffles and accessories as her mom is of simplicity. Sally may not always want to dress this way, but for now she is busy exploring her own perception of what it means to be a girl.

This sex role identification takes place even when parents are careful to minimize gender stereotypes. On playgrounds everywhere games emerge during the preschool years that focus on gender. "No boys allowed," say the girls. "Girls, ick," reply the boys with equal fervor. Although this is a natural phase, parents can still teach young children to respect all people.

Society has traditionally divided children into two categories, boys and girls. As it turns out, gender identity can be considerably more complex than this. Whatever the gender, avoid gender-based limitations.

Girls can play army, boys can play with dolls, and all can learn to develop their own special abilities. Limiting children to sex-typed roles, expecting play to fall into male or female compartments, or discouraging abilities on the grounds that they are "too feminine," "not masculine enough," or "not ladylike" may cause children to stifle their unique skills and interests. Their tastes in clothing and play will change as they grow, as will their desire to have same- or opposite-sex friends.

Children also begin to notice their physical differences during the preschool years. In these days of explicit television and advertising, questions related to sexuality may come earlier than ever before (another excellent reason for staying tuned in to what your child is being exposed to). A little boy may want to touch his dad in the shower. Watching Mom nurse a baby brother or sister may lead to all sorts of interesting questions. Both boys and girls may stuff teddy bears under their shirts and announce, "I'm having a baby!" as they simulate the growing belly of a pregnant teacher, parent, or relative.

As much as possible, try to remain calm and "askable." Use accurate terms such as "penis," "breast," and "vagina." Children don't need a great deal of detailed information about sexuality (in fact, their eyes will probably glaze over if you try), but most experts agree that it is wise to answer questions or offer explanations in simple, accurate terms, such as "Auntie has a baby growing inside her" or "Boys have penises but girls have vaginas."

Of course, children won't always get the details right.

Chelsea is four and a half. One evening, as she enjoys her bath, she carefully drapes her private parts with a washcloth. Giggling, she explains to her mother that she has to "cover her peanuts."

Make every effort to enjoy all stages of your child's development. Being open to topics involving sexuality will establish an atmosphere of comfort and trust and will enable your children to seek further information later on, when they really need it.

GENDER AND DEVELOPMENT

Research on how the brain develops has led to some interesting information about the way gender influences development. For reasons that are not clearly understood, girls gain access to the left hemisphere of their brains sooner than boys do. Each child is unique (and most of these differences disappear around the time children enter school), but be aware of the following as you raise your preschooler.

- Girls often learn language and emotional skills sooner than boys do.
- Boys may be more emotionally sensitive than girls early in life, may experience more separation anxiety when you leave, and may have a harder time calming themselves down when they become upset.
- Boys are also expected to be more physically active, more impulsive, more aggressive, and more competitive than girls. When a girl displays these tendencies, she may be referred to as a "tomboy" or told she's being "bossy"—a term rarely applied to boys.
- Girls are expected to be both nurturing and compliant, but boys can be seen as weak for displaying these traits, or girls as rebellious for not having them.

It is always helpful to pay attention to your child's unique qualities, rather than expecting (or demanding) certain behaviors based on gender.

Race and Other Differences

Just as children learn to sort objects by color, size, and shape, they notice that the people around them look and act differently too.

Randy was the child of biracial parents. When he was three, the black couple next door announced that they were expecting their first child. With the innocence of childhood, three-year-old Randy wondered aloud whether the baby would be black or white. To him, anything was possible. By the time Randy was four and a half, he had noticed that his skin looked different from some of his play-mates'. The decisions Randy makes about this fact will depend on the reactions he receives from others. If he experiences acceptance, his decision that "anything is possible" may continue. If he experiences rejection and humiliation, he is likely to make decisions related to the four mistaken goals of behavior (as discussed in Chapter 10). Preschool children are usually very accepting of differences.

Juanita and her classmates were excited when Rajid joined their class. They loved pushing his wheelchair through the halls. To them, his disability was simply part of who he was; the most important fact was that he was their friend.

Delia invited her best friend, Nora, to the dance program her Greek school was putting on. Delia was proud of the Greek songs she had learned and was excited to share her special culture with her friend.

Wouldn't life be boring if we were all the same? People are different, and the conclusions children draw about these differences will depend upon what you teach and model.

One woman remembered an event from her childhood that occurred while shopping with her aunt in the American South.

There were two drinking fountains in the store, one labeled "whites only" and the other "colored." She said, "I saw the sign 'colored' and thought it meant that the water would be colored, which I thought would be really wonderful. But when I went to take a drink, the store clerk rushed over and told me that I couldn't drink from that fountain, 'because it was for colored people only.'

"This made no sense to me, so when the clerk turned his back, I took my drink, still hoping to see lovely colored water emerge. Years later, when I thought about that experience and realized the truth, I felt deeply sad."

This story reminds us that children must be taught to discriminate and hate. Even less overt actions, such as moving to a different side of the street when a person of a different race or one wearing unfamiliar clothing passes by, sends a powerful message to a watching child. Actions speak even louder than words do.

Parents and teachers have the opportunity to teach children to value differences instead of condemning, fearing, or simply ignoring them, and to teach them that everyone is worthy of respect—even those different from themselves. Prejudice, whether it concerns race, culture, or attitudes toward different physical abilities, is learned. Even young children can learn to respect differences in race, gender, and religious beliefs. And because children of this age are learning so much about themselves, it is vital that they learn about others in ways that are respectful and positive.

Culture, Society, and Anti-Bias

Your child's development is also influenced by the culture and society within which she lives. Wise parents and teachers recognize the role of culture and respect the influence society's expectations have on children without bias or judgments.

A professor visiting the United States from her home in Singapore saw a picture of an American toddler feeding herself. The child's happy face shone with dripping blobs of yogurt, and more yogurt had been spread on the high chair tray. Shaking her head, the professor said, "Only in America." What an eye-opening statement that became for both the visiting professor and her Western colleagues. What did she mean?

Asian children are often hand-fed until they are three, four, or even five years old, for two reasons. The first is that food is never to be wasted. The second reason has deep cultural roots: in many Asian cultures the highest value is placed on relationships. Time spent feeding a child gives the child and adult opportunities to savor and strengthen their relationship, binding them closer together. In contrast, the American attitude of encouraging independence far exceeded either of these concerns for the Western educators present. For them, supporting a child's growing autonomy and helping her experience her own capability far outweigh messiness or concerns over lost food.

Skills and values differ by culture, and each family must decide on their own priorities for their children. Western cultures prize individualism, while many other cultures see collective needs as more important. This may influence the age at which a child is expected to dress or feed herself and what kinds of tasks or choices she will be given. Parents and teachers would be wise to recognize the influence of culture on development and parenting.

Birth Order

The preschool years are a time when children are making decisions about themselves and others that will influence the rest of their lives. They are asking themselves, "What must I do to find belonging and significance in this family—and with my friends? Am I good enough, or must I keep trying harder—or should I just give up?" Preschoolers will carry the answers to those questions with them, continuing to make decisions and to test what they are learning and deciding as they explore social relationships.

Beyond the influence of development and culture, Adler emphasized the importance of how each child's experiences are shaped by the family position into which she is born. Keep in mind that birth order is much more than a matter of numbers; there will be many exceptions to the behaviors associated with each birth order position. Sometimes the oldest boy and the oldest girl will each experience firstborn status because they are the oldest of their gender, and sometimes siblings are born so far apart that each feels like an only child. Overall, which birth order

BIRTH ORDER CHART

MOTTO	VANTAGE POINT	LIKELY ATTITUDES (ADVANTAGES)	CHALLENGES (DISADVANTAGES)	TIPS
Me, myself, and I	Only/first	• Independent • Self-reliant • Responsible	• Sometimes lonely • May have trouble relating to peers • Overly alarmed by conflict	• Provide time with peers • Engage in group activities • Model/Practice problem-solving
Me first!	First	• Responsible • High achiever • Take-charge, leader	• Perfectionist • Fear of mistakes • Too early adult role	• Reduce expectations and pressure • Model acceptance of imperfections (yours and theirs) • Limit responsibilities
Me too!	Second	• Team player • Innovative • Good observer	• Seldom feels "good enough" • Constant comparisons • Follower of or dependent on firstborn	• Treat each child as unique (and take photos!) • Avoid comparisons • Encourage leadership roles
What about me?	Middle	• Successful social skills • Empathetic • Champion of justice • May be a rebel with or without a cause or may be very easygoing	• Feels lacking (because of comparisons) • Vulnerable to undue peer influence • Proves worth through competition	• Recognize individual traits • Foster family involvement and contribution • Channel competitiveness into team sports
Take care of me!	Baby	• Charming • Fun and/or funny • Easygoing	• Manipulative • Defers decision-making to others • Does not feel taken seriously	• Raise expectations • Offer leadership opportunities • Ask for his ideas and opinions
Make way for me!	Youngest (not baby)	• Energetic • Focused • High achiever	• Daredevil • Ignores others' needs • Driven	• Set boundaries • Encourage teamwork • Model stress management

perspective a child will adopt is usually based on how long that position is maintained.

Birth order positions have common sets of traits associated with each one, but there are exceptions to every "rule," and those traits should not be used as labels or given mythic power. And remember, no birth order position is more advantageous than any other. Birth order is simply another means of getting into a child's world, providing additional insights into what might be motivating a child's behavior and life decisions.

Understanding birth order can give you tips for which experiences a child may need strengthened or which ones are less helpful or could cause difficulties.

Dethronement

The perceived loss of status when a newcomer challenges one's life view brings about the experience of "dethronement." The birth order position that is most likely to experience dethronement is the firstborn. Any change in the family configuration, whether a new baby or even the addition of a stepsibling, will end her status as "one and only." It's common for firstborn children to display changes in behavior when a new baby arrives, even though they may love the new baby very much.

Firstborn Children

The firstborn usually chooses to shoulder the responsibilities of trailblazer. Her view of the world is summed up in her motto, "Me first," with all its attendant benefits and burdens.

Born into a world populated by adults, firstborns may acquire language early, often becoming quite articulate (with no one around to either interrupt or interpret for them). Firstborn status may bring extra privileges in the family—but more may be expected of them too. All of this responsibility often leads to seeing oneself as "responsible." It is easy for firstborn children to become perfectionists, often seeking to do things "right." Some succeed in their quest for excellence and become high achievers, while others feel so pressured to live up to expectations that they give up or quit trying if they can't be best.

Second-Born

A second-born child arriving with a bigger, more skilled, and developmentally advanced sibling already ahead of him wants to get in on the action. It is no surprise that one of his favorite toddler phrases may be "Me too!" (And a second-born child's birth position may also be temporary, as she may become a middle child or turn out to be the youngest.) For a second-born, "Who am I?" is often a process of elimination—choosing roles and interests that the others have not. If the firstborn is a sports star, the second-born may long for trophies as well, but will pursue them in a different arena—music or dance, for example. Second-born and middle children share similar experiences, often feeling overshadowed by the siblings at either end of their family spectrum.

Middle Children

If a second child is thrust into the middle position by another newcomer, he may change his motto to "What about me?" The middle can be an uncomfortable spot, with pressure from above and behind. Middle children don't have the privileges of the oldest and have lost the fleeting benefits of being the baby (if they ever had time to savor them). With pressure from an older, more advanced sibling ahead and a cute and demanding one from behind, middle children sometimes feel unfairly cheated out of their fair share of time, attention, or material goods. Middle children often seek out peers or siblings for support and encouragement, the benefit of which is that they can develop outstanding social skills. They also have the unique perspective of learning to see in both directions, a built-in invitation to see both sides of a situation.

The Youngest

When that final family member arrives, hovered over by a houseful of older, more competent family members, he may simply coo, kick back, and live out his motto: "Take care of me!" This child may well find that the rules have relaxed for him. His parents know he is their last child and are reluctant to let go of their "baby." He can be a delightful companion with wonderful social skills. He knows how to fit into a group because he has been doing it all his life.

However, "babying" a child may not invite him to develop the skills and confidence he will need to thrive. A person who is cute and engaging (lovely attributes) can learn to apply those attributes to get others to do his bidding; that is, he may learn to manipulate others. Then his motto may become "I can get anything I want by being charming."

A youngest child may also tire of being "last in line" and reject his status as the baby. A competitive family makes this switch especially likely. Such a child becomes determined to find the quickest route to the top, galloping past his siblings while yelling his motto, "Make way for me!" He may become the family's high achiever.

Only Children

If no other children come into the family and the firstborn remains the unchallenged only child, growing up in an adult-centered environment may teach her to march to her own drumbeat. Her motto, "Me, myself, and I" or "I'm special," will fly on a banner overhead as she marshals her own parade, an experience that can be both exhilarating and lonely. Only children are the recipients of their parents' undivided love and attention, with no need to share or be flexible. On the other hand, having no one with whom to share can be very lonely—a feeling common to the only child's vantage point. They also may be more comfortable than other children with "alone time" and may identify with adults more than with their peers.

Whatever a person's birth order, remember that one's decisions about these early experiences are made on a subconscious level. Each child will choose his life attitudes based upon his unique vantage point, perceptions, and decisions. Each birth order will bring with it certain strengths (advantages), as well as traits that will be less developed or need strengthening (disadvantages). Birth order does not determine who a child will be, but it may give valuable insights about the decisions she is making—and why she does or does not behave in certain ways.

When Birth Order Gets Scrambled

Birth order can shift due to changes in family circumstances. What happens when a parent of a firstborn (or only) child remarries and there are suddenly two older children in the family? What if a child becomes ill and dies, or the older child in a family has developmental delays that alter which child accomplishes developmental markers first? Any of these situations will impact the way in which a child sees the world.

Holding a birth position for three or more years does tend to solidify that set of characteristics. Although a child may now have older siblings, her view of the world as a firstborn, with its attendant characteristics and expectations, will remain the same. The best advice is to take note of how changing dynamics are affecting your child's behavior. If she feels less important or is no longer getting the spotlight she once enjoyed, having regular one-on-one times with both parents or a new stepparent can help ease her distress.

A child in a family that suffers the loss of a sibling may not feel up to the task of meeting new and different expectations. A second-born child can feel distressed by this "out of order" experience, adding to his own grief and loss. Being gentle and never making a child feel he has to live up to the missing child's expectations are critical. No child can ever fill the place of another.

Adoption: "Should We Tell Our Child?"

One special type of family is that created when a child is adopted. Adoption is a wonderful thing, providing many children with safe and loving homes that they might not have had otherwise. (A family using in vitro fertilization or a surrogate birth mother may share similar concerns.) Most of these parents will have questions: How much should children be told about their birth circumstances? Will your adopted child truly feel like a part of your family? When should you tell your child that he is adopted, or does not share his parents' genetics?

Research does not give a clear answer to these questions. Some research says that too much information before age six or seven only confuses a child. Other researchers believe that the older a child is when told, the more upsetting the news may be. Much of human behavior relates to our feelings of "belonging." As children put together the unique puzzle of who they are, questions about adoption ("Where did I come from? Why did my parents give me away?") should be expected.

An adopted child who looks racially different from his adoptive parents will begin to notice this difference by the age of four or even younger. Knowing that a child is becoming aware of race may help parents decide when to tell him about his heritage.

There are important cultural considerations as well. Children adopted from different cultures often enjoy participating in special cultural classes during their preschool years. For example, Tory, Sarah, and Anna were all born in Korea and adopted into American families. Each summer the three girls attended a special Korean cultural camp where Korean clothing, food, art, and language were taught. Their parents wanted them to enjoy the richness of their birth culture. These girls knew of their adoption from their earliest years and were proud to wear their Korean outfits to preschool.

Attitudes toward adoption vary widely, but adoptive families are still *families*. A celebration on a child's "adoption day" encourages children to feel safe, trusting, and comfortable with adoption. If your family includes both adopted and natural children, be aware that eventually everyone will have questions. Behaving as if there is anything disturbing, secretive, or mysterious about adoption invites distrust, fear, and anxiety. If you treat all of your children with respect and create a sense of belonging and significance in your home, then the inevitable questions will not feel threatening.

All the World's a Stage

Parents constantly hear the words "It's just a stage." There's a great deal of truth in the concept. It is also true that no two children grow and develop in exactly the same way. Understanding your own child's development and other life influences will enable you to deal more effectively with his behavior, with his successes and his occasional mistakes. You can help your child learn that the world is a place where he can love, be loved, and learn about himself and the others he meets.

QUESTIONS TO PONDER

1. Think of a skill your child has developed. What opportunities can you provide for him to practice this skill? What are ways to help him build upon the skill?

2. What do you think your child's current understanding of "real" and "fantasy" is? Does this understanding (or lack thereof) affect her sense of security? How might you help her learn to differentiate between "real" and "pretend"?

3. What is your birth order position? How do you think this affects your behavior and view of the world?

CHAPTER 4

The Miraculous Brain: Learning and Development

Robbie is five years old. He loves books, knows his letters and numbers, and can write his own name and that of his dog, Comet. Robbie can hardly wait until he's old enough to join his older sister and the other "big kids" on the big yellow bus. Robbie's mom, though, has mixed emotions. She knows it will be hard to let her baby go. And while Robbie enjoys learning and displays an avid curiosity about the world around him, he is also shy and slow to engage with other children. He clings to his mom in public places. And sometimes he draws his letters backward. Robbie's mom worries that he isn't really ready for school.

"What should I do?" she asks her neighbor, whose three children attend the nearby elementary school. "Maybe I should let him have another year in preschool or at home before he starts kindergarten. I don't want Robbie to fail— but I don't want him to be discouraged either."

How (and When) Preschoolers Learn

As preschoolers approach the age of five or six, the prospect of school and formal learning looms on the horizon. The world broadens beyond home and family to include friends and teachers, all of whom will take on greater significance in a child's life as the years go by. It isn't always an easy transition for parents or for children.

We live in a highly competitive world. And because parents love their children and want them to succeed, they have many questions.

- What should we be teaching?
- When should we start?
- How much should children know about reading, writing, and math skills before they enter school?
- How important are social and emotional skills?
- What happens in growing brains that enables them to absorb and use knowledge and skills?
- How do children learn, anyway?

Research has confirmed that the academic learning so important to many parents and teachers is built on a foundation of social and emotional skills, things that are not learned from educational apps or flash cards. Play (including lots of unstructured free play) is more important than academic learning for preschoolers and kindergarteners—in fact, numerous research studies have shown that teaching academics can even be harmful for this age group.[1] Academic learning (and success on the endless tests a child will encounter in school) happens best when children possess the ability to understand and manage their emotions, calm themselves down when they are frustrated or angry, and work well with peers and other adults. Much of this essential learning happens when parents least expect it: when a child is playing.

The early years of a child's life are critically important in the formation of social and emotional skills, thinking and reasoning skills, and in the actual "wiring" of the brain itself. The way parents and caregivers interact with children during their preschool years is crucial to brain development and learning. In fact, the brain continues to develop throughout childhood and adolescence; the prefrontal cortex of the brain, which is responsible for emotional regulation, impulse control, and more adult forms of reasoning, does not develop fully until approximately the age of twenty-five.

How the Brain Grows

Stimulation from the outside world, as experienced through a child's senses (hearing, seeing, tasting, smelling, and touching), enables the brain to create or change connections and primes it to learn. While the brain is flexible and is able to adapt to change or injury, there are windows early in a child's life during which important learning (like vision and language development) takes place. If those windows are missed, it may become more difficult for a child to acquire those abilities. As early as the preschool years, a child's brain begins to prune away the synapses that haven't been used enough. So, for some functions, brain development is a use-it-or-lose-it proposition. (For others, such as social skills development, learning continues well into early adulthood.) What is used (and kept) depends in large part on the adults who shape a child's world.

What Makes Children Different?

Perhaps you are wondering where your child gets his or her particular combination of traits and qualities—and why, if you have more than one child, they can be so amazingly different. Researchers believe that genes may have an even stronger influence on temperament and personality than previously thought. Genes may influence such qualities as optimism, depression, aggression, and whether or not a person is a thrill-seeker—which may come as no surprise to parents whose preschoolers thrive on gymnastics, hurl themselves at the ball in soccer, and climb trees faster than monkeys! (We will discuss temperament further in Chapter 9.) If genes are so powerful, does it really matter how you parent your child?

The answer is that it matters a great deal. While a child inherits certain traits and tendencies through her genes, the story of how those traits develop hasn't been written yet. Your child may have arrived on the planet with her own unique temperament, but how you and her other caregivers interact with her will shape the person she becomes. (Brain researchers call these early decisions and reactions "adaptations"; they are part of an intricate dance between a child's inborn qualities and the world she inhabits.) As educational psychologist Jane M. Healy says, "Brains shape behavior, and behavior shapes brains."[2]

One key to healthy brain development is *integration*, helping the parts of the brain connect and work well together. According to Daniel Siegel and Tina Payne Bryson, "The rate of brain maturation is largely influenced by the genes we inherit. But the degree of integration may be exactly what we can influence in our day-to-day parenting. *The good news is that by using everyday moments, you can influence how well your child's brain grows toward integration.* . . . We're talking about simply being present with your children so you can help them become better integrated."[3]

Parents and caregivers, fragile and imperfect as they may be, bear the responsibility for shaping a child's relationships and environment, and therefore her development. The human brain never stops growing and never loses the ability to form new synapses and connections. Change may become more difficult as we age, but change—in attitudes, behavior, and relationships—is always possible.

What Should You Teach—and When?

There is no fast track to individual development. Underlying brain structures need time to grow. Forcing children to learn before they are ready may also have psychological effects. Children are always making decisions about themselves and the world around them. When children have difficulty mastering a concept forced upon them by loving (and well-intentioned) parents, they may decide, "I'm not smart enough," when in truth their brains just are not ready to absorb certain concepts.

There are few absolutes: each human brain is unique and it is impossible to generalize about what is right or wrong for an individual child. But some scholars, like Jane Healy, believe that our fast-paced modern culture (and our growing dependence on screens to entertain and calm young children) may be affecting children's ability to pay attention, to listen, and to learn later in life. Parents need to pay close attention to what their young children are exposed to and make sure that character and values are taught along with vocabulary and skills.

Young children learn best in the context of *relationships*, and what they most need to learn in their preschool years isn't found on flash cards (or colorful screens). Children learn best through active involvement that engages their senses: sight, smell, hearing, taste, and touch. They also need opportunities to connect what they already know to new information as they construct their understanding of the world. Isn't it interesting that play meets all of these requirements?

Preschoolers learn with their entire bodies, and they need many opportunities to move, to explore, and to engage with their environment. A preschooler playing is actually hard at work, immersed in learning and development. As the emphasis on academic testing has increased, many schools (including, sadly, kindergartens and preschools) have reduced the time available for recess, arts, and imaginative play and replaced it with worksheets, testing, and screen time. (Sometimes parents do the same thing at home.) This is not a good developmental fit for young children, who are wired to learn social and emotional skills at this age, and to explore the world around them with enthusiasm and joy. In fact, when opportunities for recess and active play are increased, academic achievement generally improves, while behavior problems are reduced.[4]

"Hardwired to Connect": What Your Child *Really* Needs

Preschoolers are such busy little people because they have so much to learn. Brain development is all about connection, and your child's brain is wired to seek connection from the moment of birth. How you and your child's other caregivers relate to her—how you talk and play and nurture—is by far the most important factor in her development. (You will learn more about emotional development in Chapter 5.)

According to Ross A. Thompson, a professor of psychology at the University of California at Davis and a founding member of the National Scientific Council on the Developing Child (developingchild.net), young children learn best when they are unstressed and when they live in a reasonably stimulating environment. Thompson believes that special stimulation, such as videos and other academic learning tools, is unnecessary; in fact, what children really need to grow and develop is unhurried time with caring adults who focus on the child and follow his cues without distraction or expectations. In preschools, dress-up clothes, dolls, blocks, props, art supplies of all types, and open spaces that allow children to interact with ease are indicators of a program that supports and encourages play.

MIRACULOUS MIRROR NEURONS

Have you ever wondered how your child learns to clap his hands, push the vacuum cleaner, or give a high five? Young children rely heavily on their mirror neurons, which perceive physical action, facial expression, and emotion and prepare the brain to duplicate what it "sees." Mirror neurons help your child figure out how to imitate you. In the same way, when you are angry, excited, or anxious, his mirror neurons will "catch" your emotion and create that same feeling within your child. Mirror neurons help explain why we weep, laugh, or get angry with each other so easily. They also explain why what you *do* (the behavior you model) as a parent is so much more powerful than your words in teaching your child.

A Word About Attachment

When you connect well with your child—when you recognize and respond to his signals, nurture a sense of belonging and significance, and foster a sense of trust and security—you help him develop a secure attachment. Securely attached children can connect well with themselves and with others and have the best opportunity to develop healthy, balanced relationships. Interestingly enough, researchers such as Erik Erikson found that an infant's development of a sense of trust in the first year of life is directly related to a mother's sense of trust in herself. *How you understand and make sense of your own history and experiences has a direct effect on your growing child.* Understanding and resolving your own struggles, challenges, and emotional issues may be one of the greatest gifts you ever give your child. (To learn more about attachment, brain development, and parenting, see *Parenting from the Inside Out: How a Deeper Self-Understanding Can Help You Raise Children Who Thrive,* by Daniel J. Siegel and Mary Hartzell [New York: Tarcher Perigee, 2013]).

Positive Discipline teaches "connection before correction": before you attempt to teach or "discipline" a child, it helps to be sure your connection to each other is strong and vibrant. Some simple ways to connect are to validate your child's feelings, offer a hug before discussion, be curious about your child's point of view before sharing yours, and have faith in your child to learn from mistakes. The importance of connection is supported by a great deal of research. For example, a 2016 study at Washington University School of Medicine found that children whose mothers were nurturing *during the preschool years,* as opposed to later in childhood, have more robust growth in brain structures associated with learning, memory, and stress response than children with less supportive moms.

THE IMPACT OF CHILDHOOD TRAUMA

There are times when a young child's life is not the peaceful ideal parents dream of. Sometimes children are exposed to physical or emotional abuse, injury, or violence in their homes or communities. Sometimes they experience medical treatment or hospitalization that is frightening or painful. These deeply stressful experiences are known as *trauma*, and they can have a deep impact on children's social and emotional development, their ability to learn in the classroom, and even their physical health and growth.

Children exposed to trauma may demonstrate a variety of behaviors:

- They may have difficulty falling asleep or they may have nightmares.
- They may seem anxious or withdrawn and may cling to parents and caregivers.
- They may have violent tantrums, triggered by something that seems meaningless.
- They may talk repetitively about what they have witnessed or act it out with toys or other people.
- They may simply shut down, showing little or no emotion.

Fortunately, the brain is resilient, and we know that the presence of healthy adults who can manage stress and adversity buffers trauma for young children and increases their resilience. Children can thrive when they have a sense of connection, belonging, trust, and security provided by at least one person in their lives. In addition, children who have a strong sense of family history and tradition (which often comes from the sharing of stories and personal experiences) often show the most resilience in the face of traumatic events.

Whenever possible, it is essential to remove the cause of the trauma. Therapy with a child therapist may also be helpful. And be sure to ask for help, for yourself as well as for your child. In order to help others cope, caregivers and family members need to heal too.

To learn more about trauma:

- Adverse Childhood Experiences Study, ACEStudy.org
- Nadine Burke Harris, *The Deepest Well* (Boston: Houghton Mifflin Harcourt, 2018)

- Nadine Burke Harris's TED talk, "How Childhood Trauma Affects Health Across a Lifetime," www.ted.com/talks/nadine_burke_harris_how_ childhood_trauma_affects_health_across_a_lifetime

How to Grow a Healthy Brain

Optimal brain development and integration happen more easily (and intuitively) in young children than most parents believe. Simply connecting well and often with your child is the best beginning. When you listen, talk about the world around you, offer a hug, and go exploring together, you are providing an environment in which your child's brain can grow and learn. Here are some ideas to keep in mind.

DEMONSTRATE AFFECTION, INTEREST, AND ACCEPTANCE

A child never outgrows the need to feel a sense of belonging and significance. It is not enough just to love your child; that love must be demonstrated daily in healthy ways. Keep in mind that rescuing, overprotecting, and overindulging are not healthy ways to demonstrate love.

Children who receive warm, consistent, loving care produce less of the stress hormone cortisol, and when they do become upset they are able to "turn off" their stress reaction more rapidly. On the other hand, children who suffer abuse or neglect early in life are likely to feel more stress with less provocation—and have less ability to turn off their reactions.

Hugs, smiles, and laughter are wonderful parenting tools and will mean more to your child in the long run than the most marvelous toys and activities. Spending special time with a child, showing curiosity in his activities and thoughts, and learning to listen well will show your child on a daily basis that he is accepted and loved and will shape and strengthen the development of his brain.

PRACTICE THE ART OF CONVERSATION

Contrary to popular belief, while children may learn words from television and movies, they do not learn *language* from even the most "educational" television shows. Children develop language by having the opportunity to speak and be spoken to by real humans. By age four, children who are exposed to healthy doses of language with the people in their lives will have a vocabulary of as many as six thousand words and can construct sentences of five or six words. By age five their vocabulary may increase to around eight thousand words—a leap of as many as five words a day, every single day for a year. Awesome, isn't it?

Conversation with any preschooler truly is an art, requiring both humor and patience. Most young children pass through the phase when every other word is "Why?" or "How come?" One weary mom, bombarded by questions from her curious four-year-old son, told him she was tired of answering questions for one day and suggested that he keep quiet for a while. The boy looked at his mom with puzzlement and informed her, "But Mom, that's how little boys learn!" And he was absolutely right.

Adults sometimes speak to young children in ways that are merely directive and that do not allow for much response:

"Put on your jammies."
"Eat your potatoes."
"Do it right now, young man!"

Such commands do not invite conversation.
Other questions do not invite real conversation:

"Did you enjoy preschool today?"
"Did you win your tee-ball game?"
"Did you have fun at the park?"

These questions can be answered with a single syllable or even with a grunt.

A more effective way to invite conversation (and to develop language skills in the process) is to ask curiosity questions (which often begin with the words "what" or "how"):

"What did you like about school today?"
"How do you think you might solve that problem?"
"What was your favorite part of playing at the park?"

These questions invite a more thoughtful response and give a child the opportunity to practice vital reasoning and language skills. Of course, they also call for focused and attentive listening from parents, something that requires putting down that smartphone and demonstrating both energy and patience. Remember, relationships and connection support brain development.

READ, READ, READ!

There is no substitute for reading when it comes to preparing for formal learning, and it's never too soon (or too late) to start. Books open new worlds to children. And because the setting and characters must be created inside a child's mind, books also stimulate thinking and learning. (If you choose to read an ebook to your child, be sure to select those without animation or other distractions.) Books can also be an effective way to counter gender stereotypes and expectations, and to invite your child's own self-discovery.

Be sure to select books that are age-appropriate and that appeal to your child's special interests—your local librarian or bookseller can recommend age-appropriate books and series, and there are numerous websites (such as www.amightygirl.com and www.guysread.com) that offer book recommendations.

When you read, make the story come alive: change your voice to play different characters, and stop to talk about the story or the pictures. Adults usually tire of favorite books and stories long before children do, so patience is essential: preschoolers learn by repetition. They may memorize favorite books and want to "read" to you themselves, turning the pages at all the right spots. Children who grow up with books often develop a love of reading and learning that lasts a lifetime and sets the stage for success in school. Many families find that reading time is also time for snuggling and connection; it remains a favorite shared activity well into the elementary school years, long after children learn to read well themselves.

Incidentally, storytelling also is a wonderful way to stimulate learning. Sharing stories from your family's history or experiences you had when you were your child's age builds closeness and trust as well as encouraging listening and learning skills. Retelling a shared memory can also help a child to expand his memory of an event.

ENCOURAGE CURIOSITY, SAFE EXPLORATION, AND HANDS-ON LEARNING

Parents and caregivers can provide lots of safe opportunities to run, climb, jump, and explore. Honor your child's interests: young children rarely appreciate (or learn from) being forced into activities they do not like or that actually frighten them. It is not necessary to sign up children for organized activities; they can learn to paint, play baseball, sing, or plant a garden by working alongside welcoming adults.

Preschoolers usually want to *do* rather than just watch, so be prepared for a few messes along the way. Remember too that some children demonstrate curiosity and talents at this age that are very real and that will be important for the rest of their lives.

Providing reasonable opportunities for children to experiment with a variety of activities will help them to build a sense of self-esteem and self-confidence and to develop into healthy, actively engaged adults.

LIMIT SCREEN TIME

Walk into many homes today and you will notice that a variety of screens have become the center of family life, with daily activities often illuminated by their flickering blue light. Unfortunately, what we are learning about the impact of screen use on young children is not encouraging. We will explore the influence of electronic media in greater depth in Chapter 19. For now, be aware that it is best to limit screen time for young children, and to encourage active play and learning.

USE DISCIPLINE TO TEACH, NOT TO SHAME OR HUMILIATE

Remember, the synapses your child will keep are the ones that are used most often, and shame, punishment, and humiliation can shape the way a young child's brain is wired. This is just one of the many reasons we emphasize that the best sort of discipline is *teaching*. Isn't it good to know that your Positive Discipline skills are also encouraging healthy brain development?

RECOGNIZE AND ACCEPT YOUR CHILD'S UNIQUENESS

Young children learn about themselves and the world around them by watching and listening; what they decide about themselves (and about you) depends in large part on the messages they receive from parents and caregivers. Learning to accept your child for exactly who she is builds her sense of self-worth, supports healthy brain development, and encourages her to value her own special abilities. Having the courage to try new things is the best insurance policy for the challenges and pressures she will face as she grows into adolescence and adulthood.

PROVIDE LEARNING EXPERIENCES THAT USE THE SENSES

Young children experience the world through their senses, and those experiences help shape their developing brains. Offer your child lots of opportunities to see, hear, smell, touch, and taste his world—with your careful supervision, of course. Your child's senses will enrich her experience and increase her ability to learn.

SPEND TIME IN NATURE TO CONNECT WITH ONE ANOTHER AND THE NATURAL WORLD

Far too many children spend most of each day indoors or in cars on their way from one activity to the next. Research has demonstrated that spending time outdoors exploring, climbing, and, yes, getting dirty nurtures healthy brain development. (You can learn more about this in Chapter 20.)

PROVIDE TIME FOR YOUR CHILD'S LEARNING THROUGH PLAY

Play is the laboratory in which a preschooler experiences his world, experiments with new roles and ideas, and learns to feel comfortable in the world of movement and sensation. Children need unstructured time in which to exercise their imaginations and their bodies.

The best toys are often the simplest: a cardboard box, some art supplies, or old clothes and jewelry. Expect—in fact, encourage—messes; you can invite your child to help you clean up afterward, and that can be fun too. Provide the raw materials, then turn your child loose to play, learn, and develop new connections in his growing brain.

SELECT CHILDCARE CAREFULLY—AND STAY INVOLVED

Childcare is critically important. Many, many children spend all or part of each day in the care of someone other than their parents. It is crucial that childcare providers and teachers also know how young brains grow and that they do their best to foster healthy development. Leaving your child in another's care may be difficult, but perhaps it will be somewhat easier when you recognize that high-quality care can support a child's development. It also underscores how important it is to be sure that the care your child receives when he is away from you truly is *quality* care. (Chapter 16 will explain what constitutes quality care and how to find it.)

TAKE CARE OF YOURSELF

You may wonder what taking care of yourself has to do with your child's brain. But nurturing and guiding an energetic, curious preschooler is demanding work. Parents and caregivers need every ounce of energy and wisdom they possess, and all too often the well runs dry just when a crisis occurs.

You will do your best work as a parent when you are rested and reasonably content. Yes, weariness and stress seem to be an everyday part of life with young children, particularly if you also have a partner or job to deal with. Still, caring for your own needs must be a priority. Exercise, eat healthy foods, and do your best to get enough sleep. Take time on a regular basis (no, once a year isn't enough) to do things you enjoy. Spend time with your partner, have a cup of coffee with a friend, sing in a choir, take a class, read a book—anything you do to refill the well will benefit your children. They will learn respect for you (and for themselves) when they see you treating yourself with respect. And they will find a calm, rested, happy adult much easier to respond to than an exhausted, grumpy, resentful one.

Keeping yourself healthy isn't selfish; it's wisdom.

Off to School: "Is My Child Really Ready?"

Kate had sworn she wouldn't cry. She was going to celebrate with Sarah on the first day of kindergarten, and then go get the shopping done without any interruptions. Somehow, though, the morning didn't work out the way she'd planned.

Oh, Sarah was fine. A bit nervous, maybe, but excited and happy. She had dressed herself in her new outfit, combed her hair neatly, and had her "big kid" backpack ready to go. Kate and Sarah had visited the classroom the week before school began, explored the playground, and met the teacher, an energetic, friendly young woman who remembered everyone's name.

Everything was fine—until Kate watched Sarah, looking suddenly very small, filing into the classroom with the other children. As she turned to walk back to her car, Kate discovered that some sort of fog had descended on the neighborhood—she couldn't see a thing. She realized with a shock that she was crying. A dad walking nearby grinned at her. "Gets to you, doesn't it?" he said. "It certainly does," Kate sniffled.

A child's first day of "real" school is a landmark event. The world will never again consist just of a small circle of family and friends; it has suddenly expanded to include other adults and children who may spend more time each day with your youngster than you do. Many parents wonder how they will know if their children are ready—intellectually and emotionally—for the wider world of school.

It is important to recognize that all children (and all schools) are different. By the time a child is ready for school, parents have had years to get into that child's world and understand the way he thinks, feels, and sees the world. Most school systems group children by chronological age, but age is not a true indicator of a child's development. Many children are eager for school to begin, and they enter the world of academic learning with hardly a backward glance. Others hover at the fringes or seem to struggle with even the simplest tasks. Assessing learning disabilities or psychological problems is beyond the scope of this book, but there are things parents can consider that will help them feel comfortable sending their children to school.

Know Your Child

No one knows a child as well as an attentive, loving parent, especially one who has made the effort to understand development and acquire effective parenting skills. Most school districts offer readiness interviews to help parents and teachers decide if a child is ready to begin kindergarten or would benefit from waiting a year.

Remember Robbie? His mother eventually decided it was best for him to wait a year until his emotional development caught up with his intellectual development. School success involves more than just academic skills; children also must be able to tolerate time away from parents, respond to a teacher, manage their emotions, and make friends with other children. There is no disgrace in waiting to begin school; in fact, children do better with academic learning when they are emotionally and socially ready to be away from home. It is less upsetting for everyone to delay the start of school rather than to be held back later on.

Here are a few simple questions that may help you assess your child's readiness:

- Does your child enjoy learning? Is he curious about the world around him?
- Does your child tolerate separation from you reasonably well?
- Is she eager to make friends and open to peer relationships?
- Is he able to pay attention to a task for an age-appropriate length of time?
- Does she express interest in school or does she seem fearful?
- Is she able to express her emotions and calm herself down when necessary?

Taking time to visit the school and meet the teacher usually resolves most of a child's anxieties. It is also helpful to talk about feelings (more about feelings and active listening skills in Chapter 6) and to share with your child that most people are nervous when they do something new. The more tuned in you are, both to your child and to the teacher, the happier the school experience will be. You and your child may feel more comfortable if you can volunteer in the classroom occasionally and attend school events and parent-teacher conferences. School will be part of your lives for years to come; getting off to a good start is worth the effort it takes.

Learning Takes a Lifetime

It has been said that "learners inherit the earth" and "the truly educated never graduate." There is always something new and wonderful to learn, both for you and for your child. The outside world may not always be kind or welcoming, and as your child moves away from your side she will experience hurts and difficulties that you won't be there to smooth away. But you can assure her that you are always on her side, that you will always listen, and that you believe in her. Regardless of the new people and experiences she encounters, your child can trust that you will always have faith in her and will always welcome her home.

QUESTIONS TO PONDER

1. Think back to a time when you saw or heard someone responding to a situation and experienced a matching emotional response. This type of experience is your healthy mirror neurons at work. Now watch your child when she sees another child experiencing a strong emotion. What do you notice? What is her facial expression? How does she respond?

2. Can you remember a time you were punished, spanked, or humiliated as a child? What do you remember about that? What lessons did you learn from it? Do you remember why you were punished? What memories and messages do you want your child to recall?

3. Consider the elements of healthy brain development. Choose three things that you are already doing well. Now choose one thing you would like to improve upon. List three ways you can improve in this area.

PART TWO

Social Emotional Learning

CHAPTER 5

Empathy, Compassion, and the Growth of Social Emotional Learning

Many of the questions parents have about preschoolers involve feelings—and how to deal with them. After all, feelings can be such bewildering things, and preschoolers have so many of them! Take a moment sometime and watch as your child giggles delightedly with a friend; her joy radiates from her entire face and body. Watch also as she tries to deal with frustration or anger. She may throw a toy across the room, fall over backward in a tantrum, or collapse in a flood of tears. In fact, she may do all of the above within the span of a few minutes.

Truly empathizing and communicating with your child means deciphering her nonverbal cues, understanding what she is feeling, and helping her to recognize and name her feelings. It means teaching her that what she *feels* is always okay, but what she *does* may not be okay. In other words, it is okay to be angry at her baby brother, but it is not okay to hit him. Learning to recognize and deal with your child's feelings is a vitally important step in understanding her behavior and interpreting her beliefs about her world.

What Are Emotions?

Emotions give us important information. Paying careful attention to your feelings—and to your thoughts—can help you decide what to do. Young children experience the same emotions their parents and teachers do. There is one significant difference, however. As you learned in Chapter 4, the prefrontal cortex (which is responsible for emotional regulation) does not fully develop until the age of twenty-five. The ability to identify and manage feelings is a skill that will take your child many years to learn; as in so many other areas of parenting, she will need your patience, understanding, and kind, firm teaching.

Just as they learn other things in life, children learn to cope with their feelings by watching adults. (Remember, you and your child both have mirror neurons, which makes it easy for you to "catch" each other's feelings.) All too often, parents are unable to deal effectively with difficult feelings, so it shouldn't surprise anyone that young children struggle as well.

Social Emotional Learning

A guiding principle in Positive Discipline is that discipline is *teaching*, not punishment. In the preschool years, bodies grow and change, as does the less visible social and emotional life of a child. Research tells us that physical and emotional growth are intertwined. The brain encodes and organizes sensory experience, the wealth of information constantly gathered from a child's eyes, ears, fingers, and body.

At first, there are no words to label what is experienced nor is the brain developed sufficiently to sort sensory input into retrievable memories. (Explicit or narrative memory, which records our experiences and activities so we can remember them, is believed to develop when a child is around two and a half years old.) Instead, early sensory experiences enter the cerebellum in a generalized fashion and are accessed at an emotional level. Eventually, a child begins to learn empathy and compassion, foundational skills for social emotional learning based, in part, on those early experiences.

Just as bodies need nutrients, exercise, and physical practice to strengthen and grow, brains need experiences to shape emotional skills. The experience of comfort, connection, and loving touch turns into the ability to connect with others and to touch lovingly.

Empathy

Like a seed, empathy grows and thrives—or shrivels and fails to develop—based upon a child's environment. The child who has his needs met, is responded to consistently, and feels loving touch will internalize those experiences, preparing him to replicate them. He will grow up feeling secure, safe, and valued. This foundation—a sense of belonging and significance—develops a child's natural tendency to feel empathy. *Empathy is defined as the ability to share in another's emotions, thoughts, or feelings.* Mirror neurons make this sharing possible, but experiences provide the environment necessary for its development.

What if a young child grows up with trauma, stress, or a lack of nurturing care? Fortunately, support can be found in a variety of settings, including extended family, preschool teachers, and other caring adults. Even severe stress can be mitigated by responsive and nurturing care. Regardless of who provides them, nurturing early life experiences help to develop a child's natural empathy.

Teaching Children the Difference Between Feelings and Actions

Throughout life, feelings play a powerful role in human behavior. They tell us whether we are safe or if there is danger present. They give us information that allows us to respond in appropriate ways. But feelings can be tricky to manage.

When a young child becomes angry and acts in hurtful ways, perhaps throwing toys or hitting others, adults may be tempted to lump his feeling and his actions together and call it simply "misbehavior." But there is an important difference.

It is vital to healthy development to teach children that their feelings are always *valid, but that some actions may not be acceptable.*

Children need to learn to recognize and name their emotions and understand that feeling and actions are different. When even uncomfortable feelings are validated, a child will learn self-acceptance, how to manage difficult emotions, and how to behave in more appropriate ways—with time and practice, of course. Self-awareness is the foundation of empathy.

Jenna sighs and takes a moment to calm herself down as four-year-old Kaitlyn stomps her foot, throws a block across the carpet, and declares, "I want to finish building my tower!"

Jenna summons a reassuring smile. "You feel disappointed that it's time for bed and you wish you could play longer. It's hard to stop doing something you are enjoying so much. It's okay to feel disappointed, sweetie, but it is not okay to throw your toys."

Kaitlyn's chin trembles as she senses her mom's empathy. She says, "It's not fair." But she is already heading down the hall to begin her bedtime routine.

Jenna follows her daughter. "What books will you choose to read tonight, Kaitlyn?" she asks. "I always look forward to our story time and snuggles."

Children must learn to identify and accept their own feelings before they can empathize with and accept the feelings of others. For a preschooler, this requires patient teaching—and lots of practice. Positive Discipline tools are helpful with this process, especially cool-offs (or positive time-out—more about this later) and curiosity questions as a means of getting into a child's world. A child needs tools to address feelings, or else chaos results. And chaos is scary.

Children often are hurtful because they are "acting out" their feelings of frustration and anger. After all, there are so many people who get in the way of a child's impulses and urges. Children need repeated support to distinguish the difference between a feeling and an action.

Three-year-old Jack was on a rampage. He had been hitting the other children at the preschool, grabbing their toys, and kicking gravel on the playground. One afternoon, Jack got angry when another child ran in front of him. He pushed her down, causing her to scrape her knee.

While her assistant helped the injured child, Miss Terry, Jack's teacher, gently led the raging Jack away from the other children and toward the book corner. As Jack calmed down, Miss Terry brought him a book that had a picture of a sad-looking boy on the cover.

"Why does he look like that?" Jack asked Miss Terry.

"Well," his teacher replied, sitting down to look at the picture, "he looks sad to me. Why do you think he might be sad?"

This question planted that first small seed of empathy, inviting Jack to experience the world through another person's perspective. Jack began to explain that the boy in the picture was sad because his favorite babysitter had gone away and he wasn't going to see her anymore—attributing his own feelings to the child in the picture. Understanding this, Miss Terry asked Jack if he would like a hug, and he scrambled gratefully onto her lap. "That little boy must feel very lonely and sad," she said. Jack began to cry in his teacher's arms.

When Jack's sobs had slowed to sniffles, Miss Terry asked if he could think of a way to help the child he had pushed feel better again. "I bet she's sad too," Jack said. "Maybe I could play a special game with her and help her put away her lunch stuff."

Miss Terry wrote a note to Jack's parents explaining what had happened and mentioning Jack's sadness over the loss of his babysitter. Jack helped by making a mark at the bottom to serve as his signature.

Jack had an opportunity to explore his feelings in safety. He also learned that he was responsible for his behavior toward other children. Identifying and accepting feelings encourages empathy.

Many adults also struggle with acknowledging and expressing their feelings appropriately. It often seems easier (or more "polite") to simply repress feelings, although those feelings often leak out in the form of resentment or depression. This mistaken pattern of denying feelings may be passed on to children. Consider this familiar exchange: An angry child says, "I hate my brother!" An adult responds, "No, you don't. You know you love your brother." It would be more helpful to say to the child, "I can see how angry and hurt you feel right now. I can't let you kick your brother, but maybe we can find a way to help you express your feelings in a way that doesn't hurt anyone."

What Is This Feeling?

Feelings are expressed by bodies and faces. When a child recognizes that hot, stinging eyes signal sadness, she can learn to recognize that feeling in the scrunched face of another. It is impossible to relate to and make sense of someone else's emotions if you are overwhelmed by your own. Empathy grows when a child understands that others share the same feelings he does. Recognizing physical sensations will help; so will learning words to describe those feelings.

Practicing Emotional Honesty

Parents (and teachers) often wonder how much of their own feelings they should share with children. As with so many things in life, children learn best by watching their adult role models. The way you manage (or fail to manage) your own emotions sends a strong message to your child. If you deal with anger by yelling, you shouldn't be surprised if the young ones in your life do too. If, on the other hand, you can find helpful ways of expressing your own feelings, you will reduce the chance of conflict and provide children with a wonderful example of how to deal appropriately with emotions.

In the course of a single day, a parent or teacher can feel love, warmth, frustration, anger, irritation, weariness, hope, and despair. Children are amazingly sensitive to the emotional state of those around them; their mirror neurons and ability to read nonverbal cues often let them know what you're feeling even when you think you're acting "normal." So, how should adults explain and express their feelings to children?

Emotional honesty is often the best policy. It is not only okay but also may be real wisdom to tell a child, calmly and respectfully, "I'm feeling really angry right now." Notice the word "you" is missing from this statement. This is very different from saying "You make me so angry." Blaming or shaming statements aren't necessary; simply explaining to your child what you're feeling and why can help you deal with your own feelings and teach your child about possible results of his own behavior. Remember too that young children are egocentric at this age and often assume that whatever you're feeling is about them. Explaining your feelings and the reasons for them may save you and your child a great deal of misunderstanding and confusion.

One helpful way of expressing feelings is by using "I statements." An "I statement" is a simple formula (formulas come in handy when you're too emotional to think straight) that allows you to explain what you're feeling and why.

An "I statement" might look something like this:

- "I feel worried when blocks are thrown in the playroom because one of the other children might get hurt. Would it help you to take a cool-off until you have calmed down, or do you have another solution to solve this problem?"
- "I feel angry when cereal is dumped on the floor because I'm tired and I don't want to clean up the mess. If cereal is dumped on the floor again, I'll know you've decided not to eat and you can either put away your bowl or I will do so for you."
- "I feel upset and frustrated because the car has a flat tire and now I'm going to be late to work."
- "I'm so angry right now that I need a time-out until I can calm down, so I don't do or say something I'll regret later."

Should I Protect My Child from Sadness or Worry?

Adults sometimes feel the need to shield children from sadness, loss, and the other unpleasant realities of life, but it is usually best to be as honest with your child as you reasonably can be. Children usually know when something in the family is amiss, and without enough information, they may assume they have done something wrong. Children shouldn't be asked to shoulder burdens too heavy for them or to take responsibility for their parents' problems, but they can be given an opportunity to understand and share in whatever is going on. (This further encourages the growth of empathy and compassion.)

If a family member or loved pet has died, it is best to provide a child with information that will help him make sense of what has happened. It is tempting to tell a young child that Grandpa is "sleeping" or has "gone away," but that may lead a child to fear going to bed or to wonder whether Mom or Dad will also "go away" unexpectedly. Death can be explained in simple but honest terms and children can be helped to grieve and to heal. (Yes, children grieve, although their grief sometimes resembles irritability rather than sadness.) It isn't necessary to tell children more than they can comprehend. You may want to explain that many adults also have difficulty understanding death, and many people have different beliefs about what it means and what happens afterward. Including children in the rituals surrounding death, such as funerals, may actually be less frightening for them than being left out. Death is part of the cycle of life; treating it as such will make coping with death easier for parents and children alike.

In the same way, if the family is undergoing financial strain or other stresses, parents can give children simple facts to help them understand and then use active listening to explore and deal with their feelings. Be aware that children will have strong feelings and reactions to traumatic events in the family, such as divorce, and it is unwise to simply assume that they'll be fine. Take time to explain, without blaming or judging, what has happened and how it will affect your child. Be sure she knows that it wasn't her fault and that she is loved and cherished. And stay tuned in; use active listening to check your child's perceptions and allow her to express her fears and feelings openly.[1]

By including young children in the life of the family, parents help them learn about feelings and deepen their ability to feel empathy. By exploring and respecting your children's feelings and by being honest about your own feelings, you will build a relationship of trust and connection, along with problem-solving skills that will last a lifetime.

From Me to Others

Books can be excellent tools for developing empathy. When you're reading with your child, pay attention to the feelings expressed by the characters in the story: "Little Bear looks pretty angry to me. What do you think?"

You might want to offer some clues: "Do you think Little Bear feels angry or surprised? How would you feel?"

You can also invite a child to empathize: "How do you think Little Bear feels right now? Do you remember a time you felt that way too?"

When a child understands that others have the same feelings he has, he will also begin to realize that the same things that help him feel better can help others as well.

Contribution (Altruism)

Researchers have demonstrated that children have an innate desire to help others. Tomasello and Warneken conducted experiments with toddlers that are adorable to watch.[2] An eighteen-month-old child is brought into a room with his mother (who is purposely passive). The child watches a researcher trying to put books into a bookcase with the door closed. The researcher keeps bumping the books into the closed door. After watching for a few seconds, the child walks over to the bookcase and opens the door, and then looks expectantly at the researcher to see if he understands that he can now put the books in the bookcase. In another experiment, the child observes the researcher pinning towels on a clothesline. The researcher drops the clothespin and attempts unsuccessfully to reach for it. The child crawls over to the clothespin, picks it up, and struggles to stand up so he can hand it to the researcher, and then displays satisfaction that he was able to help.

The implications are so important for parents and teachers to understand. When adults do too much for children, this innate desire to contribute and feel capable can be replaced by feelings of inadequacy and a desire to be taken care of. Have faith in your children, fostering their early altruism by involving them in helping as much as you can.

Empathy in Action

The Zhou family is enjoying a vacation with relatives in another state. After a busy day at the zoo followed by pizza with her cousins and several bedtime stories, something seems off for five-year-old Ting Ting. Although she had lots of fun, she seems to be feeling sad—even with Mom and Dad right there.

Dad gets down on Ting Ting's level and gazes into her eyes. "I know you enjoyed today, but right now you look like something is bothering you. What are you feeling?"

The Zhou family has been working on feelings and empathy for quite some time, so Ting Ting takes a moment to think it over.

"I feel sad," she says.

Dad smiles. "Tell me more about that."

"I miss our dog, Oggie-Oh," Ting Ting responds.

"That is sad. I bet Oggie-Oh misses you too," he says. "What can you do so you feel better?" By saying this, Dad validates the feeling and helps his daughter find ways to feel better.

Ting Ting thinks for a moment, then smiles. "I can talk about Oggie-Oh."

"That is a good plan. Let's think of some fun things Oggie-Oh might have done today."

Ting Ting is learning self-awareness and self-management as she tunes in to her feelings and tries out ways to respond to them. Now she can begin to move this skill outward.

Social Interest: The Link

Alfred Adler described "social interest" as a real concern for others and a sincere desire to make a contribution to society. As children enter into the lives of their families and schools, they want very much to feel that they belong. And one of the most powerful ways to achieve a sense of belonging is to make a meaningful contribution to the well-being of others in the family or group. When adults can help preschoolers care about and participate in their community—to feel and demonstrate compassion—everyone benefits. Adults can use everyday tasks as opportunities to teach social interest.

> While Charlene fixed the hamburger patties, three-year-old Sean happily unwrapped cheese slices and placed them on the buns. When the family sat down to dinner, imagine how pleased Sean felt when the family mentioned how good their cheeseburgers tasted, thanks to Sean's efforts.

> Five-year-old Becky reminded her grandma to use her eye drops every evening during her visit. When Grandma returned home, Becky wanted to call her every night so she could continue to remind her.

Social interest is meaningful involvement that benefits others. It provides a link between empathy and compassion.

Seeds of Compassion

Empathy puts us in touch with our emotions and grows to include others. Compassion moves from merely understanding and identifying with another's distress to wanting to do something to alleviate that distress, enabled by experiences of social interest. Children are very quick to offer help, hugs, and encouragement to others.

Compassion grows and develops in the rich soil of:
- Nurturing and loving experiences
- Recognizing and naming feelings

- Identifying appropriate responses to feelings
- Recognizing and relating to those same feelings in others
- Experiencing social interest and making a contribution
- Understanding that what helps you feel better may help someone else feel better as well

Parents (and teachers) can provide children with opportunities for social interest while encouraging the development of compassion too.

When shopping at the grocery store, Paul has the task of choosing two kinds of cereal to bring to the local food bank. Paul and his dad talk about how good it feels to eat cereal when they are hungry and how some people are hungry but don't have enough to eat. When they have a bag filled with cereal boxes, Paul helps load the bag into the car and they drive to the food bank, where he helps carry the bags inside. "These are for hungry people," Paul says as he hands them to the workers.

Each spring, Sunaya goes through her toy box with her mother's help to select toys to give to children who don't have many toys to play with. This is part of their Nowruz (Persian New Year) celebration, and Sunaya enjoys talking about how another child will have fun with each toy they select.

Part of the Ong family's tradition at Thanksgiving is to bake cookies for the people at an immigration resource center in their neighborhood. Susie loves to help shape, bake, and sample all the cookies. She knows that families new to their community will come to the center for help in adjusting to their new lives. The cookies are welcomed, and will comfort the bodies and spirits of these displaced families.

Whenever possible, you can provide opportunities to help that are personalized. Helping someone at the food bank choose a box of cereal, selecting a doll that has been requested by a child from the school's giving tree, or meeting and talking with the families at the immigration center while handing out cookies personalizes compassion. *All people—including preschoolers—react more compassionately toward a person or situation they have actually experienced than they do toward a generalized or vague one.*

The Empowerment of Helping

Children can learn and demonstrate compassion even when natural disasters and challenging circumstances intrude, bringing feelings of helplessness and chaos. Rather than being overwhelmed, even preschoolers can experience compassion and find ways to express it.

When an emergency occurs nearby, such as a flood, the teachers at Pinetree Childcare Center talk about what the affected children might need most. The children talk about what being wet would feel like and how cold it would be. They decide to help by collecting children's jackets to send to the affected families.

All week the children bring in outgrown or newly purchased jackets. They help bake cupcakes to sell to their parents; the money collected will pay for shipping the jackets. Both activities give the children opportunities to contribute to the well-being of others and to feel helpful in a situation that might otherwise foster feelings of helplessness.

There are many more ways to give children opportunities to contribute to those around them, enhancing both social awareness and responsible decision-making. Empathy and compassion are not likely to happen unless adults value and make time for this growth, incorporating critical social emotional learning opportunities both at home and in childcare settings. What contributions will your child and his generation make to the world around them?

1. Think of a strong feeling your child experiences. Consider ways you can name and validate that feeling, and work with your child to discover ways to feel better.

2. Choose a book at the library or bookstore that shows characters experiencing different emotions. Read it with your child (or class) and talk about the characters' feelings. Name the feelings. Discuss how the character does or could respond to his feelings.

3. If your child is an older preschooler, think of one activity you could do together to give her an opportunity to practice compassion (to identify with and alleviate another's suffering). How can you introduce this experience? When could you try it? What additional discussion would expand and enhance the experience?

CHAPTER 6

Recognizing, Naming, and Managing Emotions

Adults and children express emotional energy (and energy speaks louder than words) on their faces, in their voices, and in the way they move or stand. Because preschoolers are still developing their language skills, they trust the message of this nonverbal communication far more than they do mere words.

Three-year-old Kyle scampers into the kitchen where Linda, his mother, late for a meeting, is preparing dinner.

"Look, Mommy, look—I drew an airplane!" Kyle bubbles, waving his paper excitedly.

"That's great, sweetie. You're quite an artist," his harried mother replies without glancing up.

Linda undoubtedly means well, and there is certainly nothing wrong with her words. Still, Kyle notices that her hands never stop grating cheese for the casserole and her eyes never quite look at his airplane.

Five-year-old Wendy is helping her dad make lunch. Wendy's little brother is cranky, and Dad is trying to watch the football game on television while he makes the grilled cheese sandwiches. Wendy is valiantly pouring milk when the heavy carton slips from her grasp, sending a half gallon of foamy liquid across the kitchen floor.

Wendy looks up timidly into her father's face. "I'm sorry, Daddy," she says. "Are you mad?"

Dad's eyebrows lower ominously, his jaw tightens, and when he speaks his voice is thin and tense. "No, I'm not mad," he says. When Wendy bursts into tears, he wonders why.

Ms. Santos is reading a naptime story to her class of four-year-olds. She hasn't had a break because her replacement didn't show up and no substitute teacher is available. Little Allie looks at her teacher and asks, "Don't you like this story?" Ms. Santos looks at Allie in surprise and answers, "Of course I do. Why?"

Allie answers, "Because your face is all scrunched up."

What messages do you think these children received?

The Power of Nonverbal Communication

You will be more effective at connecting with your child if you are aware of the messages you are sending him—and whether your words and your actions agree. For instance, saying "I love you" may not be the most effective way to communicate that message to your child. Saying the words often (and meaning them) is important, but words alone won't communicate this vital message to your young child.

THE ELEMENTS OF NONVERBAL COMMUNICATION

- Eye contact
- Posture and position
- Tone of voice
- Facial expressions and touch

EYE CONTACT

Try an experiment sometime. Stand back-to-back with someone and try to tell him or her about something that happened to you or explain how you're feeling. If you're like most people, you'll find yourself wanting to crane your neck and turn around to look your partner in the eye.

In most Western cultures, eye contact signals attention. A good public speaker will catch the gaze of audience members and by doing so will involve them in what he or she is saying. In the same way, making eye contact with your child signals to him that he is important, captures his attention, and increases the effectiveness of your message.

Toni Morrison once asked a poignant question on an *Oprah* show: Do your eyes light up when your child walks into the room?

Unfortunately, parents often reserve eye contact primarily for certain occasions. Can you guess what those are? If you are like most adults, you tend to make direct eye contact with your child most often when you are angry or lecturing her, saving your most powerful communication for your most negative messages.

It is important to recognize that in some cultures, making direct eye contact is regarded as a sign of disrespect. One teacher thought a child was being "sneaky" by avoiding eye contact but changed her mind once she understood the respect this young child's lack of eye contact conveyed in his native culture. Her attitude shifted and she communicated far more effectively with this child and his family throughout the rest of the year.

POSTURE AND POSITION

Making eye contact with your child may not be as simple as it sounds. Without help, your child will tend to look you right in the knees! If you want to communicate, get down on his level. Kneel next to him, sit beside him on the sofa, or (as long as you hold on to him) set him on a counter where his eyes can meet yours comfortably. Now, not only can you maintain eye contact while you speak to him, but you've eliminated the sometimes overpowering difference in size and height. Be aware of the signals your posture sends: crossed arms or legs, for example, can indicate resistance or hostility. Your child will be quick to notice.

Susan was trying to coax her daughter, Michele, into sharing what was upsetting her.

"Come on, honey," Susan said gently, "I really want to help."

Michele hesitated, then said, "But you might get mad at me."

Susan smiled encouragingly and replied, "Michele, I promise I won't get mad. I care about you, and I want you to be able to tell me anything."

Michele thought for a moment, then looked up into her mother's face. "I'll tell you if you promise not to look at me with your lips all tight."

Poor Susan—she was trying hard to be unconditionally accepting and loving. Her daughter, however, was able to read the body language that betrayed her true feelings. When Susan's words and her expression match consistently, Michele will feel more comfortable talking honestly with her mother.

TONE OF VOICE

Your tone of voice may be the most powerful nonverbal tool of all. Try saying a simple sentence, such as "I can't help you," emphasizing a different word each time. How does the meaning change? Even inoffensive phrases like "Have a nice day" can become poisonous if you choose a particularly cold tone of voice. It is often the way you say something, rather than the words you use, that carries the message. Remember, children are especially sensitive to the nuances of nonverbal communication.

FACIAL EXPRESSIONS AND TOUCH

When you're feeling particularly blue, does it help when a friend smiles and gives you a pat on the shoulder or a friendly hug? The way you look at your child and the way you use your hands can communicate very effectively without a single word being spoken.

> Tommy is curled up on the couch under a blanket, suffering from a bad case of the flu. Dad walks by, adjusts the blanket, and gently ruffles Tommy's hair.

Has anything been communicated? Chances are Tommy knows without words that his dad cares about him, wants to help, and hopes he'll soon feel better.

Think about all the aspects of nonverbal communication. How might you say "I love you" to your child now? Imagine how powerful it will feel if you kneel in front of him, look him directly in the eye, smile, and in your warmest tone of voice say, "I love you." Now the words and nonverbal cues match up—and a big hug may be on the way! Nonverbal communication teaches children about connection, feelings, and, eventually, the words that go with them.

Validate Feelings

Validating feelings requires active (or reflective) listening. This is an effective tool of communication that will serve you well as you parent your child and (sooner than you may think) the adolescent that child will become. Active listening is the art of observing and listening to feelings and nonverbal messages, then validating them. Validating does not require that you *agree* with your child's feelings, but it allows your child to feel connected and understood—something all people need— and provides an opportunity to explore and clarify those mysterious impulses known as emotions.

> Four-year-old Chrissy ran through the front door, slamming it so forcefully that the pictures rattled on the wall, and promptly burst

into tears. "Tammy took my ball," she wailed. "I hate her!" Then Chrissy threw herself onto the sofa in a storm of tears.

Her mom, Diane, looked up from the bills she was paying. Resisting the impulse to scold Chrissy for slamming the door, she said quietly, "You seem pretty angry, kiddo."

Chrissy pondered for a moment. "Mom," she said plaintively, sniffling a little, "Tammy is bigger than me. It isn't fair for her to take away my stuff."

"It must be pretty frustrating to be picked on by a big girl," Diane said, still focusing on reflecting and validating her daughter's feelings.

"Yeah. I'm mad," the little girl said firmly. "I don't want to play with her anymore." She sat quietly for a moment, watching as Diane put stamps on envelopes. "Mom, can I go play out in the backyard?"

Diane gave her daughter a hug—and a great deal more.

By simply reflecting back her daughter's underlying feelings and validating them, Diane refrained from lecturing, rescuing, or discounting those feelings. She allowed Chrissy the opportunity to explore what was going on for her, and in the process, to discover a solution to her own problem. Later on, Diane might be able to engage in some problem-solving with Chrissy about avoiding future problems—and, perhaps, ask her what she could do to express her anger instead of slam the door.

Diane also showed respect for her daughter's feelings. Parents often do not agree with (or completely understand) their children's emotions, but active listening does not require you to agree or completely understand. It invites children to feel heard and lets them know it's okay to feel whatever they feel. Validating a child's feelings with love and understanding opens the door for real connection and problem-solving and works toward building a lifelong relationship of love and trust. It also nurtures a child's developing sense of empathy and compassion.

Pretend these statements are made by a child. How would you validate feelings and convey empathy?

- "No! I won't take a nap!"
- "I want a bottle like the baby has."
- "I hate going to the doctor."
- "Nobody will let me play with them."

Parents often try to argue a child out of her feelings in hopes of changing her mind or helping her "feel better." These attempts may sound like this:

- "Of course you need your nap—you've been up since six. I know how tired you are."
- "Don't be silly. Only babies use bottles. You're a big boy now."
- "I keep telling you, you have to go to the doctor to feel better."
- "Why, sweetie, you know you have lots of friends. What about . . ."

Each of these examples may leave the child feeling misunderstood and defensive.

Active listening that demonstrates empathy might sound like this:

- "You look disappointed that you have to stop playing with your toys. You were having a lot of fun."
- "Sounds like you're feeling left out in all the fuss over your new baby sister. Is there more you can tell me?"
- "Sometimes I feel a little afraid of going to the doctor too."
- "You seem pretty sad about being ignored by the older kids."

These responses make no judgments and open the door for children to go further in exploring their feelings. Asking "Is there more?" indicates a willingness to listen and may help a child discover deeper, buried feelings.

What About Anger?

Like adults, children feel angry and frustrated from time to time. After all, there is so much that a young child cannot understand or do. Unfortunately, young children do not yet have the skills or maturity to express anger and frustration in ways that are acceptable to adults—which is why angry children are usually viewed as misbehaving children. Adults and children alike need to find acceptable, positive ways of dealing with feelings—even the difficult ones.

When you become angry, an interesting thing happens in your brain. The prefrontal cortex—the part responsible for emotional regulation, impulse control, and good judgment—essentially "disconnects," leaving you with physical sensations and feelings. (This is commonly known as "losing it," something all parents experience eventually!) Remember, mirror neurons make it easy to catch strong emotions; when you lose it your child is likely to do the same—and vice versa. It is impossible to solve problems effectively without the use of your connected prefrontal cortex, which is why it is so important to take a positive time-out to cool off *before* attempting to deal with problems.

When a child becomes angry, adults usually call it a "tantrum." Instead, offer a hug or a positive time-out (and keep in mind that a young child simply can't deal with strong emotions in a mature manner yet). Sometimes it is most helpful to simply allow a child to feel angry (without rescuing her or trying to "fix" her feelings). Her anger will eventually dissipate and she has learned a lesson in resilience in the process. When adults jump in to rescue children or punish them for their anger, they miss this opportunity to allow their children to experience their own capability. Later you can follow up with curiosity questions to help your child understand her feelings and figure out solutions.

Positive Time-Out: The Fine Art of Cooling Off

You may wonder where the common parenting tool time-out fits in the Positive Discipline approach. Most parents use it (in one study, 91 percent of parents of three-year-old children admitted to doing so), but few really understand what it is or how best to use it with young children.

Positive time-out can be an extremely effective way of helping a child (and a parent) calm down without feeling shame or pain by allowing time for self-regulation. Punitive time-out is past-oriented, making children suffer for what they have done. Positive time-out allows for cooling off until both of you can access the rational part of your brain, and it is future-oriented because when children feel encouraged, they can learn to make positive decisions about self-control and responsibility.

It may be helpful to rename these time-outs, taking away the implication of punishment or restriction. Let your child decide what to call her positive time-out. She may decide on "cool-off," or "feel-good place," or even "my comfy fort."[1] You can invite your child to help you create a positive time-out area, supplying this special spot with items that help your child soothe himself (soft or squeezable toys, a favorite blanket, etc.). It is best not to allow screens.

Some parents and teachers believe that making a time-out area inviting and pleasant rewards children for misbehavior. Wise adults realize that all people have moments when they are too upset to get along, and a few moments of positive time-out (when it's not shaming or punishing) provides a cooling-off period.

One childcare center used the "cooling-off" image literally. The children helped to set up a corner of the classroom with pillows and cuddly toys and named it "Antarctica." Any child could choose to go to Antarctica to cool off when she needed to. The whimsy of this space appealed to the children, taking away negative connotations and allowing cooling off to become a positive life skill. (Wouldn't it be great if adults had a handy Antarctica too?) Make sure children know they're welcome to return from their cooling-off period when they are ready.

Here are several essential points to consider regarding cool-offs for young children:

- **Time-outs should not be used with children under the age of three or four.** Until children reach the age of reason, which starts around age three (and is an ongoing process that even some adults have not fully mastered), supervision and distraction are the most effective parenting tools.

- **Do not "send" children to their positive time-out area; allow them to "choose" it.** When your child is feeling discouraged (misbehaving), you can ask, "Would it help you to go to your feel-good place?" If your child refuses, ask if she would like you to go with her. (Remember, the purpose is to help her feel better.) If she still refuses, go yourself, to model calming down until you feel better.

- **Positive time-out is most effective when it is offered as one of several choices.** Ask, "Would it help you to go to the comfy area or for us to do some deep breathing together?" When children don't have a choice, even positive time-out can turn into a power struggle, with an adult trying to make a resistant child stay in an area that feels like punishment to him, no matter what the adult calls it.

- **Children do better when they feel better.** Strong emotions can feel overwhelming to a young child. Positive time-out gives them an opportunity to calm down and catch their breath, so they are able to work with you to solve the problem. Remember, the purpose is for both of you to feel better so you can choose better behavior—eventually.

- **No parenting tool works all of the time.** Be sure to have more than just time-out in your toolbox. There is never one tool—or three, or even ten—that is effective for every situation and for every child. Filling your parenting toolbox with effective, non-punitive alternatives will help you avoid the temptation to punish when your child challenges you—and he undoubtedly will.

- **Always remember your child's development and capabilities.** Understanding what is (and is not) age-appropriate behavior will help you not to expect things that are beyond the ability of your child.

Time-out can be an effective and appropriate parenting tool when it is used to teach, encourage, and soothe.[2]

The Importance of Emotional Literacy

Michael Thompson, Dan Kindlon, William Pollock, and other researchers have discovered that while no child is born with an "emotional vocabulary," it may be even more important for parents to use words that describe emotions with their sons. Boys often develop emotional skills more slowly than do girls; in addition, Western cultures often label feelings such as fear, sadness, or loneliness as "weak" and encourage boys to suppress them, sometimes leaving no emotional alternative but anger. Using simple, accurate language to reflect and describe emotions teaches your child to identify what he feels, and it enables him—with time and practice—to use words rather than behavior to express them.

HOW TO HELP A CHILD RECOGNIZE AND MANAGE FEELINGS

Here are some ways you might help a young child explore and express strong emotions.

- Invite the child to draw a picture of how the emotion feels to him. Does it have a color? A sound?
- Ask the child to talk through rather than act out what she is feeling. Because most children are not consciously aware of their feelings and may lack words to describe them accurately, you might try asking simple yes-or-no questions about the feelings: "Sounds like you might be feeling hurt and want to get even." "Are you having a hard time holding your anger inside?" When you are correct in guessing her feelings, your child will feel validated and relieved at being understood.
- Ask the child what she notices happening in her body when she gets really angry. Because anger triggers physical reactions (adrenaline is released, heart rate and respiration increase, blood vessels expand, and so on), most people actually feel anger *physically*. If your child reports that her fists clench, or she feels a knot in her stomach, or her face feels hot (all common responses), you can work together to

help her recognize when she's getting really angry and provide ways to cool off before anger gets out of control. (Adults too can benefit from paying attention to their body's cues.)

• Keep a Feeling Faces chart handy and refer to it with the child, asking, "Does one of these faces show how you feel?"[3] This is especially helpful in caregiving settings, where it can serve as a learning tool for all the children.

• Provide an acceptable way to deal with anger. You may help your child express her feelings physically by running around the yard, punching a "bop bag," or even pretending to be a ferocious dinosaur. (Stay nearby to talk through those strong feelings as your child expresses them.) Some preschools have an "anger box," a knee-high cardboard box where an angry child can go to stand, jump, or yell when upset. (Sometimes the teachers use it too.)

• Teach a slow-breathing technique. One of the handiest tools of all is slow, focused breathing, something a child (or adult) can do anytime and anywhere. Practice breathing in and out while you count slowly to four on each inhale and each exhale. Do this for several breaths. A younger preschooler can learn to breathe in as if she's sniffing flowers and breathe out as if she's blowing out birthday candles. An older child can learn to take his pulse and discover how slow breathing actually slows his heartbeat too. What an exciting and empowering discovery!

• Use books and pictures to initiate discussions about anger and other emotions. Two excellent books on anger and emotions are *Sometimes I'm Bombaloo* by Rachel Vail (New York: Scholastic, 2002) and *The Way I Feel* by Janan Cain (Seattle: Parenting Press, 2000). Pictures of people displaying different feelings are helpful because they teach children to recognize facial and body language cues (which help in the development of empathy) as well as to name those feelings. (This technique is best when you and your child are calm and can talk together about what you learn.)

• Help your child create an anger Wheel of Choice. Then he can choose something from the wheel that he feels would help him express his anger in a nondestructive manner. Use any of the ideas listed here and add your own. (One word of caution: Be sure all the choices on your anger wheel are acceptable to you.) Here is a sample anger wheel.[4]

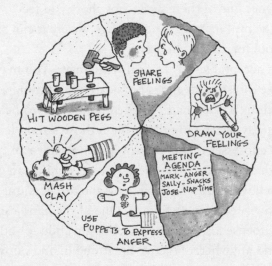

- Let your child have the last word. It isn't helpful to try to talk a child out of her feelings or to try to fix things for her. Have faith in your child; let her feelings run their course and, when she is calm, focus on teaching skills so she can look for solutions to her problems. Your silence provides a means to end the discussion and keep it from escalating, and it models self-control.

Conflicts have a way of escalating quickly when many small children are involved. Teachers may find it helpful to practice ways of defusing anger or to allow groups of children to play "Let's Pretend" about what happens when they feel angry. Talking in advance about emotions and actively teaching skills to manage them can give everyone, children and teachers alike, a plan to follow when strong feelings erupt. A classroom anger Wheel of Choice (see illustration) is a helpful tool to model and discuss appropriate behaviors and to provide ideas for coping with this strong emotion.

Anger isn't the only difficult emotion young children must learn to deal with. By practicing active listening, validating feelings, taking time to understand, and using some of the ideas above, adults can also help children develop self-awareness and deal honestly with their feelings.

Connection Before Correction

Parents and teachers can also practice separating a child from his behavior. You can reassure your child about his place in your affections and encourage his efforts to understand his world, while still teaching him that certain behaviors or actions are not acceptable. We call this "connection before correction." For example:

- "I love you, and I can't allow you to kick me when you're angry."
- "I'm glad you want to learn about the kitchen, and you can't melt your crayons on the stove."
- "I appreciate your help, and you're not quite old enough to fix the vacuum cleaner."

Action is a more effective teaching tool with young children than words. If your child is at risk of injury or harm, act first—with kindness and firmness—and talk later.

The Time You Spend

Another way in which parents communicate love and caring is by how they spend their time. Your child needs to know that you consider her important enough to spend time with—and it doesn't take large doses of time to do this. Spending regular, focused one-on-one time with a child, something we call "special time," is one of the most important things you can do for your child.

If you're fortunate enough to be the parent of a young child, you have a golden opportunity. The best time to begin building a relationship of trust and openness isn't after your child has become an adolescent and you suddenly realize how serious the issues are; the time is *now*, while he's young. Time spent talking to your child, listening to his daydreams and thoughts and feelings, teaching him about life, and simply being human together is an investment in the future you will never regret.

If you are a preschool teacher, remember that the time your young students spend with you shapes the way they view their world—you truly do touch the future when you teach young children. For parents and teachers alike, taking the time to understand emotions and to express them in positive ways will help you build relationships where love and trust can flourish.

QUESTIONS TO PONDER

1. Notice what happens when you talk to your child. Ask yourself these questions:
    - Am I on his level?
    - Do I make eye contact?
    - In what way have I engaged his attention before speaking?

2. Without trying to fix or change your child's emotions, reflect back what she may be feeling.

    Tip: Imagine that you are holding a mirror and as your child expresses her distress, use this mirror to reflect back whatever she is experiencing.

3. Create an anger Wheel of Choice with your child, listing things he might do when he feels angry. See example on page 106, or for more ideas see "Anger: Everybody Simmer Down" in *Top Ten Preschool Parenting Problems* by Roslyn Ann Duffy (Redmond, WA: Exchange Press, 2007). Using art supplies, design and decorate the chart together. Display the completed chart in a convenient place where both of you can refer to it when upset.

CHAPTER 7

"You Can't Come to My Birthday Party": Social Skills for Preschoolers

"Will you be my friend?" Every preschool teacher has heard this plea. A child's need for friendship and social skills is one of the most important parts of social and emotional learning. Caring adults can offer training, patience, and encouragement during this period, a time often fraught with tear-streaked faces, thrown toys, and grim tugs-of-war.

What Does Friendship Mean to Young Children?

When children are two or younger, they don't really have friends, even though they may find themselves surrounded by classmates at childcare, the children of parents' acquaintances, or neighbors with whom they are plopped down to play while the adults socialize.

Around the age of three, friendships begin to emerge; they are often organized by adults and may be fleeting, but the seeds of real relationship have been planted and some children do begin to build real connections with peers. By age four, children will begin to build more lasting friendships, often with two or three favorite playmates.

Learning for preschoolers often seems to involve opposites—they learn one skill and its opposite at the same time. In the case of friendship, this means that the blossoming of connection through friendship also brings with it a negative side—that of exclusion. There is no greater statement of friendship from a preschooler than "You can come to my birthday party." She is saying, "I like you enough to share the most important day in my world: the celebration of me!" Unfortunately, pre-schoolers also learn that leaving another child out provides a sense of power or the opportunity for revenge.

Friendly (and Not So Friendly) Dynamics

Rose is four and a half years old. It is June and her birthday is not until December. Even so, hardly a day goes by that Rose does not invite—or uninvite—someone at her preschool to her birthday party. When a parent wanders in to discuss enrolling her daughter, Rose immediately goes up to the new girl and says, "I'm going to be five. You can come to my party." A short while later, however, when Rose's friend Ilsa won't share the dress-up clothes, Rose sticks out her lower lip and announces in a voice of doom, "You can't come to my birthday!" Ilsa trembles at such a threat and quickly hands over one of the scarves.

Birthday invitations (or the threat of their withdrawal) are an early social tool. They represent an offer of mutual companionship and acceptance—and its opposite, momentary rejection. Because children at this age are unskilled at identifying and saying how they feel, this birthday threat (and others like it) serves two purposes. It says, "I am mad, sad, or upset in some way." It also serves as a tool to manipulate others to do one's bidding: "If you don't let me use the swing, you can't come to my birthday." As children mature and gain social and emotional skills, they learn to interact cooperatively—especially when parents and teachers model respect, cooperation, and kindness for them.

Sergio and Kenneth are five years old, and they are best buddies. Each watches for the arrival of the other at the childcare center in the morning. They greet each other by rolling around on the floor in mock combat, or they quickly run off to begin a new Lego tower. They want to sit next to each other at group time, and their teacher sometimes has to remind them that if they can't sit together quietly, they will have to sit apart. Sergio and Kenneth are together all through the day; theirs is a wonderful and important early friendship.

A common problem evolves when three children are friends and one gets left out. By the next day, the hurt feelings are usually resolved and the friendship continues to thrive, while parents may still be suffering from the "rejection" of their child. Interestingly, gender also appears to influence social interactions. Several studies have shown that girls are more likely to use relationships and rejection as forms of aggression, while boys are more likely to fight or argue—and make up quickly.

 Hal, Aaron, and Shelley chase one another around the playground and are an inseparable team. Shelley is the clear leader of this threesome; she is frequently the one who chooses the game to be played and makes the rules. The wise teacher knows that if he wants to get these three interested in a new activity, the one to convince is Shelley.

Special friendships form important foundations for many of life's relationships and provide a way for children to experiment with different roles. Just because Aaron chooses to follow Shelley's lead now, for instance, doesn't mean he will never be a leader. It's merely one of the roles he's trying on for size.

Social skills do not come without practice, and there will be many yelps of complaint and tearful faces. If adults focus on helping children feel influential and capable, rather than rescuing or refereeing, those children will acquire the social skills they need to achieve a sense of belonging in a world of relationships.

FRIENDSHIP DEVELOPMENT "YOU CAN COME TO MY BIRTHDAY PARTY!"

AGE	LEVEL OF FRIENDSHIP	DETAILS
2 or younger	No real friendships	Surrounded by classmates or children of adults' friends Mostly solitary play and exploration
2–3	Some interaction Some parallel play	Others are objects of curiosity Beginning of social skills and earliest friendships
3	Friendships take form and strengthen	Most interactions organized by adults Connection to peers begins
4	More lasting friendships	Often friends with 2-3 favorite children Desire to initiate and sustain play with friends
5	Genuine friendships	Self-chosen friends Special closeness to 1 friend (or circle of friends) Strong emotions; rocky dynamics, including exclusion

Playtime: A Stage for Socialization

Children's play is actually a laboratory where intensive research about roles and relationships is taking place. Still, there will be rough spots, and most parents and caregivers can tell stories like this one.

Four-year-old Amani came home with a scraped and bleeding knee one afternoon; her best friend, Jamie, had pushed her off the swing. Her mother's first instinct was to call the preschool teacher and complain. After all, weren't the staff supposed to be watching the children?

Fortunately for Amani, her mom was more interested in helping her learn life skills than in blaming others for social conflicts. She sat down next to Amani and asked, "Honey, can you tell me what happened?"

"Jamie got off the swing and I got on. She wasn't using it anymore," Amani whined.

Mom suppressed a smile, suddenly realizing where this story might be going. "Do you know why Jamie got off the swing?"

"To get her jacket," was the calm response.

As Mom suspected, when Jamie came back with her jacket she found Amani on "her" swing and pushed her off.

Mom took a moment to validate her daughter's feelings. "I'll bet it was scary when Jamie pushed you. Maybe you felt that she wasn't your friend anymore."

Amani's lip quivered. "Uh-huh," she said, and burst into tears. When her crying had subsided and she felt better, Amani and her mom explored what had happened. Mom asked if Amani might have done something other than get on the swing when Jamie got off. Amani thought for a moment and decided that she could have held the swing for Jamie until she got back.

"What might have happened if you held the swing for Jamie?" Mom asked.

"Jamie would have gotten back on," Amani said.

"Would Jamie have pushed you off?"

Amani shook her head. She could see that the results would have been different if she had behaved differently. Mom agreed that it was wrong of Jamie to push Amani, and she helped her daughter understand that she could have told Jamie clearly, "No pushing."

Mom has helped Amani understand that she has choices that can affect the outcome of a situation. In other words, Amani has personal power and influence. By talking this through with Amani rather than rushing in to rescue her, Amani's mother has helped her to feel capable.

It is important that parents avoid training children to see themselves as victims, helpless to change or affect what happens to them. Rushing to call (and blame) her daughter's preschool might have encouraged her daughter to develop a "victim mentality." Amani is learning how to interact in social situations, and parents and teachers can help her explore for herself what is happening, how she feels about it, what she is learning from it, and what ideas she has to solve the problem. *Adults can help children learn from these early friendship experiments that they are not powerless and that the choices they make in life affect what they experience.*

Victims and Bullies

As early as preschool, however, children learn to use exclusion and physical threats to gain and maintain control over others. These behaviors plant the earliest seeds of bullying. When adults rescue, they may unintentionally encourage children to become victims. And bullies need victims to be successful.

Marcie learned that she could get lots of attention when she complained to her mother that another child had hit her. Her mother would hug her, call her "my poor baby," and then call the preschool or neighbor (if the incident had happened at a friend's house), enraged that there had not been adequate supervision to "protect" Marcie. The teacher or neighbor would promise to be more vigilant.

One week Marcie's teacher, Joe, saw something very different happen on the preschool playground. As Joe watched from a corner of the yard, he saw Marcie trip and fall. When Joe went over to help her, Marcie said, "Bobby pushed me." Joe was astounded. Bobby had not been anywhere nearby. Marcie had decided that she liked the pity and attention of being a victim and was prepared to lie to get it.

How can Joe help Marcie? Marcie needs tools that empower her.
• She can learn to say, "Stop! Don't hit me."

- She can ask an adult for help, and the adult can coach Marcie in expressing her feelings: "That hurt me. I feel angry."
- The adult can help Marcie say what she does want: "I want to play without being hit or hurt."

By focusing on healthy problem-solving methods and teaching children to understand and express their feelings, you can prevent bullying instead of reinforcing it.

Other problem-solving skills include naming and expressing one's feelings in words and learning to have empathy for others. Children can also learn the important skill of focusing on solutions (rather than blame). Empathy and compassion will continue to develop throughout childhood and adolescence and can be encouraged during these early friendship encounters. Many of these skills are enhanced through family and class meetings (see Chapter 17).

The preschool years are a good time to talk openly about bullying. During a family or class meeting you can invite children to talk about how others feel when someone is unkind to them, why they think someone might choose bullying behavior, and how they could solve the problem.

In one preschool, the children often expressed anger at Joshua for knocking down their block towers and stomping on their sandcastles. Joshua was relatively new to the school and had made few friends because of his aggressive behavior. One day Joshua was absent, and the teacher decided to use this as an opportunity to help her students practice compassion and problem-solving. During a class meeting she asked, "Why do you think Joshua does things that hurt other people's feelings?"

One observant little girl said, "Maybe he doesn't have any friends."

Another said, "Maybe he hasn't learned to use his words."

The teacher then asked, "How many of you would be willing to help Joshua?" Every child raised his or her hand. (Children love the opportunity to help.)

The teacher said, "I'll talk to Joshua and ask if he would be willing to join us in brainstorming for solutions to this problem. Meanwhile, what could you do to help Joshua?"

Several children suggested that they would be his friend and would invite Joshua to play with them. They also decided that they could use their words and tell him how they felt when he destroyed things and ask him to stop—or ask him to help them rebuild and play together instead.

The teacher decided to see how their plan worked before talking with Joshua and found that the problem diminished so profoundly that she didn't have to bring it up again. Joshua's aggressiveness began to blossom into leadership; he offered many suggestions for solving other problems that came up on the class meeting agenda. He learned to feel belonging through the children's efforts at friendship, and to use his power in helpful ways.

"But Nobody Likes Me"

Children's friendships are social skills laboratories—and not all of their experiments turn out well. Hurt feelings come with the territory. When you can help children learn from their mistakes, you will be teaching them to feel capable and competent.

Carla is four. One day when her mother is getting her ready to go to preschool, Carla resists. She says she doesn't want to go because she has no friends and no one likes her.

In addition to asking curiosity questions to find out more about why she believes this, Carla's parents and teachers must figure out what is really happening. If, in fact, Carla does not have playmates, the adults in her life can help her understand why. A child who is hurting others or who refuses to cooperate in games is not a welcome playmate, but such children can be taught more effective ways of relating to their peers.

Children who are successful at social relationships often have learned to watch a game in progress and then join in by creating a role for themselves. Angela, for instance, spends a few moments watching her playmates play house, then offers to bake cookies for the others. She smoothly blends into the game in progress.

Erica is less skilled at doing this. She bounces over to a group of children and says, "Can I play?" She is often told no because the others don't want to be interrupted by having to create a role for Erica. Helping a child develop social skills will help her find belonging in her peer group—a need that, if not met, can result in the mistaken goal behaviors of attention, power, revenge, and inadequacy (more about these in Chapter 10).

A child like Carla may actually be a welcome playmate who simply does not see herself that way. Class meetings may be helpful in dealing with this situation at preschool, but a parent confronted with this dilemma might need a different approach. For instance, Carla's dad might ask her, "What makes you believe that the other children don't like you?" or "What do you think it means to be someone's friend?" Together they can explore Carla's perceptions of friendship and then examine her experiences. "I noticed that today Adrian asked you to play on the swings with him. Why do you think he did that?" Carla now has an opportunity to compare her perceptions with what has actually happened. Teachers may also be able to offer information about positive experiences that happened during the day.

Playdates

The playdate has become part of modern life. Children often do not have lots of siblings or other children living nearby, and inviting a child over to play is a way of nurturing friendships and providing social skills practice. Children feel a greater sense of kinship when they share time together in different settings. Carla's parents could invite one of her schoolmates to go to the zoo with them or perhaps to spend a Saturday afternoon playing with Carla's new playhouse. The increased closeness that results often will translate into more playtime at preschool as well.

Six-year-old Leyla burst through the door announcing, "My friend is here for a playdate!" She was breathless with excitement and so was her friend, Zoya. They raced through the house and Leyla joyfully showed her friend each room. Even Leyla's mom, Fauziah, was excited, though a bit anxious. Zoya was in Leyla's kindergarten class at her new school. Fauziah usually knew Leyla's friends from their mosque or because they were family friends. This was the first time Leyla had formed a friendship all by herself. Leyla's playdate with Zoya marked an important benchmark in Leyla's social development.

The Less-Than-Lovable Friend

Children sometimes choose friends who pose a problem for parents. Sometimes your child will actively dislike or quarrel with a friend—or you may not care for the way your own child behaves when with a particular playmate. If your child's friendship results in exceptionally rowdy behavior or aggressiveness, it is helpful to set clear expectations.

Ben loved to play with Marty, who lived down the street. Marty was a wild little guy who was very physical. The pair of four-year-olds inevitably wound up running recklessly around the house or wrestling on the lawn, and more than once toys were broken and Ben returned scraped, bumped, and bruised. Ben's mother wasn't happy about this friendship, especially since Marty was the only child with whom this sort of play occurred. Ben's mom decided not to rescue Ben but to establish clear guidelines about what she would allow when the boys played at her house.

One quiet morning, Mom sat down with Ben and explained her feelings and her concerns for the boys' safety. She then clearly explained her expectations to Ben, gently having him repeat them back to her to be sure he understood.

She established three rules: no bad names, no making fun of people, and no hurtful play. Mom and Ben agreed that when Ben or Marty chose not to follow the rules, Marty would have to go home. Marty would wait in the den and Ben would wait in his room until Marty's mother could come to get him.

The plan was discussed with Marty and his mother, who agreed with the rules. Now both moms needed to plan ways to follow through when necessary. It is the nature of learning (and young children) that Ben and Marty would need to see if the plan was for real. They might play nicely once or even twice, but eventually the rules would have to be tested.

Sure enough, the day came when Ben joined Marty in climbing on the countertop. Ben refused to get down when his mother asked him and threw in a "You're a butthead" for good measure.

Ben was given the choice of walking to his room or being carried there. Mom pointed kindly but firmly to the sofa, where Marty could wait for his mother. There was no reminder or warning necessary, since both boys knew the expectations and consequences. Marty's mom arrived at the front door quickly and escorted Marty home. Now both boys had learned that their parents really meant what they said and that their behavior would have to change. If it didn't, Ben and Marty would lose the opportunity to play at each other's house.

"Hey, Look at Me!": Showing Off

Some children seem to have inherited "peacock genes." They act as though strutting their stuff is the best way to succeed with others.

Q. *My four-year-old son seems to totally forget everything we have taught him when he gets together with his peers. He is so excited to be with them that he tries to show off by misbehaving intentionally in their presence. He turns a deaf ear to all grown-ups and will only stop goofing off if we raise our voices very loud. What action can we take to stop this behavior?*

A. Your son is becoming more interested in interacting with his peers than in paying attention to adults, which is developmentally appropriate. Understanding this fact will help you decide how to respond to your young "show-off."

It would probably be good to stop using your loudest voice. When you want your son's attention, kindly and gently take him aside, get down to his eye level, and establish eye contact. Explain the problem, what you would like him to do, and what *you* will do.

For example, explain that the yelling indoors must stop. If it continues, you will have to take him home. If you are not willing to actually leave, perhaps you can go into another room with him where he can calm himself before rejoining the play. This plan will work only if you can speak to him respectfully and privately, so that he is not tempted to continue misbehaving out of embarrassment—and if you follow through.

Sibling Fights

The family is often the laboratory where children first experiment with social skills—and brothers and sisters are the guinea pigs. It is heartwarming to see eighteen-month-old Timmy go up to his four-year-old sister and say, "Wuv you, Bef." It isn't so heartwarming to watch Timmy pull Beth's hair when she tries to rescue her favorite book from his clutches. When children are three to six years old, sibling fighting is the result of their immature social skills, mistaken ways to find a sense of belonging and significance in the family, and the reactions of the adults involved.

Social skills training is important for siblings, especially because of the unique aspect that sharing (and vying for) a parent's love and attention brings to their conflicts. (Keep in mind that sibling fighting is not the same as sibling rivalry. Sibling rivalry is about the decisions each child in the family makes based on his or her birth order and role in family life—and can be a hidden basis for sibling fights.)

It is helpful when parents learn to see sibling fighting for what it usually is. Young children sometimes tussle as they investigate their relationship with each other. Parents can stay out of the rescuer role by simply leaving the room. Taking a quiet moment elsewhere eliminates the audience—and sometimes the struggle.

If the noise level and fear of mayhem is too great to ignore, try giving the children a big hug. "What?" you may say. "Reward them for fighting?" Not exactly. If your children are competing for your attention, try giving it in an unexpected way. While hugging them, say, "I bet the two of you would like my attention right now. Next time, try telling me with your words instead of hurting each other." Acting in an unexpected way can cause children to pay more attention to your words—and hugs are almost always welcome.

It is important to treat squabbling siblings the same way. Invite both children to take a positive time-out to cool off. Don't try to be judge and jury; worry about whodunit when you read a mystery, not when you raise a preschooler. When your children are calm and ready to get along, they can both come out. You have shifted the message from "who is loved more" to "hurting each other is not okay."

A PARENT WITH ARGUING CHILDREN CAN USE ONE OF THE FOLLOWING THREE OPTIONS

- **Beat it.** You can choose to leave the area. It is amazing how many children stop fighting when they lose their audience. Don't be surprised if they follow you. This is why Rudolf Dreikurs suggested that the bathroom is the most important room in the house—it's sometimes the only room with a lock on the door. If your children pound on the door, you may want to jump into the shower or stuff your ears with tissues while you read a good novel. (If you choose these methods, it is a good idea to tell your children, in advance, that this is what you will do when they fight.) You then may want to discuss fighting and problem-solving at a family meeting.

- **Bear it.** This is the most difficult option because it means staying in the same room without jumping in to stop the fight or fix the problem. When children are fighting in a car, "bear it" may mean pulling to the side of the road and reading for a while, telling your children, "I'll drive as soon as you are ready to stop fighting." The hard part is keeping your own mouth shut until they say they are ready.
- **End the bout or boot 'em out.** If things are simply getting too heated and you're worried about their safety, you can send both children to cool off somewhere, or they can go outside (provided it is safe to do so) if they want to continue their fight. Or they can "end the bout," an option they have at any time.

Family Meetings

Sibling fights will be significantly reduced when you have weekly family meetings. There are many reasons for this. When children are fighting, you can interrupt and say, "Which one of you would like to put this problem on the family meeting agenda?" Often, this is enough to end the fight, as one chooses to add it to the agenda. It is especially effective when family meetings are consistent and effective (meaning parents avoid lecturing and instead involve children in brainstorming for solutions), giving children regular skill-building practice at problem-solving and focusing on the things they appreciate about each other during compliment time. You will learn more about family meetings in Chapter 17.

The Social Skill of Sharing

Sharing isn't easy. Most of us know adults who struggle with the concept, and for preschoolers, sharing is an ongoing challenge in the development of social skills. Sharing is also affected by societal and cultural attitudes. In Western cultures, we expect children to take turns, or to be willing to give up playing with a favorite toy (often without much training or encouragement). These skills are counterbalanced by attitudes of ownership and the high value placed on individualism. Expectations often accelerate during the late preschool years. Older preschoolers are beginning to suspect that they are not the center of the universe—and the idea is not entirely welcome.

Many adults do not have much patience with children who have not mastered the social skill of sharing, and in many cultures such "selfishness" would be unthinkable. Still, learning to share is an ongoing, developmental process that requires training, lots of practice, and lots of patience from adults.

Q. *My three-year-old has been acting up lately in childcare, fighting with the other kids. He doesn't hit them, but he can't agree about sharing toys. He is not listening to his teacher. One day he seems okay, but the next day he refuses to allow any children near "his" playthings. How can I get him to understand that what he is doing is not acceptable behavior?*

A. This is a typical challenge for three-year-old children. They are just learning how to share, and sharing is a difficult skill to master. Most of us are unhappy when we do not get to have what we want when we want it.

A child needs clear and firm guidance and he needs teaching rather than lectures or punishment. Remember, he does not yet know how to negotiate, compromise, and discuss problems with others. When children argue over a toy, adults frequently take the toy away from both children. There is more, however, that parents and caregivers can do to help children learn this important skill.

Children need to learn how to use words to ask for what they need. For example, the adult can take two children aside after a dispute. When everyone is calm, try practicing how to ask to play with a toy. For instance, a child may ask, "May I use the blocks?" One possible response to a playmate's request is "I am not done with them yet." You can then teach negotiation skills: "You can play with them in five minutes" or "Would you like to play with me?" Such training is vital to learning to share.

MORE POSSIBILITIES FOR PEACEMAKING

- Invite children to put the problem on the family or class meeting agenda.
- After a cooling-off period, use curiosity questions (which often begin with "what," "why," or "how") to help children explore what happened, how they feel about it, what they learned from the experience, and how they can solve the problem now.
- Teach children to use their words. This means that adults act as coaches—not lecturers or referees.
- Use a timer to help children share. Set the timer for a short period of time (perhaps two minutes) and give the timer to one child. The other child gets to play with the contested toy. When the timer rings, the children exchange the toy for another two minutes.
- Invite children to look at the "Wheel of Choice" to choose solutions (see page 106).

Quarreling

Have you ever watched a litter of puppies wrestle, nip, and fight? You probably laugh at puppies and see their aggressive behavior as normal and even cute. When children argue and fight, however, parents are a bit less enchanted. Yet testing limits and disagreeing are as normal for young children as for puppies.

When children between the ages of three and a half to six years of age quarrel, just as with sibling fighting, it may be effective to ask if it would help them to go to their "cool-off" place, or to put the problem on the family (or class) meeting agenda, not as punishment but as an opportunity to cool off and calm down. Later you can then ask them to explore and name their feelings, and invite them to identify ways they could handle the situation next time. It is not helpful for adults to lose their own tempers; offer blame, punishment, and lectures; or leap into the fray themselves.

Teaching social skills with the same attention you give to other types of skill development will produce children who can play together peacefully—at least most of the time. When children experience continual modeling and training, they can learn to get along quite well with other members of the world around them.

Mr. Conners found another creative way to deal with fighting when he saw two five-year-olds wrestling with each other at their preschool. He grabbed a toy microphone, rushed up to the boys, and said, "Excuse me. I'm a reporter for the six o'clock news. Would you each be willing to take thirty seconds to tell our listening audience your version of what this fight is all about?" He handed the microphone to one boy and told him to look into the make-believe camera.

The boy caught the spirit of the game and started telling his story. When thirty seconds were up, Mr. Conners took the mike and handed it to the next boy. When his thirty seconds were up, Mr. Conners looked into the imaginary camera and said, "Well, folks, tune in tomorrow to find out how these boys solved their problem."

Then Mr. Conners turned to the boys and said, "Would you boys be willing to come back tomorrow and tell our listening audience how you solved this problem?" With big grins on their faces, both boys agreed and went off together to work on a solution—which was reported the next day to the imaginary camera. Mr. Conners turned an argument into an opportunity to learn social skills.

Hitting and Aggression

Older preschoolers who are hitting or pulling hair should be firmly separated. A parent or teacher can say, "I can't allow you to hurt others," and can help the combatants explore other ways of acting when they feel angry or frustrated. It is important to understand that behavior often contains a coded message about how a child is feeling; while some behaviors are inappropriate or hurtful, the feelings themselves are not wrong. Interpreting the beliefs a child has about himself will provide clues about how parents and teachers might respond. Patient repetition, modeling, and guidance will help children learn more quickly the pleasures of getting along; it won't turn them into angels!

Tip: Social skills "mistakes" can always be turned into opportunities to learn.

When Children Hurt Adults

Sometimes a child's aggression and anger aren't directed only at other children. Some preschoolers have learned to hit, kick, bite, or yank the hair of their parents and caregivers when life doesn't go their way. And even little fists and feet can hurt. Parents often do not know what to do with an aggressive child and may inadvertently reinforce the very behavior they are trying to change.

Q. *I'm the mother of a three-and-a-half-year-old boy. My son has been calling me names and hitting me when he doesn't get what he wants. I think he picked this up at his preschool. We've always tried to use the most humane methods of discipline; we don't hit, yell, or humiliate him in any way. We always try to reason with him. I'm at a loss in this situation. Please tell me the best way to deal with such behavior.*

A. It is unlikely your child picked up this behavior at preschool. Preschool simply exposes him to more children and adults with whom he must share, to whom he sometimes has to defer his demands, and over whom he tries to establish his right to territory. At home he may simply redouble his efforts to get his way, where the odds are a bit more to his liking.

There are several things a parent can try to help a child change aggressive behavior. The following sections provide suggestions; choose the one that fits you and your child.

DECIDE WHAT YOU WILL DO

Let your son know that every time he hits you or calls you a name, you will leave the room until he is ready to treat you respectfully. After you have told him this once, follow through without any words. Leave immediately.

SHARE YOUR FEELINGS

Tell him, "That really hurts (or that hurts my feelings). When you are ready, an apology would help me feel better." Do not demand or force an apology; children must be helped to understand and express genuine remorse.

The purpose of this suggestion is to model sharing what you feel and asking for what you would like—not to make your child feel guilty. You can show respect for yourself by sharing your feelings and wishes in nondemanding ways.

USE A POSITIVE TIME-OUT

Create and name a positive time-out area with your child. When your child hits or hurts, ask, "Would it help you feel better to go to your cool-off place for a while?" It is helpful to teach your child that people do better when they feel better and that everyone needs time to calm down and cool off. If your child doesn't want to go, you might model for him by saying, "I'm very upset right now. I think I'll go to a quiet spot until I feel better."

ASK CURIOSITY QUESTIONS

Curiosity questions help a child explore the consequences of his behavior: "What happens when you hit people or call them names? How does it make you feel? How does it make others feel? What could you do to help them feel better? How else could you get what you want?" Be sure to ask these questions in a kind and firm manner and with a sincere desire to hear what the child has to say, and remember that your child must calm down before she can respond.

OFFER LIMITED CHOICES

You can let your child know what he *can* do by offering limited choices. You can say, "Hitting and hurting others is not okay. You can stop hitting and stay here with me, or you can go to your room and have your feelings in private. You decide." Be sure that all of the choices you offer are respectful and are acceptable to you.

PUT THE PROBLEM ON THE AGENDA

When the problem of hitting and name-calling appears on the family or class meeting agenda, it can be discussed during a regular family or class meeting when everyone is feeling calm. Everyone can work together for solutions.

STOPPING VIOLENT BEHAVIOR

Q. *How do you handle a child who feels that violence is the only way to solve a problem?*

A. This question raises several more: What is going on in this child's life? Where is this child learning violence? Too much television? Too many video games? Too much punishment? A child's environment and the role models he encounters provide many clues about that child's violent behavior.

As a wise person once said, if you want to understand the fruit, look at the tree. (However, any parent with more than one child can tell you that they come into this world with different temperaments. Many loving, kind, and firm parents struggle daily with a child who has an aggressive temperament.)

Children do indeed learn what they live, and changing angry, aggressive behavior is best accomplished through kind, firm teaching and respectful, nonviolent ways of solving problems, as well as watching adults practice what they preach.

Disruptive Behavior in the Classroom

It is especially important in group settings to provide opportunities for learning about social skills. Teachers face the ripple effect of behavior daily: Everyone sits down to group time and one child starts to make "raspberry" noises. Within moments, the entire group is buzzing and spitting.

Sit quietly until the class calms down. Model the behavior you want. Some teachers decide to join in the noisemaking, which usually makes everyone laugh—and which may be the easiest way to help children settle down. When disruptive behavior causes repeated problems, ask the children for help.

129

Use a class meeting to explain that it causes a problem for you when children continue to make noise after the group gathers together. Discuss what happens, invite the children to comment on what they notice, and then come up with a proposed solution. A hand signal, clapping pattern, or lights out might be decided upon as a way to indicate that classroom noise should stop. The sound of a bar chime resonates for quite a long time. Ask children if they can become silent before the vibrations end.

Class meetings can be used to explore many possible problems. Ask, "What would you do if . . . ?" or describe a situation and ask the children what they think went wrong. Storytelling, flannel boards, and books are other ways to introduce social skills. Help children identify the skills you are teaching, and take time to discuss what happened and why.

Relationships: The Ties That Bind

Like it or not, relationships form the fabric of our lives. We live in families; we go to school with peers; and eventually we work, live, love, and play with other people. Helping your young child get along with others prepares him to experience the best that life can offer: connection and contentment with friends and family. Disagreements and conflict are inevitable, but he can learn to handle those too with dignity and mutual respect.

QUESTIONS TO PONDER

1. Think of a time that your child complained about the behavior of a friend. How did you respond? What messages do you think your response sent? What skills did your child learn from this situation? What skills could you help her develop in future situations?

2. How can you determine if another child's behavior is bullying? If bullying is involved, what skills can you help your child develop

in this situation? Name two ways that you can teach your child to feel empowered, instead of being a victim.

3. Name a social skill that your child is struggling to learn—for example, sharing toys or playing with others peacefully. What would mastery of this skill look like? Have a conversation with your child in which you share your thoughts about what this skill would look like. Ask him what is hard for him, and ask what kind of help he could use from you.

CHAPTER 8

"I Can Do It!": The Joys (and Challenges) of Initiative

Preschoolers have so many ideas of their own—and so much energy with which to implement them! It's not surprising that parents sometimes feel overwhelmed by their offspring's ingenuity, vitality, and determination. Take this little fellow, for example:

Q. *My son doesn't walk anywhere—he gallops. He chases the birds at the beach, leaps into the wading pool for his swim lesson, and this morning I found him trying to saddle the dog with a blanket because he wanted to ride him. I had to explain that dogs are not strong enough to carry people on their backs. He gave up the riding plan, but I know he will come up with something else any moment. He seems so fearless, and I worry that he will get hurt. I'm worn out trying to keep track of him. Should I allow him to do these things?*

A. You sound exhausted by the effort of supervising and guiding your active young child. Never fear; most parents have had moments when they wondered why three-year-olds have so much more energy and creativity than their parents. Think for just a moment, though: your son is demonstrating a number of wonderful qualities. He is courageous and not afraid to try new things. He is able to connect ideas and actions, and he hurtles through life with excitement and curiosity. The same traits that exhaust you today may be just the traits that will make him a successful, capable adult later on.

Erik Erikson, a pioneer in understanding human development, tells us that from about the ages of two to six, children experience a crucial stage in their development that Erikson called "initiative versus guilt."[1] Initiative seems to be innate in preschoolers. They are little scientists exploring the world to discover what and how things work. Some may not be as rambunctious as the little one described above, but it takes initiative to discover their full potential. Guilt is instilled when parents and caregivers use language that indicates these children are doing something bad: "No!" "Don't touch that." "You are in time-out for doing that." "You will be punished for that."

Children need initiative. Those who are not able to nurture and develop a sense of initiative can turn into adults who struggle with life's challenges, who have a lingering sense of guilt, and who may believe that nothing they do is good enough.

Children need secure boundaries and limits within which they can explore, experiment, and learn to believe in their own competence and capability. *Creating a balance between safety (and appropriate behavior) and creativity and courage is the essence of parenting three- to six-year-olds.* Parents can create this balance and avoid instilling a sense of guilt by enforcing boundaries with kindness and firmness rather than humiliation or punishment. It is kind and firm to say, "Climbing on the bookcase is dangerous. Where is it safe for you to climb?" It is humiliating to say, "I can't believe you would be so careless. You could hurt yourself!"

Encouraging language sounds like this:

- "Let me show you what you can touch."
- "You are a good problem-solver. I'll bet you can figure out what to do instead of hitting."
- "What could you do to help Joel feel better?"
- "I need your help."

These are the years when parents are apt to hear a great deal of the phrase "I can do it!" Your children are trying to let you know that they are more capable than you think they are. Children in the early pre-school years want to try everything: they want to push the vacuum, wash the dishes, and dig holes in the garden. All too often, parents stifle their would-be helpers by telling them, "No, you're too little. Wait until you're bigger. It is easier and faster for me to do it." It usually *is* easier (and less messy) for adults to do these tasks, but denying a child the opportunity to learn and practice new skills may plant the seeds of guilt instead of initiative and capability. And years later, those same adults may find themselves wondering why their child "just won't do *anything*!" The drive to develop a sense of initiative versus guilt and shame continues throughout the preschool years.

Initiative in Action

Michael's mom took him to a nearby park. Michael, who had just turned three, was eager to play on the jungle gym. He scrambled up the lower rungs easily enough, but then he looked down and his stomach did a flip-flop. Michael whimpered for Mom to rescue him and lift him down, but Mom just smiled and placed an encouraging hand on Michael's back. She spoke reassuringly to her frightened son, helping him find his way back down. When he was on the ground his mother gave him a big hug and congratulated him on getting down "by himself." Michael beamed a proud smile. Mom and Michael returned to the same park regularly, and by the end of the second week Michael was scampering up and down the jungle gym with ease.

Margaret's mother faced the same dilemma but responded much differently. When Margaret, also three, cried out from the top of the same playground equipment, her mother ran up and gathered Margaret into her arms. She cuddled her and told her firmly how dangerous it could be to climb up so high. Margaret cried a little, then went over to play in the sandbox. Even though they visited the park often, two months later Margaret still avoided the jungle gym, clinging to her mother's leg whenever anyone invited her to climb it.

Preschoolers usually see the world as an exciting and fascinating place, especially as they develop more initiative and a greater physical and intellectual capacity to explore. When adults interfere, children may feel frustrated and withdraw, adopting a sense of guilt about their inabilities, while others give up and allow their anxious parents to smother them, keeping them from experiencing the frustrations needed to stimulate growth. In either case, their developing sense of initiative and capability may be thwarted. Margaret's mother wanted to protect her daughter from injury but ended up convincing her to avoid climbing at all. Later in life, Margaret may still find it difficult to take risks—even those that could benefit and enrich her life.

Adults can choose to encourage children as they face challenges, just as Michael's mom did. Michael's mom showed faith in his ability to master a new skill, and his experience told him "I am capable" in a way his mother's words never could. When Michael and Margaret face challenges as they grow, what will they believe about their own abilities?

Initiative—or Manipulation?

A child who is discouraged from developing initiative sometimes responds by developing manipulation skills instead. This is the child who withdraws into helplessness and insists that you do everything for her. Instead of developing the attitude "I can do it," she seeks belonging and significance through an attitude of "I can't." She "can't" walk to the car; she "can't" put on her socks; she "can't" pick up her toys. Whenever your child misbehaves, you might ask yourself, "Could this behavior be founded in discouragement and mistaken ideas about how to belong?" Consider the dilemmas these two parents face:

Q. *My three-year-old daughter screams and cries when I say no. She never eats what we give her: she asks for bread with peanut butter and licks off the peanut butter, refusing to eat the bread. Then she will insist on putting more peanut butter on the bread. If I don't do as she says, she will start whining or crying. She's at childcare during the day and behaves well there.*

Q. *I believe that no means no, but my daughter doesn't realize that yet. I used to put her in a corner where she couldn't see us until she stopped crying, but it only worked for a while. Now my husband puts her in our small bathroom with the light off. I believe that this will make her claustrophobic. She does sleep in her own bed, but she wets almost every night. Bedtime is a hassle, as she won't stay in bed. I have to pat her on the back until she falls asleep. I hate the constant battle with my child, but she won't do what I say.*

A. Situations like these are heartbreakingly common. Many of these battles could be eliminated if adults understood developmental and age appropriateness, the mistaken goals of misbehavior (see Chapter 10), and non-punitive methods of discipline that set limits while inviting cooperation.

The mother in the first example could let her daughter spread the peanut butter on the bread instead of doing it for her (and teach her to clean up afterward). Involving this child in meal preparation will increase her drive for initiative, will help her feel more capable by teaching her a life skill, and will motivate her to eat what she helps prepare, including the bread beneath all that peanut butter.

Punitive time-out—putting a child in a corner or in a room without a light—is never helpful and may teach unintended lessons. These punitive time-out experiences create doubt, shame, and guilt. Instead, parents can say no and then allow the child to have her feelings. When she cries, they can empathize: "I know you feel disappointed." If parents can't stand the crying, they can leave, saying, "It is okay to feel sad as long as you want to. Come find me when you are ready."

Preschoolers need to know that you mean what you say and will follow through with kind and firm action (instead of lectures). Children "listen" to kind, firm, and consistent action more than they listen to words.

When Your Child "Doesn't Listen"

One of the most common complaints parents have about young children is the mysterious hearing loss known as "my child won't listen." What parents really mean is, "My child won't obey." There are many reasons why children don't respond to adults' instructions—few of which have anything to do with their hearing.

Three-year-old Brianna, for instance, is grabbing her playmate's blocks and barely pauses when her teacher tells her to stop. Gregory's dad tells him it's time to leave the park and go home, then gets no response—until he raises his voice and grabs Gregory's elbow. Yesenia's mom tells her calmly and clearly before they enter the store that there will be no treats or toys today, and Yesenia nods when asked if she understands, but as they wait at the checkout stand, Yesenia howls loudly for candy anyway.

Sound familiar? The problem usually isn't that children don't listen but that what you are asking of them runs counter to some more basic need. Brianna, for example, is very young and is still working on her social skills. She needs to learn language and be encouraged to use it, and if she continues to refuse to share blocks, she should be removed calmly to another place with different play equipment. Gregory is experimenting with his initiative and autonomy, which unfortunately don't match his dad's concept of what he should be doing. He can learn from limited choices and from kind, firm action. Yesenia is simply too young to remember instructions that were given an hour earlier—especially when they're contrary to what she wants now.

Understanding age-appropriate behavior will help; so will avoiding yelling, punishment, or nagging, which only invite power struggles. You can invite cooperation instead of insisting on obedience: "Gregory, it's time to leave now. Would you like to run or hop to the car?" Children usually cooperate when they feel empowered to choose.

REASONS CHILDREN "DON'T LISTEN"

- Adults yell, lecture, or nag, which does not invite listening.
- Adults tell children what to do instead of asking. "Pick up your toys" invites resistance. "Where do your toys go before story time?" is more likely to invite cooperation.
- Adults set up power struggles that make winning more important than cooperating.
- The child is programmed by her instinct toward development to explore, and the voice of a child's instinct is usually louder than the voice of an adult.
- The child cannot comply with a request because it demands social skills or thinking skills that have not yet developed.
- The child is overwhelmed by strong feelings, which drown out your words.
- Children don't have the same priorities as adults.

How to Encourage Initiative and Discourage Manipulation

Encouraging the development of initiative is a tricky task precisely because parents and caregivers find it so challenging and inconvenient. Still, adults at home and school can help develop preschoolers' confidence and initiative by providing a range of opportunities, time for training, and encouragement for the many things children *can* do. When supported in this way, children learn to trust themselves and to feel capable.

One of the best ways to help children develop initiative is through family meetings or preschool class meetings, as discussed in Chapter 17. Other ways include playing "let's pretend," teaching the child to assess risk, stating clear expectations, offering limited choices, and following through, along with other Positive Discipline methods.

PLAY "LET'S PRETEND"

Children love to play, so "let's pretend" (what adults sometimes call role-playing) can be a fun way to teach them skills and help them understand the difference between effective (respectful) and ineffective (disrespectful) behavior.

One way to set up "let's pretend" is to say to your child something like this: "You be the daddy, and I'll be the little boy. We are at the pancake house. How should I behave? Should I cry and run around and throw my food? Or should I sit quietly in my seat and eat, or perhaps color quietly while I wait?" Then demonstrate by pretending you are sitting in the restaurant and having your child supervise your behavior. Let your child demonstrate the appropriate behavior. This will help to reinforce his understanding of expectations. (Acting out inappropriate behavior can be confusing, especially for younger children who do not yet distinguish between fantasy and reality. Using puppets or stuffed toys to act out behaviors can help overcome this developmental challenge.)

LEARNING TO ASSESS RISK

With help, a child can develop the ability to assess risk. Adults can point out things that might pose problems in a given circumstance and, most important, help the child decide what to do about that potential problem.

While on a walk through the park, Ari sees a large boulder ahead and wants to climb it. Ari's dad stands with her at the base of the boulder and says, "That looks pretty high. Do you see any places where you could stop to rest while you climb? Are there grasses or small plants that you could hang on to? Does that boulder look rough or smooth to you?" After considering these questions, Ari and her dad agree that the climb is safe to try.

What if they identify a problem? Perhaps they could agree that when Ari reaches the small shrub partway up, she will need to climb back down. Or if the risks cannot be managed safely, the climb might not be possible. Ultimately, Ari's dad will have to decide what is safe for his daughter to try. Ari might feel disappointed if he says no, but she would not feel less capable. Instead she will be learning a valuable skill about how to make responsible choices.

STATE CLEAR EXPECTATIONS

One of the oldest bits of parenting advice is still one of the best: say what you mean, and mean what you say. How should you establish clear, appropriate expectations for young preschoolers? Let's listen in as Cody's father gives it a try:

Even though he is only four, Cody loves baseball. He's been collecting baseball cards since he was tiny, loves to play wiffleball in the backyard with his dad, and knows the entire starting lineup of the San Francisco Giants. Tim, Cody's father, is planning to take his small son to his first real baseball game. Previous experience has taught him that in order to enjoy the day with his curious, active preschooler, some preparation and groundwork will be necessary.

First, Tim decides to take Cody to the local park for a Little League game. As they sit in the bleachers together, Tim asks Cody how he thinks they should act at the "big stadium." Cody considers this question thoughtfully, furrowing his small brow in concentration.

"We should sit still?" he offers tentatively, knowing this is a tough rule for him to follow.

"Well," his dad says with a smile, "we can stand up sometimes. And we can walk together to get a cold drink or a hot dog."

"We can do seventh-inning stretch!" Cody shouts excitedly, and begins to sing "Take Me Out to the Ball Game."

Together, father and son explore the guidelines for the big day. Tim makes it clear that lots of people will be at the game, so Cody will have to hold his hand when they walk anywhere. Tim and Cody agree that Cody can have a hot dog, a cold drink, a snack, and one souvenir of his choice—as long as it costs ten dollars or less. And they agree that if Cody runs away or climbs on the seats, they will have to return to the car.

Tim knows his son well: when Cody's curiosity gets the better of him, a firm hand on his shoulder (without scolding or a lecture) draws him back to Dad's side. And when Cody decides he wants to climb down a row (and over three people) to see better, Tim only has to ask him what their agreement was for Cody to plop quickly back into his seat.

Because Cody is four, his dad knows that the day will not be perfect. He also knows that Cody may not be able to follow the guidelines for nine full innings and is prepared to leave if necessary. Or they may need to sit in the car for a while until Cody is ready to try again. But by setting clear and reasonable expectations (in advance) and by following through on these simple limits, Cody's first baseball game will be an occasion father and son will remember for years to come.

OFFER LIMITED CHOICES AND FOLLOW THROUGH

Parents sometimes believe that giving children what they want and not burdening them with rules will show them that they are loved. However, permissiveness is not the way to help children develop initiative—or any other valuable social or life skill. One alternative to permissiveness is offering limited choices with kind and firm follow-through. Limited choices are effective when they are related, respectful, and reasonable.

Five-year-old Elena's family went to the zoo with another family from their neighborhood. Elena asked for cotton candy, snow cones, and everything she saw other children enjoying. Her father told Elena she could have either a snow cone or popcorn. Elena chose popcorn. Her father purchased the popcorn and then told Elena that if she continued to ask for other treats, she would need to return to the car with him, where they would wait until the others finished viewing the exhibits.

Partway through eating the popcorn, Elena saw a child with a snow cone and began to ask for one. Elena was determined: she emphasized her demand by flinging the remaining popcorn down, spilling it all over the walkway. Her father calmly asked Elena if she wanted to hold his hand on the way to the car or be carried. (He decided to ignore the spilled popcorn, since the pigeons were already taking care of that problem.) When she refused to move, her father picked her up and left for the car. He did not scold, spank, or remind her why they were leaving. He treated her respectfully, and when she began to wail that she wanted to see the monkeys, he assured her that he was confident that next time they came to the zoo, Elena would make better choices—and would be able to visit the monkeys.

Giving a child a chance to try again is reasonable and encouraging. It is not reasonable to say, "I'm never taking you there again—or anywhere else, for that matter!" Most parents do not follow through on such threats—which only teaches children that they can safely disregard both the rules and their parents.

You have a choice. Which is more important, a family outing or the self-esteem, initiative, and confidence your child will develop by learning appropriate social skills? When you follow through with kindness and firmness, you won't have to miss many outings before your child learns that you say what you mean and will follow through. Of course, follow-through requires that adults think before they speak.

If you can't actually do it, don't say it!

Positive Discipline in Action

Ted and Lamar decided they would teach their son Mark to dress himself when he was three years old (excellent training for budding initiative). They purchased pants with easy-to-pull-up elastic waists, wide-neck T-shirts, and sneakers with Velcro fasteners. Mark was a willing student and soon mastered the art of dressing himself (even though he put his shoes on the wrong feet about half of the time).

Mark attended preschool, and his morning routine included getting himself dressed, helping with breakfast, and being ready to leave by seven-thirty, when Lamar would drive him to school on the way to work. Mark and his dads had created a special morning routine chart with a picture of him doing each task—which Mark followed enthusiastically for several days. Ted and Lamar also knew that Mark might use his initiative to "test" the routine. They worked out a plan with Mark in advance that included a limited choice and follow-through. Together they decided that anytime Mark was not dressed in time to go, they would put Mark's clothes in a paper bag so he could finish dressing at school. They weren't sure how much Mark really understood about their discussion of choices and follow-through, but they had faith that he would learn if they ever had to carry out their plan.

Sure enough, after several weeks of smooth mornings, the day arrived when Ted noticed Mark wasn't following his routine. When it was time for Lamar to leave for work, Mark was still in his pajamas. Ted had prepared the sack of clothes, so Lamar kindly and firmly picked Mark up under one arm, took the sack of clothes in his other hand, and walked to the car through pouring rain—just as a neighbor was out picking up his newspaper.

Lamar sighed and reminded himself, "Oh well, taking time for training with Mark is more important than what the neighbors think."

Mark cried and complained that he was cold while they were driving to school. Lamar pointed to Mark's coat on the seat beside him and suggested he would be warmer if he pulled it over him. Lamar also reminded Mark that he could get dressed as soon as they got to school. Mark continued to complain. When they arrived at the school, Joyce, the preschool director (who understood these moments well), smiled as the pair approached.

"Oh, hi, Mark!" she said warmly. "I see you didn't get dressed this morning. You can take your bag of clothes into my office and come out as soon as you are dressed."

Mark got himself dressed. A month later, he decided further research was in order and tested the routine again. Lamar responded matter-of-factly, carrying the clothes bag to the car. When they arrived, Mark's teacher invited him to get dressed, reminding him that he would need to be dressed for outside playtime. He refused and began to play with the blocks, nattily attired in Mickey Mouse pajamas. Mark played happily until it was time to head outside. Mark's teacher assured him that as soon as he was fully dressed he could join his classmates on the playground. After a moment of reflection, Mark decided that proving his point was not worth missing recess, and he scrambled into his clothes.

Mark's parents and teacher did not nag, lecture, or remind Mark about getting dressed. They simply did what they said they would do—carry his clothes to the car for him, limit his ability to play outdoors until properly dressed, and allow him to dress himself at school. (It's important to note that this plan would not be appropriate for an older child who might feel humiliated by arriving at school in pajamas. Adult actions should never cause shame or embarrassment.)

Lamar could have made this experience humiliating to Mark by "piggybacking," which means adding blaming or shaming lectures to his kind and firm actions. Lamar did not say, "It serves you right! Maybe next time you'll hurry up. The other kids will laugh at you for not getting dressed." Instead, Lamar and Joyce treated Mark kindly and firmly, which helped him learn the benefits of using his skills to help himself and cooperate with others.

"Oops, I Made a Mistake!"

By now you might be thinking that you have to be a perfect parent and raise a perfect child. There are no such things. Isn't that wonderful? It doesn't matter how much you learn or how much you know; you will never stop making mistakes. Once you understand this, you can see mistakes as the important life processes they are: interesting opportunities to learn. Instead of feeling discouraged when you make a mistake, you can say, "Terrific! I've just been given another opportunity to learn!"

Wouldn't it be wonderful if you could also instill this attitude in your children so they wouldn't be burdened with all the baggage you carry about mistakes? How many adults developed a greater sense of guilt than of initiative because they were shamed and punished when they made mistakes? Of course, preschoolers will not do things perfectly. But which is more important, perfection or helping your child develop healthy initiative and strong life skills? Sometimes the deepest learning grows out of failure.

Asking Curiosity Questions

Children do not develop a strong sense of initiative when parents and teachers spend too much time lecturing: telling children what happened, what caused it to happen, how they should feel about it, and what they should do about it. Telling instills guilt or rebellion because it sends the message that children aren't living up to adult expectations. Perhaps most important, telling children what, how, and why teaches them *what* to think, not *how* to think.

Children will develop thinking skills, judgment skills, problem-solving abilities, and initiative when adults ask them curiosity questions:

- What happened?
- What were you trying to do?
- Why do you think this happened?
- How do you feel about it?
- How could you fix it?
- What else could you do if you don't want this to happen again?

When Mark, who wouldn't get dressed in the morning, complained about being cold in the car, his dad might have used it as an opportunity for asking questions. "Why do you think you are cold? What might you do to feel warmer?" These questions would have helped Mark make the connections between clothing and warmth. He might also have discovered why pajamas aren't a good choice when it is cold outside. Perhaps Mark does not truly understand this connection and would have answered, "Because I didn't eat all my toast." This would have given his dad an opportunity to help Mark learn that clothes affect whether we feel warm or not.

Believe it or not, children do not always understand the reasoning that seems so obvious to adults. That is why it is so important to understand development and age-appropriateness—and encouragement.

It's All About Encouragement

Rudolf Dreikurs said over and over, "A child needs encouragement as much as a flower needs water." So what is encouragement?

The word "encouragement" comes from a French root that means "to give heart to." Encouragement helps children develop courage: the courage to learn and grow, the courage to learn from mistakes without blame and shame, the courage to develop social and life skills. Children develop courage when their parents and other adults in their lives create a safe place where they can practice their developing initiative and learn from their mistakes.

Remorse is not the same as guilt. Children will feel remorse when they make a mistake and hurt others, especially if they are developing compassion. Remember, though, that you cannot force a child to feel genuine remorse. Adults offer encouragement when, through curiosity questions, they help children explore the consequences of their choices instead of imposing consequences on them. Curiosity questions also help children understand what they feel, why they feel that way, and how they can make amends. In this way, children will feel encouraged to learn from their mistakes.

As Dreikurs said, "A misbehaving child is a discouraged child." This is why adults need to understand the long-term effects of what they do.

Vague Praise Is Not Encouraging

Vague "attaboys" aren't the best way to encourage young children—keep your encouragement specific. For instance, if a three-year-old at the childcare center brings you his latest drawing and you tell him, "Oh, it's the most gorgeous picture I've ever seen—I'm going to frame it and hang it on the wall," you may not be helping him as much as you think. You may have taught him that the most important thing he can do is to please people, which can be a dangerous creed to live by. Telling that same child, "I see you really like red and yellow. Can you tell me about these shapes?" opens the door for talking and learning together.

Another way to determine if something is true encouragement is that it can only be said to that person at that time, whereas praise is more general. You could say "That's a great project" to most anyone at any time. You could only say, "You built a very tall block tower. Look how high you had to reach to place those top blocks on it—it's taller than you are!" to a particular child in a specific situation. This child will feel you noticed what she did and that you were speaking uniquely to her.

This chart will make these distinctions clearer:[2]

DIFFERENCES BETWEEN PRAISE AND ENCOURAGEMENT

	PRAISE	ENCOURAGEMENT
Dictionary definition:	1. To express favorable judgment of 2. To glorify, especially by attribution of perfection 3. An expression of approval	1. To inspire with courage 2. To spur on: stimulate
Addresses:	The doer: "Good girl."	The deed: "Good job."
Recognizes:	Only a complete, perfect product: "You did it right."	Effort and improvement: "You gave it your best" or "How do you feel about what you learned?"
Attitude:	Patronizing, manipulative: "I like the way Suzie is sitting."	Respectful, appreciative: "Who can show me how we should be sitting now?"
"I" message:	Judgmental: "I like the way you did that."	Self-directing: "I appreciate your cooperation."
Used most often with:	Children: "You're such a good girl."	Adults: "Thanks for helping."
Examples:	"I'm proud of you for getting an A" (robs person of ownership of own achievement).	"That A reflects your hard work" (recognizes ownership and responsibility for effort).
Invites:	Children to change for others; becoming "approval junkies"	Children to change for themselves; becoming inner-directed
Locus of control:	External: "What do others think?"	Internal: "What do I think?"
Teaches:	What to think; dependence on the evaluation of others	How to think; self-evaluation
Goal:	Conformity: "You did it right."	Self-discovery: "What do you think/feel?"
Effect on sense of worth:	Feel worthwhile when others approve	Feel worthwhile without others' approval
Long-term effect:	Dependence on others	Self-confidence, self-reliance

Helping Children Reach Their Full Potential

Joyce, the director of the preschool Mark attends, believes in the importance of using encouragement and skills training to help children develop initiative and capability. Her staff look for every opportunity to let children experience how capable they are by taking time for training and then letting the children do as much as they can for themselves.

When Joyce goes shopping for groceries, she lets the children take turns going with her to help her put items in the grocery cart. When she returns to the childcare center, she backs the van into the play yard and calls the children to help take the groceries to the kitchen. The cook helps the children remember where to put the items.

During lunchtime, the children dish up their own food. One little fellow named Matt would consistently take too much food. After about a week, his teacher helped him explore what was happening by asking, "What happens when you take too much food?"

Matt responded, "I can't eat it all and I have to throw some away."

The teacher continued: "What would happen if you took smaller helpings of food?"

Matt looked like he had made a great discovery as he said, "I could eat it all."

The teacher said, "I'm sure you could." Then she asked, "If you took less food, ate it all, and were still hungry, what could you do then?"

Matt beamed as he said, "I could take some more."

The teacher asked, "When will you start doing that?"

Matt looked like he could hardly wait as he crowed, "Tomorrow!"

After lunch, the children each scrape any leftover food from their plate into a plastic dishpan, rinse their own plate in another dishpan, and then put the dish in the dishwasher. This routine is definitely more time-consuming than having an adult clean up after lunch. But Joyce and her staff of teachers are more interested in helping children

149

develop their full potential than in getting chores done quickly. They also love the children, enjoy them, and feel privileged to be part of their growth and development.

The more you know about what is developmentally appropriate, how to enhance the environment in which children grow, learn the skills that will encourage them to reach their full potential, and forgive yourself when you make mistakes, the more you can relax and just enjoy watching your children grow, knowing that they're learning to trust their own abilities, to believe in the support of the adults in their lives, and to experience the wonder of life all around them.

QUESTIONS TO PONDER

1. Think of an ineffective limit you have set for your child if she behaves in a certain way. How did you follow through (or not)? What lesson have you really taught? What might your child decide about herself, and about you? What could you do differently?

   Tip: If you can't do it, don't say it.

2. When was the last time that you made a mistake? How did you handle it? Is this the attitude toward mistakes that you want to instill in your child?

3. Consider a time you were hard on yourself for making a mistake. Choose three curiosity questions from the list on page 146. Now apply those questions to your situation. How do you feel after doing this? Try using those same questions with your child the next time she makes a mistake.

PART THREE

Understanding Behavior and New Tools

CHAPTER 9

Accepting the Child
You Have: Understanding
Temperament

Most parents can't help but notice differences between their children and those around them, privately if not publicly: their siblings, other children at the preschool, the neighbors' kids, nieces and nephews. And differences often lead to judgments: Bobby is "such a good boy"; Miranda is "a little monster."

You have already learned that preschoolers are passing through some interesting developmental stages; you know that experimenting with autonomy and initiative can lead them to behave in ways that adults perceive as "bad." Is there such a creature as a "perfect child"? Would you really want one?

The Myth of the Perfect Child

A "perfect child" is often pictured as the one who quietly obeys his parents, doesn't fight with his brothers or sisters, does his chores without complaining, saves his money, does homework without being reminded, gets good grades, is athletic, and is popular.

Frankly, we worry about the child who fits this fantasy description. This is usually the child who does not feel secure enough to test power boundaries and find out who she is apart from her parents and teachers, or who is afraid to make mistakes or risk disapproval. We say "usually," because a few children do fit the fantasy description yet still feel secure and aren't afraid to make mistakes.

Most researchers believe that temperament traits are inborn, part of each child's "wiring." How your child interacts with you and her other caregivers appears to have a strong effect on how these inborn tendencies actually develop. It's a complex process, one that we don't yet fully understand. While attitudes, behavior, and decisions may change with time and experience, temperament appears to be part of us for life. Understanding your child's unique temperament will help you accept the child she truly is and work *with* her to learn, to grow, and to thrive.

Goodness of Fit

There are several approaches to temperament. Stella Chess and Alexander Thomas emphasize the importance of "goodness of fit," which is the depth of understanding parents and teachers have of a child's temperament and their willingness to work with that child to encourage healthy development.[1] Children experience enough stress in life as they struggle for competency and belonging. *It does not help to compound that stress by expecting a child to be someone he is not.*

Positive Discipline provides many respectful tools for helping parents and children "fit" well together. For instance, a child with a short attention span will still need to learn to accept some structure and to stay focused. Offering limited choices is one way to be respectful of the child's needs and of the needs of the situation (meaning the behavior appropriate for the present environment).

Working out a match between parents and children that meets the needs of both is critical to goodness of fit. If your child has difficulty adapting to new situations while you are the life of a party, you have a poor fit. The good news is that, with understanding, you can find balance and create a good fit. Your child may not make friends quickly, but she can learn social skills that will help her find one or two good friends. She may feel discouraged if you push her to be like you, but she will find it encouraging if you gently teach her that it is okay to take her time while being open to the friendly overtures of other children.

Finding the balance between your needs and those of your child can take some time and practice, but learning to accept and work with the individual, special temperament of your child will benefit you both.

The Berkeley Studies

Each child is born with a unique style of processing sensory information and responding to the world around her. Stella Chess and Alexander Thomas investigated the miracle of personality in a longitudinal study they conducted in the late sixties and seventies. The Berkeley Studies revealed that there were two basic orientations, active and passive, and that these were lifelong characteristics; in other words, passive infants grew up to be passive adults, while active infants grew up to be active adults. In fact, activity levels can be measured in the womb.

The nine temperaments found by Chess and Thomas—the qualities and characteristics that contribute to individual personalities—serve to describe three types of children: the "easy" child, the "difficult" child, and the "slow to warm up" child. All are good; some are just more challenging than others.

The Nine Temperaments

All children possess varying degrees of each of the nine characteristics studied by Chess and Thomas. These characteristics resemble a continuum; each child (and each parent) falls somewhere along the line between either extreme. (You may want to think about a child you know as you explore these aspects of temperament.)

The following nine temperaments shape a child's personality and approach to life:

1. Activity level
2. Rhythmicity
3. Initial response (approach or withdrawal)
4. Adaptability
5. Sensory threshold
6. Quality of mood
7. Intensity of reactions
8. Distractibility
9. Persistence and attention span

ACTIVITY LEVEL

Activity level refers to a child's level of motor activity. A high-activity preschooler might delight in energetic running games, while a low-activity child chooses something quiet, like drawing or looking at a book.

Q. *My three-year-old son doesn't know what the words "Wait, please!" mean. He never slows down. I am worn out. My sister's child seems so much calmer. Am I doing something wrong?*

A. Have you ever noticed how often parents and teachers of preschoolers use the phrase "worn out"? Most preschoolers have a high level of physical energy—after all, there's so much they have to do and learn each day—but some youngsters seem to have far more than their share. If you have one of these highly active little ones in your home, rest assured: there is nothing wrong with you or your child. An active child is not "bad." He simply is busy being who he is. The key to living peacefully with your active preschooler is to find a way to meet his needs without abandoning your own. Here are some suggestions:

- **Plan ahead with your child's needs in mind.** Provide him with space, challenging activities, and opportunities to run off excess energy. Take him to parks, enroll him in swim classes or gymnastics, and provide plenty of time for energetic play. It may also be wise to skip, for now, the ballet class, the music recitals and plays, and the four-course restaurant meals. Do your best to match your expectations to your child's abilities.
- **Schedule time for yourself.** Get a sitter, enroll your child in preschool or other classes to give yourself a break, or ask a friend or partner to spend time with your child on a regular basis. This is not selfishness; it's wise parenting. You need lots of energy to deal calmly and effectively with an active preschooler, and you need time to rest and refresh yourself.
- **Learn to love your child for who he is.** He did not choose his temperament. Rejoice in his strengths. There is much he can accomplish later in life with his abundant energy.

Monica has learned to plan her days with her twins' different temperaments and activity levels in mind. One Sunday afternoon at the community swimming pool, three-year-old Ned and Sally keep Mom company while their older sister takes swimming lessons. As the hour progresses, Ned plays with the bag of plastic animals that his mother has brought along. The entire hour passes with Ned happily absorbed in his play.

Sister Sally is a different story. She begins coloring in the book her mother has brought along, but within ten minutes has marked up all of the pages and wants her mom to read to her. Halfway through the story, Sally decides she is thirsty, so Monica takes her to the drinking fountain. Then Sally begins to climb on the bleachers. Before half an hour has passed, Sally has colored, heard a story, gotten a drink, and explored the bleachers. Monica knows her daughter well and is already expecting to take a walk to the swings—and she knows they'd better be ready to leave the minute lessons are over.

Ned has a low activity level, while Sally's is high. Monica used to feel frustrated by the differences between her twins, especially since she thought she treated them the same way. Information about temperament helped her understand them better. She decided she might as well relax and simply enjoy (and plan for) the uniqueness of each child.

RHYTHMICITY

Rhythmicity refers to the predictability (or unpredictability) of biological functions, such as hunger, sleeping, and bowel movements.

Karen and Leah could set their clocks by the routine of their younger son, three-year-old Martin. He woke up at six-thirty every morning, wanted the same lunch every day, always chose to play with the same toys, insisted on his nap every afternoon at one-thirty, and went to bed every night at the same time.

Martin provided a needed rest for Karen and Leah after their experience with his five-year-old brother, Stanley, who was as unpredictable as his younger brother was predictable, with everyday activities in constant flux. While Martin's style was easier to live with, Karen and Leah learned to be patient with Stanley and to avoid showing preference for Martin's style. They got both boys involved in planning morning and bedtime routines (even though Martin didn't need one). Stanley was usually happy to follow routines that he had helped create.

Understanding rhythmicity can help parents and caregivers plan a child's schedule in ways that ease conflict and stress for everyone.

INITIAL RESPONSE

This temperament describes the way a child reacts to something new, such as a new food, toy, person, or place. Approach responses are usually easy to see: a child will smile, or run to join a new playmate. Withdrawal responses look more negative and are expressed by crying, a worried expression, or even running away from a new activity or person. Learning to parent your child means recognizing these cues and responding in encouraging, nurturing ways.

> Amanda came to her new childcare center when she was three years old. Whenever the children gathered for a group activity, Amanda would hang back and refuse to join in. Because her teacher was sensitive to her temperament, she did not insist that Amanda join the group, although she made sure that Amanda knew she was welcome. For two weeks, Amanda held back, watching what happened and gradually moving closer. By the third week, she was happily playing with the others. Amanda's initial response was withdrawal, and her teacher wisely honored this aspect of her temperament.

Again, temperament is inborn, and research indicates that these deeply ingrained personality traits are not easily changed by anxious parents.

> Bonny worried about her five-year-old son, Jason: she feared that his shyness would keep him from ever having happy relationships or enjoying the activities that she and his father had always loved. Bonny found that when she pushed him forward, urged him to speak to or play with someone new, or signed him up for a sport or activity, he only retreated further, hiding behind her leg and burying his head against her side.

When Bonny realized that Jason might always be wary of new situations, she decided to accept her son for who he was—and to find ways to help him feel more comfortable and confident. She learned to provide opportunities for Jason to watch other children playing tee-ball before signing him up. She learned not to push him to speak to new acquaintances but to carry on a friendly conversation herself, keeping a gentle hand on her son's shoulder as reassurance.

Bonny made time to stay a while with Jason in new situations, accepting that he felt comfortable more quickly when she was with him. Most important, she offered him acceptance and encouragement without requiring that he "get over" his shyness. Jason may always be slow to warm up to new people and circumstances, but his mother's patience and loving encouragement will help him to believe in—and accept—himself.

ADAPTABILITY

Adaptability describes how a child reacts to a new situation over time—her ability to adjust and change. Some children initially spit out a new food but accept it after a few trial tastes. Others accept a new food, a new article of clothing, or a new preschool far more slowly, if at all.

When four-year-old Maria's parents decided to file for divorce, her dad found an apartment a few blocks away. Any child finds divorce painful, but Maria's slow-to-adapt temperament increased the stress associated with such a major change. Although both parents agreed to share parenting duties, with Maria spending several nights each week with her dad, they decided to take a gradual approach at first.

When Maria's dad moved out, he invited her to help him carry things to his new apartment. Over the next few weeks he took Maria to his apartment several times, increasing the length of these visits. After three weeks, Maria was spending full days with Dad and eating dinner at his new apartment but returning to her familiar bedroom at the family home to sleep.

Gradually, Maria and her dad set up a bedroom for her at his new home, picked out some furniture, and selected clothes she could move to her new room. A month had passed before Maria and her parents felt comfortable with overnight visits at Dad's apartment.

Maria's parents put her needs first and gave her time to adjust to this change.[2]

If your little one struggles with rapid transition and change, then recognizing and allowing for her temperament may save you both discomfort and unhappiness.

SENSORY THRESHOLD

Some children wake up from a nap every time a door opens, no matter how softly, while others can sleep through a hurricane. Some children complain about tight clothes or rough sheets, while others scrape their knees or thump their heads without even slowing down. The level of sensitivity to sensory input varies from one child to the next and affects how they behave and view the world.

Alice was celebrating her fourth birthday. She opened a present containing a beautiful flowered dress and smiled in delight. The smile changed to dismay, however, when she noticed that the puffy skirt was held in place by a layer of stiff nylon net. "Do I have to wear this part?" she asked in alarm. "It'll scratch my legs."

Such minor details didn't faze Andy. He loved to walk barefoot and took off his shoes at every opportunity. His parents would point with concern to the gravel playground or exclaim about the hot pavement, but different textures and temperatures didn't bother Andy at all.

Time and experience will teach you about your own child's sensitivity to physical sensation and stimulation. Does your child like noise and music or does he become irritable? Does he gaze at bright or flashing lights, or does he turn his face away? Does he like to be touched and hugged, or does he wriggle away from too much contact?

If your child is more sensitive to stimulation, you will need to go slowly when introducing new toys, new experiences, and new people. Soft light and gentle music may help him calm down; he may become nervous or irritable in noisy, crowded places (such as birthday parties, amusement parks, or busy malls). A less sensitive child may be more willing to try new experiences. Discover what engages his attention; then create opportunities for him to explore and experiment.

SENSORY INTEGRATION DYSFUNCTION

Some children are overwhelmed by sensory input; in fact, in some cases, a child's brain may have difficulty integrating sensory information. A child may find his socks "painful" or his shirt "too tight"; he may insist on the same foods and routines because others are uncomfortable or "bad." Other children do not respond strongly to any stimulation; they may rock, spin, or bang their heads in an effort to generate sensory input, which they find comforting. Such children may have sensory integration dysfunction and can benefit from a variety of therapies that will help them make sense of sensory information and feel more comfortable.

If you suspect that your child reacts differently to sensory input than other children the same age, it may be wise to ask your pediatrician for an evaluation.[3]

QUALITY OF MOOD

Have you ever noticed how some children (and adults) react to life with pleasure and acceptance, while others can find fault with everything and everybody? One child might favor her family with sunny smiles, while another feels compelled to pout or scowl, "just because."

Parents of less sunny children can take heart. If your child wears a frowny face more often than you would like, remember that those scowls are not in response to you or your parenting skills. It can be discouraging for parents and teachers to deal with a child who always looks on the dark side, but there are ways to both accept this temperament and help a child to face life more positively.

> Stephen came home from his parenting class with a new idea: he would ask his five-year-old son, Carl, about the happiest and saddest moments of his day. Stephen looked forward to making this a part of their bedtime routine and having a chance to get into his son's world. When Stephen asked Carl about his saddest moments, he often had a long list of troubles to relate, but when asked about his happy moments, he couldn't think of any. Stephen began to feel real dismay that Carl was so miserable.
>
> When Stephen learned about temperament, he was able to stop getting hooked by Carl's negative mood. He would listen to his son's list of troubles, then share some of his own sad moments. Then he would share his happy moments. As Stephen continued to show Carl that it was okay to see both negatives and positives, Carl started sharing happy times too. He still sees lots of negatives, but he is learning to see the positive things as well.

Carl simply has a negative quality of mood and sees the world from that perspective. By accepting his temperament, Stephen learned more about his child and how to help him broaden his perspective.

INTENSITY OF REACTIONS

Children respond to events around them in different ways. Some smile quietly or merely take a look, then go back to what they were doing; others react with action and emotion. For instance, the tantrums of your high-intensity child can be heard throughout the apartment complex, while your neighbor's son retreats into quiet sulking when faced with disappointment.

Veronica was getting ready for art time with her class. While the children played quietly, Veronica set out paper, markers, pastels, and scissors. She was carrying the box containing the trays of watercolors and brushes when she tripped over a forgotten block and the box of painting supplies crashed to the floor.

The group of children reacted in a number of interesting ways. Some looked up, startled, then returned to playing. Steffi and Adam began to cry loudly. Mark got up to poke through the debris with his toe, while Angie ran around the room giggling.

The children responded differently to the same situation because their intensity levels were different. Understanding that children react to stimuli with varying degrees of intensity can help both parents and teachers deal with behavior more calmly.

DISTRACTIBILITY

Distractibility describes the way an outside stimulus interferes with a child's present behavior and his willingness (or unwillingness) to be diverted.

It is naptime at the childcare center when Melissa makes the unfortunate discovery that her special teddy bear has been left at home. The teacher holds her, talks with her, and offers one of the center's toys as a substitute, but nothing helps. Melissa spends the entire naptime sitting on her mat whimpering for her teddy.

Melissa has low distractibility, which will be a real asset someday when she's hired to be an air traffic controller. But for now, Melissa is not a child who should be brought to childcare without her precious teddy. In fact, it might be wise to have two teddy bears, one for home and another for school, so this sort of crisis can be avoided.

Aaron, on the other hand, is perfectly happy to curl up with whatever toy is available. Today he has forgotten his stuffed dinosaur, but when his teacher offers a blue rabbit, Aaron smiles and contentedly drifts off to sleep.

Later on in life, Aaron may prove to be an easygoing person who can do many things at once. It is encouraging to adults and children when parents and teachers remember to focus on the assets of a child's temperament.

PERSISTENCE AND ATTENTION SPAN

Persistence refers to a child's willingness to pursue an activity in the face of obstacles or difficulties; attention span describes the length of time he will pursue an activity without interruption. The two characteristics are usually related. One child who is threading beads on a string might give up if a bead doesn't go on immediately; another will try again and again until she succeeds. These children are demonstrating different levels of persistence. Again, no temperament is necessarily better than another; they're simply different, and they present different challenges in parenting and teaching.

Mitchell has been tracing the same map from his children's atlas every morning for a week. He has carefully continued his work, adding details and humming contentedly to himself as he draws. Mitchell's best friend, Erica, comes over to play, and she sits down to help him—for a while. Within half an hour, Erica has three hastily completed drawings and turns her attention to a new container of Play-Doh. Someday Erica may be discovering new strains of bacteria or innovative medications with her ability to detect and investigate, while most of us would be very comfortable with the future Dr. Mitchell performing our six-hour open-heart surgery.

It is important to understand that a child with a short attention span and little persistence does not necessarily have the condition known as attention deficit hyperactivity disorder (ADHD). ADHD (which can occur with or without hyperactivity) is a neurological condition that should be diagnosed by a pediatric neurologist or a pediatrician trained to recognize its special symptoms. It is not usually wise to act on a "diagnosis" offered by another parent or a caregiver—although such suggestions may be worth investigating with your child's physician.

Most physicians are reluctant to diagnose ADHD until a child is at least five or six years old; before that time, impulsive behavior, high activity levels, and short attention spans may be due to temperament, trauma, or developmental differences. If you're concerned, check with your child's pediatrician or a child therapist trained to evaluate young children (more about special needs in Chapter 18). Understanding development and temperament, being both firm and kind, and using Positive Discipline skills will help you and your child experience success at home and at school no matter what other conditions may be present.

Temperament: Challenge or Opportunity?

If asked, most parents and teachers would probably prefer children with a long attention span and high persistence; they're easier to teach and entertain. However, few children fit this ideal description. In fact, most families include children of different temperaments, and teachers can find themselves working with a large assortment.

Each child—and every temperament—possesses both assets and liabilities, strengths and weaknesses. None is "good" or "bad," and as you've already seen, comparison and judgments can lead to discouragement and disappointment. All parents must eventually recognize and accept the ways in which their children's dreams and temperaments are different from their own.

Evan's parents are artistic people who design beautiful wall hangings and nontraditional clothing. They became concerned that Evan wasn't being given ample opportunity for artistic expression at his preschool, as Evan never came home with paint on his clothes or clay under his fingernails. In fact, Evan had many opportunities to explore the world of art. He just wasn't interested. Evan was a precise, orderly youngster who preferred to work quietly putting together puzzles or building with blocks. He didn't like the slippery feel of paint on his hands or the gooey mess of clay. Evan's parents were viewing their son in light of their own temperaments, not his. When Evan's teacher explained his temperament, his parents were grateful. Now they could accept Evan for the unique person he is and encourage him to follow his own dreams, not theirs.

Needs of the Situation

An awareness of temperament will help you understand why different methods are more effective with some children than with others. There are some universal principles, such as everyone's right to dignity and respect.

You cannot make your child respect you, but you can treat yourself with respect. If your child is behaving disrespectfully, you can choose to leave the room or find another Positive Discipline method to deal with the behavior. It is neither effective nor respectful to withdraw love or acceptance from a child because her behavior needs work.

Aaron did nothing in half measures. His mother described her four-year-old son as "passionate," an admirable trait—in the right circumstances. One afternoon, Aaron's mom told him it was time to put away his crayons. Aaron did not want to stop coloring. His face scrunched up in anger, his jaw jutted out, and in a burst of anger he launched his crayons at his mother. Aaron's mom recognized that his frustration was understandable, but his feelings and his intense temperament did not give him permission to mistreat others. Aaron's mother took a calming breath to control her own anger, then proceeded to leave the room without any comment.

Aaron yelled. His mother remained calm, going to her own room. A few minutes passed, and Aaron began to realize that tantrums feel pretty silly when there is no one around to witness them. Aaron went in search of his mother.

When he found Mom in her room, Aaron climbed onto the bed with her and snuggled wordlessly against her side. Now Mom has a choice: she can lecture Aaron about his unacceptable behavior and march him into the next room to pick up the crayons, or she can respond to his desire to be close. Aaron's mom chose to give her small son a hug.

After they had established a good connection, Mom told Aaron that it was okay to feel angry sometimes, but it was not okay to throw things at her or anyone else. He snuggled closer to her and nodded to indicate that he knew he shouldn't throw things. After a few quiet moments, Mom asked whether he wanted help picking up the crayons that he had thrown or whether he could do it on his own. Aaron bounced off the bed and with one more hug dashed off to gather his crayons.

Did Aaron "get away with" misbehavior by throwing crayons at his mother? Actually, Aaron's mother chose to deal with the situation in a manner that allowed for both her own temperament and her son's. Had she yelled, demanded immediate compliance, or punished Aaron, the situation would likely have grown passionate on both sides. Instead, she respected her needs by removing herself as a target, modeling self-control, and taking her own cool-off moment. She let Aaron know that he was still loved by returning his hug, then invited him to correct the situation by picking up the crayons when he had calmed down.

Temperament and strong emotions are not an excuse for inappropriate actions. Taking into account a person's natural tendencies simply provides perspective, guides your responses, and reminds you that your child always needs your love, especially as he struggles to improve his life skills.

Positive Discipline Skills for Parents and Teachers

Many of the Positive Discipline skills we suggest are appropriate for children of all temperaments, because they invite children to learn co-operation, responsibility, and life skills. However, an understanding of temperament helps us understand why different methods may be more effective, depending on the temperament and needs of an individual child.

For example, positive time-out, when properly used, can be an encouraging way to help children who need time to calm down and cool off. Family and class meetings are essential to help children learn problem-solving skills and cooperation (see Chapter 17). Asking curiosity questions encourages children to focus on personal accountability as they explore what happened, what caused it to happen, how they feel about it, and what they might choose to do differently next time. Parents and teachers can help children develop into the best people they can be when they understand and respect differences, individuality, and the creativity of each child.

Parents who understand their child's temperament can be knowledgeable consultants to teachers and other people who may be working with that child. For example, if your child is slow to adapt, ask for a conference and explain to the teacher that your child adapts slowly but responds to patience and kind firmness. If your child has a short attention span, look for a program or a teacher who appreciates creativity and provides a variety of experiences during the day. Avoid authoritarian teachers and programs where children are required to spend a great deal of time sitting still and where children who do not conform to expectations are punished. Be sure that it is your child's temperament and not your own that motivates you. You should always be your child's best advocate and supporter.

Individuality and Creativity

One of the primary motivators for Chess and Thomas's study of temperament was the desire to stop society's tendency to blame mothers for the characteristics of their children. Chess and Thomas state, "A child's temperament can actively influence the attitudes and behavior of her parents, other family members, playmates, and teachers, and in turn help to shape their effect on her behavioral development." In this way, the relationship between child and parents is a two-way street, each continuously influencing the other.

Parents and teachers don't discourage individuality or creativity intentionally. An awareness of temperament underscores the diversity and individuality of all children.

Loving the Child You Have

Most parents have dreams for their children. You undoubtedly want your child to be healthy and happy, but more than that, you want her to fulfill all the potential you see in her. You may cherish visions of your child as a star athlete or musician, a Nobel-winning scientist, or even president of the United States.

Michael had dreamed of the day his son would be born. He proudly carried his newborn into a room decorated with pennants and some of Dad's own trophies, and he placed a tiny blue football in the infant's crib. As little Kevin grew, he was signed up for every sport. His dad was never too busy to toss the football or to take some batting practice. Kevin played tee-ball with the other five-year-olds and soccer with the youngsters' league. He had a miniature basketball hoop and a perfectly oiled baseball glove. His dad never missed a practice or a game.

There was only one problem: Kevin hated sports. He did his best, but he had little natural ability and he loathed competition. Alone in his room, he dreamed of being an actor or a comedian, of standing on a stage before smiling, applauding people. He lined up his stuffed animals and told his favorite stories and jokes, hearing in his mind the enthusiastic response. He regaled his neighborhood buddies with tall tales.

As Michael talked eagerly to his son about the major leagues, Kevin only sighed. Shattering his dad's dreams would take more courage than he possessed. Afraid of losing his father's love and approval, Kevin played on, growing just a little more discouraged with every game, feeling disappointed that he would never be the son his father really wanted.

All parents have dreams for their children, and dreaming is not a bad thing. If you are to encourage your child, though, and build her sense of self-esteem and belonging, you must take time to teach and encourage her dreams—not your own.

Work for Improvement, Not Perfection

Even with understanding, parents struggle occasionally with their child's temperaments and behavior, especially when they lose patience, focus on their own ego, or get hooked into reacting to behavior instead of acting thoughtfully. You and your children are all too human: you will have good days and days when you're just cranky. Awareness and understanding do not mean you become perfect; mistakes are inevitable. However, once you have had time to cool off after you make a mistake, you need to resolve it with your child. Children are usually more than willing to hug and offer forgiveness, especially when they know you'll do the same for them. It is important to help your child work for improvement, not perfection; you can give this gift to yourself as well.

1. Look at the list of nine temperaments and pick one. Determine where you fall in terms of each of these temperament traits using a scale of 1 to 10, where 10 means you very strongly express this trait and 1 means you don't strongly express this trait. Now do the same for your child. Are your numbers the same? Very different? Somewhere in between? Think about a situation where you and your child conflict. Can you find at least three respectful ways to improve your "goodness of fit"?

2. What does "needs of the situation" mean to you—and to your child? When going to the zoo, having a meal at a restaurant, or visiting a friend's house, what are the expectations and guidelines? How might your child's temperament affect his ability to comply?

   Tip: Refrain from "telling." Ask instead, with connection and encouragement.

3. Which aspects of your own temperament are most different from your child's? How can you practice self-awareness and take care of yourself so you can minimize disagreements and conflict?

CHAPTER 10

"Why Does My Child *Do* That?": The Messages of Misbehavior

Understanding your preschooler's development and filling your tool-box with Positive Discipline parenting tools will go a long way toward resolving conflicts with your young child. It also helps to know that temperament, birth order, brain development, physical and intellectual abilities, and skill acquisition underlie much of your child's behavior in these early years. Still, even the most delightful preschooler isn't perfect, and misbehavior can be frustrating. Why *do* children misbehave? And what should parents do about it?

Carly is playing happily on the floor while her mom pays the bills. The phone rings, Carly's mom answers—and suddenly Carly is glued to her mother's leg, whining for juice. No amount of whispered urging will make Carly return to her play. Why?

Alberto knows that brushing his teeth is part of his bedtime routine. He also knows that this procedure is extremely important to his fa-ther. When Alberto's dad approaches with a loaded brush, Alberto folds his arms, furrows his brow, and clamps his mouth tightly shut. Alberto's dad threatens, pleads, and even tries to wiggle the tooth-brush past Alberto's lips, but Alberto keeps his mouth sealed. Why?

Are these children misbehaving? Well, it certainly seems so. Most parents have experienced moments like these and have struggled to find a solution. As you will learn, before you can help your child behave differently, you must understand the beliefs *behind* your child's behavior, and why his behavior makes sense to him.

In addition to behaviors that are age-appropriate or age-typical, behavior can also be a coded message that reveals a child's underlying beliefs about himself and about life. When your child misbehaves, he may be telling you in the only way he knows that he is feeling discouraged, or that he feels like he doesn't belong. As you learn to decipher this code, you will find that your responses (and eventually, your child's behavior) will change.

There is a parable that urges us to walk a mile in someone else's shoes before we condemn or criticize his actions. When you can get into your child's world (and walk in his small shoes), his behavior may begin to make sense.

What Is Misbehavior?

Parents sometimes view any atypical behavior as misbehavior. For just a moment, put yourself in your child's place; make an effort to get into his world.

Four-year-old Randy was at home with his mom, recuperating from the chicken pox. Mom had had to take a few days off from work and needed to spend some time on the phone keeping up with business. One afternoon, after a particularly long phone call, she walked into Randy's room and found him absorbed in using the permanent marking pens. The imaginative little boy had looked at his chicken pox spots and been reminded of his dot-to-dot coloring book. Randy had removed his clothes and was busily drawing lines from one spot on his body to the next with the marking pens. He was covered with brightly colored lines connecting his red spots.

Randy's mom was wise enough to realize that this was not misbehavior. He was not trying to get attention or make a mess; he had decided that his body was a large dot-to-dot drawing! What did his mom do? She let her sense of humor take over. She went and got the washable markers and finished connecting the dots with him.

It would have been easy for Mom to scold and humiliate Randy. The entire event could have disintegrated into tears and misery. Instead, Mom made room for one of childhood's treasured moments. When Randy is a dad himself, sitting with his children around Grandma's table telling "Remember when . . ." stories, Randy and his mom will both laugh as they remember Randy's dot-to-dot chicken pox!

When three-and-a-half-year-old Elsie's dad picked her up from preschool one evening, he immediately noticed that Elsie's hair was significantly shorter in the front than it had been that morning. "Did someone cut Elsie's hair today?" he asked Elsie's teacher.

"No, she did that herself," the teacher replied. "Elsie has been practicing a lot with the safety scissors lately."

Was Elsie misbehaving? When Dad entered Elsie's world, he realized that Elsie was actively exploring the wonders of using scissors. Today she had discovered that hair could be cut. Dad may not like his daughter's new hairstyle, and he will surely explain to Elsie that he would prefer that she not cut her own (or anyone else's) hair. He might also tell his intrepid daughter, "Let's find some things you can cut." This dad knows that Elsie's experiment was a learning experience. Hair grows back. Elsie made a mistake, and her dad will help her to learn from it.

Both of these children were behaving in ways that are developmentally appropriate—and quite creative. Yet it would have been easy to interpret both situations as misbehavior.

So, how do you know when a behavior is misbehavior? The key is the child's need for belonging and her feeling of discouragement. Children who feel discouraged about their ability to belong are more likely to misbehave. Neither Randy nor Elsie was discouraged; instead, both children were exploring the world around them (and their parents and teachers might want to increase their supervision of permanent markers and scissors!).

Randy's behavior could have been misbehavior if he had been trying to get his mother to play with him but he was so engrossed in his body art that he wasn't even aware his mom was on the phone. If Randy was trying to get his mom to notice or respond to him, his behavior might have been intended as a mistaken way to feel a sense of belonging. When a child believes he doesn't belong (even momentarily), he feels discour-

aged. Out of that discouragement he chooses what Rudolf Dreikurs, author of *Children: The Challenge*, called a "mistaken goal of misbehavior."[1] They are considered "mistaken" goals because the child mistakenly believes the behavior will help him regain a sense of belonging. As Rudolf Dreikurs said, a misbehaving child is simply a discouraged child who wants to belong and has a mistaken idea about how to achieve this goal.

Misbehavior or Coded Message?

Four-year-old Mary is visiting her grandparents' house on Thanksgiving, with all the other aunts, cousins, and members of her family. When Grandma goes to see what's taking Mary so long in the bathroom, she finds Mary tearing a roll of toilet paper to shreds.

Is Mary misbehaving? It would be understandable if her grandmother's first response was to feel hurt and disappointed. How an adult feels is the first clue to identifying mistaken goal behavior.

Getting into a child's world is a bit like looking through a kaleidoscope. Pretend that you are Mary's grandmother. What do you see when you look through the kaleidoscope? You may see piles of shredded paper everywhere, dulled by the shadow of your own disappointment. Now turn the kaleidoscope slightly and look again. Look at Mary, who has just been chased away from the kitchen because she was "underfoot." Look at Mary, who just got told by her big sister Joan that she was too little to play Monopoly with Joan and her older cousins. Look at Mary, who wanted to show Grandpa how to do "Itsy Bitsy Spider" but was abandoned when he had to go help move chairs into the dining room. What might Mary really be saying with her toilet paper? What is she thinking and feeling?

Understanding Mary's world does not mean that deliberately making a mess is okay. But understanding some of what Mary is experiencing is likely to affect how her grandmother responds. Mary will still have to pick up all the tiny bits of paper. Armed with love and understanding, Grandma may be more likely to help Mary pick up the pieces and maybe to invite her to help roll out pie dough afterward.

Misbehaving children are discouraged children, and encouragement is like rain to their parched souls. It is important to create opportunities to help children feel encouraged and valuable, to let them know they belong.

Let's turn the kaleidoscope together and take a look at the four coded messages of discouraged children.

Remember, your attitude matters. New tools won't be effective unless your attitude communicates connection, encouragement, kindness, and firmness.

Breaking the Code

If you can learn to read the code behind your child's behavior in different situations, you can deal effectively with his *beliefs* instead of just the behavior itself.

There are three specific clues that will help you break the code. Let's examine the clues that help you decode the message behind a child's misbehavior—and, finally, what to do that will encourage your child and help him change his behavior.

EARLY CHILDHOOD MISTAKEN GOAL CHART

THE CHILD'S GOAL IS:	IF THE ADULT FEELS (THINKS):	AND TENDS TO REACT BY:	AND IF THE CHILD'S RESPONSE IS:	THE BELIEF BEHIND THE CHILD'S BEHAVIOR IS:
Undue attention (to keep adults occupied or to get special service).	**Annoyed, irritated** ("I'm overwhelmed by how much you are demanding of me"). **Worried, guilty** ("What if I'm not doing enough for you?").	Reminding. Coaxing. Doing things that the child could do for himself.	Stopping temporarily but resuming the same (or another) challenging behavior. Stopping when given one-to-one attention or something special is given.	"I belong only when I'm getting noticed or getting special service." "I'm important only when I'm keeping you busy with me."
Misguided power (to be the boss or to make sure the adult isn't).	**Challenged, threatened** ("You are *not* getting away with this! I'm going to make you do what I say"). **Defeated** ("It's just not worth fighting you over this").	Pushing back harder. Setting rigid limits. Giving in just to avoid the battle.	Being angrily defiant. Escalating the battle. Throwing a tantrum.	"I belong and am capable only when I feel powerful on my terms." "You can't make me do anything, and you can't stop me either."
Revenge (to get even and hurt others).	**Disbelieving, hurt, disappointed, embarrassed** ("I can't believe you actually did this"). **Enraged** ("I'm going to hurt you back so you know how it feels").	Retaliating and punishing angrily. Feeling personally injured. Worrying about what others might think.	Retaliating back. Hurting others. Damaging property. Escalating and perhaps finding an even more hurtful behavior.	"I do *not* belong. This hurts me so deeply, I want to hurt you and others to show how it feels to be unloved and unvalued."
Assumed inadequacy (to give up and simply be left alone).	**Despairing, hopeless** ("I don't have a clue what to do"). **Helpless, inadequate** ("Nothing is helping and nothing will help").	Backing off and leaving the child alone. Giving up. Overhelping. Showing a lack of faith in the child.	Withdrawing even further inward. Showing no improvement or response. Refusing to try.	"I can't belong and I am not capable. I can't live up to your expectations, so why try?" "It's no use trying because I won't do it right anyway."

THE ADULT MAY CONTRIBUTE BY THINKING:	CODED MESSAGES	HOW THE ADULT CAN HELP AND ENCOURAGE:
"I'm afraid I will hurt you by not giving you enough attention." "I feel guilty when you're not happy." "You won't feel supported if I don't clap and cheer for you." "It hurts to watch you struggle so I will do things for you."	Notice me and involve me usefully.	Redirect into contributing behavior ("I could really use your help."). Allow the child to experience feelings, including disappointment. Strengthen routines. Use more encouragement and less praise.
"This is a power struggle that I have to win!" "If I give in even an inch, this child will never learn that adults are in charge." "I can't bear the screaming. Just do what you want."	Let me help. Give me choices.	Use asking instead of telling. Seek cooperation and contribution instead of compliance. Model withdrawing from the conflict to calm down. Find developmentally appropriate ways for the child to be powerful. Stay focused on finding solutions together (instead of arguing or giving in).
"This child is just *mean!*" "If I don't come down hard on this, the child will never learn." "If I don't come down hard on this, others will think I'm weak."	I'm hurting. Validate my feelings.	Validate hurt feelings *first* even when that seems difficult. Help the child manage emotions until he or she can do it without you. Use physical closeness as silent encouragement. Help make amends to those who have been hurt.
"What is the problem? This isn't that hard." "I expect you to live up to my expectations." "I know you can't do this. Let me just take care of it."	Don't give up on me. Show me a small step.	Teach skills by breaking them into small steps. Do *with* but don't do *for* the child. Use physical closeness as silent encouragement. Build on strengths and interests.

YOUR OWN FEELINGS IN RESPONSE TO THE BEHAVIOR

How *you* feel in response to a child's misbehavior is the first important clue to understanding the child's mistaken goal. For instance, when the child's goal is undue attention, her actions invite adults to feel:

- Annoyed
- Irritated
- Worried
- Guilty

When a child seeks misguided power, adults usually feel:

- Challenged
- Threatened
- Defeated

When the child's mistaken goal is revenge, her actions invite adults to feel:

- Disbelieving
- Hurt
- Disappointed
- Embarrassed
- Enraged

When a child is so discouraged that she gives up completely (the mistaken goal of assumed inadequacy), adults feel:

- Inadequate
- Despairing
- Hopeless
- Helpless

As you examine the Mistaken Goal Chart on page 178, you can usually find one set of feelings in the second column that best describes your feelings when faced with a misbehaving child. Note that you don't need to *do* anything about your feelings; simply notice and use them to help you understand your child. Also notice that your child's behavior does not "cause" you to feel a certain way. Your feelings flow from your interpretation of your child's behavior. When your understanding changes (and you recognize the coded message), your feelings also will change.

YOUR USUAL (INEFFECTIVE) ATTEMPTS TO STOP THE BEHAVIOR

Another clue is your usual response to your child's behavior. Adults often respond to the behavior of each mistaken goal in predictable ways. For instance, Dad and Ryan are constantly battling over something, whether it's what to wear, how much to eat, or how long Ryan can play at the computer. Their struggles reveal an ongoing battle for power: Dad gives a command, Ryan resists, and Dad reacts by fighting with Ryan, thinking, "You can't get away with this; I'll *make* you do it." Some adults just give in. In either case, there is a power struggle with a winner, a loser, or a slight pause while each gathers strength and ammunition to continue the battle. The third column of the mistaken goal chart lists the common reactions of adults to each of the four mistaken goal behaviors.

YOUR CHILD'S RESPONSE TO YOUR INEFFECTIVE ACTION

The third clue in deciphering a child's mistaken goal is how a child responds when the adult tries to stop the misbehavior with punitive or permissive methods (instead of Positive Discipline methods).

When the teacher at his childcare center tells five-year-old Matthew, "Behave yourself," Matthew usually responds by damaging toys or knocking over other children's blocks. Sometimes he even yells, "I hate you!" Matthew's mistaken goal is revenge. The goal is revenge when a child reacts to an adult's actions by hurting others, damaging property, or retaliating in some other way, such as using insulting words.

The fourth column of the mistaken goal chart lists a child's typical responses to ineffective intervention by adults for each mistaken goal behavior.

Stick to the Spirit of the Principle

Sometimes it is hard to determine a child's mistaken goal. Don't be overly concerned about getting the "right" answer, and don't get hung up in the "paralysis of analysis." The Mistaken Goal Chart is one tool of many in the Positive Discipline toolbox. Observe carefully, and do the best you can. Learn to see your mistakes as opportunities to learn and grow.

Misbehavior never happens in a vacuum (whether you're a child or an adult); there is a message behind the behavior, and the message involves some form of discouragement. No matter what the goal, it is always wise to use encouragement through unconditional love, hugs, patience, and letting children know you have faith in them.

Seeing the Possibilities

No matter how hard you try, you can never force someone to change his behavior, at least not more than superficially. And when behavior is tied to deeply held beliefs, those beliefs will have to change before the behavior will. You may be able to make a child stop banging his spoon against his cup by removing the cup, but if that child believes he is important only when he is getting attention, he will surely be banging his leg against the chair within the next five minutes.

Stopping a symptom provides only temporary relief from the condition. When a child's deep need to feel belonging is satisfied, his mistaken method of reaching that goal is no longer necessary. One of the most powerful ways to create a sense of belonging is to spend special time together.

Special Time

Since a misbehaving child is a discouraged child, the obvious solution for misbehavior is encouragement. Often it is not necessary to deal with the misbehavior directly. Instead, help the child feel encouraged and the misbehavior will disappear.

Each of us needs time with those we love. Quality time together affects the health of family relationships.[2] What do we mean by "special time," and what makes time together special? The 3 A's of Special Time will help you create meaningful special time with your child.

The 3 A's of Special Time are:

- Attitude
- Attention
- Alone

The first A is *attitude*. When you begin with an attitude that special time is valuable and worthwhile and you take time to really connect with your child, the time you spend together takes on a truly special quality. It is this quality of specialness that will help you create long-remembered and treasured memories. Attitude (yours and your child's) makes special time a powerful tool in strengthening each child's sense of belonging, the sort of feeling that comes from meaningful connection to others.

The second A, *attention*, means that special time will be more effective when you focus on being fully present with your child. Special time is a time to engage in an activity without any outside competition for your attention: no other family members, ringing phones, or scheduled commitments. Imagine filling up your child's heart and spirit, as well as your own, with this special sharing of attention and love. Even a trip to the grocery store can become special when you devote your full attention to being together.

The final A, *alone*, underscores the idea that special time is time spent away from other family members, a shared time between one child and one adult. No matter how big or small a family might be, time spent alone with a parent (or aunt, uncle, or grandparent) is a treat. A bit of creativity helps.

Jenny's mom, Rose, is a public defender whose days are long, with work often extending into weekend hours. But Jenny and her mom do have one time together each day—their car trip to Jenny's child-care. Rose decided to turn this time into their special time. Each morning, she and Jenny stop at a nearby coffee shop. While Jenny sips her hot chocolate and Rose enjoys a latte, they talk about the day ahead. Jenny looks forward to having her mom all to herself each morning, and Rose enjoys reliving these moments throughout her busy day.

Elaine needed to get creative too. When her husband is deployed at sea for months at a time, she is alone with their two children. So first she asked her daughter, five-year-old Maria, to be her special grocery buddy, a task Maria loves. Each week, while her younger brother, Johnny, is at preschool, Maria helps find the items on their list, while explaining new soccer moves or choosing cereal for a cousin's upcoming visit. Elaine gets a needed task done and enjoys uninterrupted time with Maria.

Next, Elaine made three-year-old Johnny her library pal. While Maria is at soccer practice, Elaine and Johnny walk to a nearby library. But it is actually the walk that has become their real special time. They discover mushrooms or new flower buds, gather leaves, or stop to watch a column of ants march across the sidewalk. Johnny loves to ask questions; even more, he loves having his mom's full at-tention on their weekly walks.

The other part of special time is *time*. For busy parents, this may be the most difficult part. Still, a wise person once said that "love" is spelled T-I-M-E. If something is important to you, chances are good that you will find time for it. Even in the busiest of lives, there is time for what matters.

One mother of five reads to each child for ten minutes every night—less than an hour of time spent reading. She cuddles with each child in the rocking chair in the corner of her bedroom while the other children help with after-dinner chores. Each child knows when her ten minutes are coming and is willing to honor the time Mom spends with the others. Interruptions are rare—and Mom spends her evenings lovingly connected with her children instead of all alone in the kitchen, scouring the sink.

Plan It and Name It

You can let your child know you look forward to your special time as much as she does: "I am glad we can have this special time together" or "It is a special treat for me to go swimming with you." You can validate your child's unique skills: "Isn't is great that you are older and can do so many things now that you couldn't do when you were a baby?" (For an older child still adjusting to the arrival of a new baby, such words will be balm, indeed!)

When your child wants some attention and you truly are too busy, it can be comforting to your child when you say, "I can't right now, but I sure am looking forward to our special time after dinner."

Satisfaction

Misbehavior requires a lot of energy from both children and adults and generates some pretty intense feelings. Being chased around the playground or carried kicking and screaming to bed might just seem better to a discouraged child than feeling unimportant, unnoticed, and powerless. There are a number of ways to invite a child to form a new belief, depending upon the goal of her behavior. Possible solutions for each mistaken goal are shown in the last column of the Mistaken Goal Chart.

(You may find this chart a useful addition to the front of your refrigerator.) There are many other Positive Discipline tools for encouragement—only a handful would fit in the last column.

Getting into a child's world will help you interpret the meaning of your child's behavior, especially if you can remember that undesirable behavior is not always *mis*behavior. When a discouraged child does misbehave, you can practice compassion and discover more effective ways to respond. In Chapters 11 and 12 we will examine what each of the four mistaken goals looks like at home and in childcare settings. When you understand the message behind a child's misbehavior, you will be better able to deal with it in loving and truly effective ways.

1. Plan some special time with your child. (It can be as simple as a walk outdoors or a trip to the library.) Turn off all devices and focus on this time together. What do you notice?

2. Think of a favorite memory from your childhood of time spent with a parent, grandparent, relative, or friend. What do you remember? What about it made you feel special? (If you can't recall a memory like this, what do you wish you could remember?) Now think of things that you and your child might do together to create a lasting and special memory.

3. Think of the past week. Was there a time you might have turned an unpleasant event into a positive one by using humor? How might seeing the situation from your child's perspective (getting into his world) have transformed your response?

CHAPTER 11

Mistaken Goals at Home

To understand the coded messages behind your child's actions and to work with him effectively, it is helpful to learn to recognize mistaken goals in real life. Let's see what happens when behavior is viewed from the perspective of the mistaken goals. (Refer to the Mistaken Goal Chart on page 178 as you learn.)

Undue Attention, or "I'll Keep You Busy with Me!"

Mom, Catherine (age seven), and Ann (age five) are in the doctor's office because Catherine has a fever and cough. Mom gets Catherine settled in the waiting room and gently tucks her coat around her. She feels her forehead for fever and tries to help her feel as comfortable as possible. Mom then sits down and begins to look through a magazine. Ann comes over with a children's book she has found and asks her mom to read it to her. Mom says, "Not right now." She reminds Ann that she was up most of the night with Catherine, and now she just wants to look at her magazine.

Ann wanders away, but a few minutes later she begins to bounce up and down on the couch. "Stop bouncing and sit quietly, Ann,"

Mom calls out. Ann stops bouncing but within minutes she asks if she can sit on Mom's lap. Mom says, "No, of course not. You are much too big a girl for that!" Mom gets up and goes over to Catherine to check on her fever again.

Then they are called into the examining room. As the three of them are waiting for the doctor, Ann complains of a stomachache. Mom looks at her anxiously and feels her forehead. When the doctor arrives to examine Catherine, Ann starts tugging on Mom's sleeve, saying she has to go to the bathroom. Mom sighs loudly, gets up, and takes Ann down the hall to the bathroom.

Children are not consciously aware of their mistaken goals. They aren't even aware of their beliefs. This is why it is helpful to become a "mistaken goal detective." What might Ann believe that prompts her to act this way? Well, Ann has noticed Catherine getting a lot of attention. Ann may have decided that Mom loves Catherine more. It certainly looks that way from her perspective. Ann's behavior is saying, "I want attention too. I want to be noticed and to be a part of what is going on." Ann believes that she belongs or matters only when she is being noticed or when Mom is busy with her. This is the first of the four coded messages (or mistaken goals): undue attention.

Put on your detective hat and make some guesses. How do you think Mom is feeling right now? Annoyed? Irritated? Guilty? She probably wishes she'd left Ann at home. How would Mom feel if she got into Ann's world? What might she do differently?

Identifying the Goal of Undue Attention

Feelings listed under the second column of the Mistaken Goal Chart are the first clue to help you identify the mistaken goal. The second clue is how the adult reacts to the misbehavior. When Mom and her daughters were at the doctor's office, what sorts of things were taking place and how did Mom react (column three of the chart)? Mom asked Ann to sit quietly and stop bouncing on the sofa. Mom coaxed Ann out of sitting on her lap by reminding her that she is a "big girl" now. Finally, she walked her down the hall to the bathroom, which Ann may have been able to do on her own. All of these were reactions to Ann's behavior. Children whose mistaken goal is undue attention successfully keep the adults in their lives busy with them most of the time. All children need their parents' attention, but they may not be seeking that attention in positive, encouraging ways.

Look at the next column on the chart. What was Ann's response to her mother's actions? Ann stopped each behavior when her mother told her to, but quickly discovered another attention-seeking behavior. The feelings and reactions of Ann's mother and Ann's responses to her mother are important clues that reveal the mistaken goal of undue attention.

The child who sends a coded message by seeking undue attention is willing to accept any attention, even negative attention, to achieve this goal. Peer through your kaleidoscope and picture this child wearing a large sunbonnet covered with feathers, fruit, flowers, or flying dinosaurs. There is a colorful banner that says, "Notice me. Involve me usefully."

"But wait a minute," parents often say when they learn their children's behavior is focused on getting attention. "We give our kids lots of attention. We spend all our free time with them; we read to them and play with them. How could they possibly need *more* attention?" Actually, giving children excessive attention (even in the name of love) may be part of the problem. Children with special needs or children who simply are loved a great deal may receive huge amounts of adult attention. Children love this—as long as it continues. When something happens to deflect adult attention, even momentarily (a telephone call, a doctor's appointment, a conversation with a friend), children perceive this as a loss and do whatever they can to regain the usual amount. In other words, it isn't necessarily true that children whose mistaken goal is undue attention aren't receiving enough attention; they may actually be receiving so much that it creates a need for special service—all of the time.

Responding to the Message

How can you give your child the attention and feeling of belonging he needs without giving in to an endless stream of small annoyances? Now that you understand the belief that prompts your child's mistaken goal of undue attention, you can respond in ways that will encourage your child instead of reinforcing the mistaken belief "Love means I must be the center of attention all the time." Here are some things you can do.

ENCOURAGEMENT FOR UNDUE ATTENTION SEEKERS

- Use active listening to deal with the belief instead of the behavior.
- Notice and compromise.
- Involve the child to gain useful attention through contribution.
- Give a reassuring hug.
- Encourage the child's ability to entertain and soothe himself.

USE ACTIVE LISTENING TO DEAL WITH THE BELIEF INSTEAD OF THE BEHAVIOR

Let's go back to the doctor's office. Mom could have chosen to deal with Ann's *belief* that Mom loved her sister more rather than attempting to control Ann's behavior. One possibility might be to practice "active listening" with Ann.

Mom could say, "It must be hard for you to see me giving so much attention to Catherine. You might feel that I don't have any love left for you." If Mom has guessed correctly, Ann will feel validated. She may even cry from relief as she acknowledges the truth of her mother's guess. She might then be able to give up her belief that she doesn't have significance—and her need to misbehave.

NOTICE AND COMPROMISE

Mom might tell Ann that she will read her one book when Ann agrees to look at another book quietly afterward and let her mother look at a magazine. This form of limited special time offers appropriate attention while setting a boundary on undue attention. By asking Ann to honor her need for some quiet time, her mother has not just "given in" to Ann's demands for attention but has understood Ann's needs, respectfully stated her own needs, and then reached a compromise.

INVOLVE THE CHILD TO GAIN USEFUL ATTENTION
THROUGH CONTRIBUTION

Mom could invite Ann to help care for her sick sister. (Do you remember the banner that said, "Involve me usefully"?) She could ask Ann how they might help Catherine feel more comfortable, involving her in the process of caring for Catherine. Mom then might ask for Ann's support by explaining how tired she is, and Ann might offer to give her a neck rub, or even read her mother a story. When adults ask children for their help, children can be remarkably thoughtful. These choices could create a sense of caring and connection, rather than inviting further misbehavior.

GIVE A REASSURING HUG

Another choice might be to hug Ann and tell her that Mom loves her very much. It can be very powerful to forget about the behavior and give a reassuring hug that says, "You belong and you are significant in my life." This is often enough to stop the misbehavior. A hug feels much better for everyone than nagging and lecturing.

ENCOURAGE THE CHILD'S ABILITY TO ENTERTAIN
AND SOOTHE HIMSELF

None of us is born knowing how to amuse ourselves; it takes time and encouragement from parents and caregivers for children to learn this skill. Children usually expect adults to provide constant entertainment and diversion, but if adults comply, children may never learn how to occupy quiet moments or cure boredom for themselves.

Encourage your child to learn to entertain herself. When Ann demanded undue attention, her mother might have suggested that Ann watch where each fish in the office tank spends most of its time. "Does the orange one only go to one corner? Does the striped one stay near the bottom?" Helping a child to learn to tune in to details by giving her a prompt for doing so is a wonderful way to develop valuable life skills. Keen observation skills open up a world of discovery. When a child does seek undue attention, saying "I love you, and I have faith in your ability to entertain yourself right now" offers a message of encouragement.

Misguided Power, or "You're Not the Boss of Me!"

Four-year-old Beverly is standing beside the computer, gazing curiously at the keyboard. Interesting pictures and patterns move across the colored screen; Beverly has watched Mom and Dad do this and is determined to try. She's been warned not to touch the computer, so she looks carefully around her and, seeing that Mom's not in sight, gives the keyboard several taps.

Mom turns the corner just in time to see this. She flies across the room, grabbing Beverly firmly by the elbow, totally hooked by her small daughter's misbehavior. "I've told you not to touch the computer! Now you've messed up my work," she says angrily, and lightly slaps Beverly's hand. Beverly responds by twisting free of her mother's grip and smashing her small fist down on the keyboard.

Mom, exasperated beyond belief, picks Beverly up and puts her into her room for a punitive time-out. Beverly launches into a major tantrum; Mom storms out to repair her damaged files. Right now, Mom is feeling angry—she has been defeated by a four-year-old!

Beverly's behavior may have begun as a lack of controlling her inner scientist. She knew she was not supposed to touch the computer—but that rule could not override her impulse to explore, touch, and learn. Mom's swift reaction changed things at once, triggering an intense power struggle. Beverly's discouraged message becomes her misbehavior: Beverly is saying, "I don't believe I am important unless I have power—or at least I don't let you boss me around."

Identifying the Goal of Misguided Power

It is important to remember that it takes two to engage in a power struggle. When Beverly and her mom were struggling over the computer, her mom first felt provoked and then defeated. Beverly's mother reacted with some power-filled statements: "I've told you . . ." and "You've messed up my work!" Beverly's response to her mother's ineffective interventions was to intensify her own behavior. And the battle raged on.

The problem with power struggles is that if there's a winner, there also has to be a loser. When the loser is a child you love, the victory may not be worth the price.

There is another interesting thing going on here. Power struggles generate a lot of energy, and the harder the adult tries to win, the more obvious it becomes just how much power the child has. This is a thrilling discovery for children beginning to experience their own initiative.

If you have heard an impassioned "You're not the boss of me!" shouted by a child, you might well suspect that the goal involved is misguided power. This child can be imagined wearing a bright orange hard hat. Printed in bold letters on this hat is the command "Let me help; give me choices."

Responding to the Message

When Beverly and her mom fought over the computer, they were involved in one of a series of power struggles that might set the tone of their future relationship. Fortunately, Beverly's mom learned about her own responsibility in fueling their power struggle. She changed *her* behavior first, and thus opened the way for Beverly to change her belief system and her behavior.

ENCOURAGEMENT FOR SEEKERS OF MISGUIDED POWER

- Offer limited choices.
- Turn misguided power to useful power by asking for help.
- Shut your mouth and act—kindly and firmly.
- Ask if a positive time-out would be helpful.
- Make a date for problem-solving.

OFFER LIMITED CHOICES

Beverly's mom sought out a parenting class and eventually learned how to empower Beverly by giving her power in appropriate ways. She learned to give Beverly limited choices and ask curiosity questions instead of demanding obedience: "Mommy's work is for Mommy to do. Would you like to read a book or play with your Legos?" or "What would you like to do while I work?"

TURN MISGUIDED POWER TO USEFUL POWER BY ASKING FOR HELP

A power struggle can often be defused by asking a child for her help. Mom could let Beverly know how much she needs her. "Honey, we are a family and you are so important to me. I know you really want to touch the computer, but computers are easy to damage. Mommy needs to be the only person who touches the computer. But I'll bet there are ways you could help me with my work. Let's see what we can find!" Asking for help or involving a child in the solution redirects both the child and the parent away from a power struggle and toward the positive power of cooperation. Demands invite resistance. Curiosity questions invite co-operation.

SHUT YOUR MOUTH AND ACT—KINDLY AND FIRMLY

Another way to disengage from a power struggle is to be firm and kind *at the same time*. When Beverly pounded the computer keyboard, she was throwing down the gauntlet, challenging her mom to fight. Instead of picking up the gauntlet, Mom can stop talking and act. She can kindly but firmly pick Beverly up and take her into another room (this time Mom's energy is kind and firm, instead of combative). There need be no further mention of the computer until after a cooling-off period, which is often necessary before a child will listen to a limited choice or an appeal for help.

By not lecturing or shaming her daughter, Mom does not invite further resistance. Even if Beverly chooses to have a tantrum, Mom has defused the power struggle by refusing to become engaged (or throwing her own mom-size tantrum). Children's tantrums are less likely when children feel the energy of kindness along with firmness. This does not mean that tantrums can be entirely avoided, but avoiding a tantrum is not the goal. The goal is to kindly and firmly act upon what you have said. You can also help your child find ways to cool off when strong emotions erupt.

ASK IF A POSITIVE TIME-OUT WOULD BE HELPFUL

When adults and children engage in power struggles, both have stopped thinking rationally and are reacting irrationally. The neuronal connections needed for logical thought and objectivity actually become unavailable when the brain is flooded by strong emotion. Until everyone can cool off, effective problem-solving will need to be postponed; positive time-out may be required before win-win solutions can be found. Invite your child to help you create a positive time-out area (see Chapter 6). Then, when power struggles occur, you can ask, "Would it help you to go to your cool-off spot until you calm down?" If your child has helped create a place to cool off and understands that this kind of time-out is not punitive, she will often choose this option. If your child says no, you might say, "Well, then I think *I'll* go to my room until I feel better." What powerful role modeling that would be! *Remember, it takes two to have a power struggle. When you choose to calm down, your child can too.*

It is appropriate to follow up a positive time-out by working on a solution together. Beverly and her mom might agree that Beverly can play her own computer games when Mom is there to help, that Mom needs uninterrupted time to work (and will help Beverly find an appropriate activity for these times), and that Beverly must ask Mom when she wants computer time.

MAKE A DATE FOR PROBLEM-SOLVING

Problem-solving with preschoolers can be accomplished by using curiosity questions to help them explore what happened, what caused it to happen, and what ideas they have to solve the problem. Four- and five-year-olds are also very good at participating in family meetings (see Chapter 17). After a cool-off period (or even at the time of conflict), it might defuse the power struggle to ask, "Would you like to put this problem on our family meeting agenda, or would you like me to?" Not only does putting the problem on the family meeting agenda give everyone a cooling-off period, but you can then work together on solutions at the meeting. One of the most obvious solutions they might think of is for Mom to put her computer out of reach so Beverly doesn't have to deal with the temptation.

Revenge, or "I'll Make You Feel as Bad as I Do!"

It is bedtime, and Dad is helping three-year-old Alice get ready. Dad says it is time to put on her jammies, but Alice is having great fun playing with bubbles in the sink and doesn't want to stop. Dad takes Alice's arm, perhaps a bit more firmly than he had intended, and says in a threatening tone of voice, "Alice, put on your pajamas now!" Alice begins to cry: Dad is hurting her feelings and her arm. As Dad becomes more impatient, Alice says, "You're mean. If you hadn't been such a crummy dad, Mom wouldn't have left." And Alice breaks her father's grip on her arm, runs to her room, and slams the door.

Dad feels terrible; he can't believe his sweet little girl would say such a thing. He is hurt and disbelieving.

Alice's coded message might be, "Daddy hurt my feelings, so I'll hurt him back," and she does so in the only way she knows. This is the third of the four mistaken goals: revenge.

Identifying Revenge

Dad was shocked that Alice would resist him and then say something cruel. He didn't feel good about grabbing her arm, but he was exhausted by his ongoing divorce from Alice's mom and didn't know how else to respond to her behavior. Both Alice and her dad wound up feeling deeply hurt.

Whenever an adult feels hurt by the behavior of a child, it is likely that the child is feeling hurt too. As you examine Dad's feelings and reactions and Alice's response, you will see the clues that indicate the mistaken goal of revenge. When you picture the child whose goal is revenge, imagine a black baseball cap turned backward. On the back is written the plea "I'm hurting; validate my feelings."

Responding to the Message

When adults can begin to see a child who is hurtful as a hurting child, they feel motivated to respond to that child differently. Instead of giving in to the instinctive desire for retaliation and punishment, they can choose to offer care and support. If a child is feeling hurt, does it make sense to make that child feel worse?

ENCOURAGEMENT FOR REVENGE SEEKERS

- Deal with the hurt feelings, then wait for a cooling-off time and work on a solution together.
- Apologize if you caused the pain.
- Listen to your child's feelings.
- Make sure the message of love gets through.
- Make amends, not excuses.

DEAL WITH THE HURT FEELINGS

First of all, Dad can move to the heart of the matter by dealing with Alice's hurt feelings. Dad could say, "It looks like you're feeling very hurt right now. I'll bet it hurt your feelings as well as your arm when I grabbed you." The adult getting into her world and acknowledging her feelings is validating for a child, and she is likely to feel understanding, belonging, and significance. Once they have both calmed down, they could work together to find solutions for dealing with the problem (or to prevent it from happening in the future).

APOLOGIZE IF YOU CAUSED THE PAIN

Alice's dad really does love his daughter, and he immediately regretted his actions. When he takes responsibility for his own behavior by apologizing, his attitude may invite Alice to change her beliefs. Dad can reassure her that it is wrong for people to hurt each other, even when they're angry or hurt.

Responding to the belief behind a child's behavior (instead of reacting to the behavior itself with punishment or lectures) will require that you give up the notion that you can or should control your child. You must also decide for yourself that teaching and encouragement are more effective responses than punishment. Making this change—especially if you were raised with old-fashioned ideas—will take some time. Be patient with yourself, acknowledge your mistakes, and be willing to learn from them.

If you have never had the experience of apologizing to a child, swallow your pride, admit that adults aren't always right, and apologize the next time you make a mistake with your child. Children are delightfully quick to forgive, and you may discover that the hugs that follow apologies bring you even closer. And you have modeled a life skill that will improve all future relationships.

LISTEN TO YOUR CHILD'S FEELINGS

Dad might take a moment to observe his small daughter closely. He may notice Alice's jutting lip, trembling chin, and the tears beginning to fill her eyes. And he can ask Alice—with genuine interest—what she is feeling. If she is too young to articulate her feelings, he can ask her if she thinks that Daddy doesn't love her, or if she is missing her mother. Alice will probably respond with a verbal (or nonverbal) signal that lets her dad know he has understood correctly. When Dad and Alice have this kind of conversation, they are developing a new sense of connection and trust.

When a child is feeling hurt, it is difficult for her to move beyond her emotions to solutions. Therefore, it is important to address the feelings first.

MAKE SURE THE MESSAGE OF LOVE GETS THROUGH

Dad has a chance to tell Alice how much he loves her and how important she is to him. When a child is feeling hurt, this message can do so much to heal the pain. Dad also can share how he felt. When Dad can listen to and respect Alice's feelings and then explain his own, each will learn a great deal about the other. The love connection is rekindled. Children always need "connection before correction." When children feel loved and connected, they often will stop misbehavior, or at least be willing to work with you to find solutions.

If Dad tries these new ideas, he just might find himself snuggling close to his precious daughter as they read a bedtime story together. Even a painful and damaging experience can be healed when the message of love and caring gets through.

MAKE AMENDS, NOT EXCUSES

Once Alice and her dad have dealt with their feelings, they will still need to complete their bedtime routine. Dad might offer to help her put on her jammies with a special song. If Alice resorts to tears or retreats into hurt feelings again, her dad can make this encounter an opportunity to teach (rather than continuing the revenge cycle) by kindly and firmly continuing with her regular bedtime routine.

"HELP ME PUT THINGS RIGHT"

Q. *My four-year-old threw his cup of juice onto the floor when I told him it was time for his nap. The cup cracked and broke. I think his feelings were hurt because he didn't get to go to the park this morning. I want to respond to his hurt feelings, but I don't think his behavior should go unpunished.*

A. Sometimes adults take the approach that if a child misbehaves "for a mistaken purpose," he is no longer responsible for his actions. *Ignoring misbehavior does not teach life skills. Nor does punishment, which, translated, usually means "You must suffer to learn." What does help is to give children the opportunity to make amends.*

If an item is damaged, first help children understand that mistakes are opportunities to learn. Then it is appropriate to work out a way for the child to replace or repair it. That might mean doing a few helpful tasks to earn the money—even four-year-old children can do some small job—or taking the money out of his piggy bank. Or it might mean helping come up with a plan to repair the damage, such as patching a tear in a book.

All of these solutions focus on teaching responsibility. Spanking, shaming, yelling, or taking away television for a week does not achieve the same life lesson. With those punishments, a child might learn fear of retaliation, escalate to more hurtful behavior himself, or decide that he is a "bad" person. None of these outcomes includes learning to take responsibility for his actions.

Children feel so much better about themselves when they deeply believe that mistakes are opportunities to learn, and are then given a chance to put things right. If this is done in a spirit of love instead of anger, a child can regain a measure of self-esteem in the process. Few children feel pleased with themselves when they lose control of their behavior. They need encouragement to learn from their mistakes and tools to repair the damage, while parents need to change their attitude of shame and blame to one of support and true discipline.

Assumed Inadequacy: "I Give Up"

Jean lives with her grandparents and today is her fifth birthday. When she enters the kitchen, her grandparents eagerly watch for her reaction to the brand-new bike proudly displayed in the center of the room. Jean looks anxiously around and doesn't comment on the bike. Grandmother impatiently asks, "Well, what do you think? Do you like it?" Jean doesn't respond. Grandma then says in a coaxing voice, "Jean, look at your wonderful new bike." Jean shakes her head and mumbles, "I can't ride a bike." Grandpa rushes over to reassure Jean. "That's no problem, sweetie, you'll learn in no time." Jean says nothing and does not go near the bike. Her grandparents look at one another in exasperation and shrug their shoulders. "What's the use?" they think, and Grandpa dejectedly begins to pour Jean's cereal and milk for her.

Jean's grandparents have been convinced to give up on her. They feel hopeless about themselves and about Jean. Somehow Jean has come to believe that she is not "good enough," that she is truly help-less. She acts upon this belief by convincing others of her inadequacy. Jean's grandparents love her, but they mistakenly believe that the best way to show that love is to do things for her, such as pouring her cereal and milk, which she could easily do for herself.

Of all the four goals or messages, children displaying assumed inad-equacy are often the most overlooked—and the most discouraged. They usually don't create the havoc that children acting upon the other three goals do. Children communicating this message may become nearly in-visible.

This goal is rarely found in children younger than age five unless they are given little or no opportunity to develop a sense of autonomy. It can be especially baffling when highly productive and goal-oriented parents see this behavior in their child. What parents value as personal drive and determination may overwhelm their children and convince them that they are truly incapable—that they can never measure up to expecta-tions. This creates the fourth mistaken goal: assumed inadequacy, or giving up.

Identifying Assumed Inadequacy

Jean's grandparents try not to feel hopeless, but Jean looks so discour-aged. They do their best to protect her and to make up for the fact that her parents aren't around. Grandma and Grandpa react to Jean's helpless behavior by doing things for her. Grandpa pours her milk and cereal; Grandma dresses her every morning. They supply Jean's every need. They buy her things and make plans and choices without her participation. Jean's response is to retreat further, to act passively, and to refuse to try anything new. The feelings, reactions, and responses all give clues that the behavior is assumed inadequacy.

Criticism may also cause feelings of inadequacy. It is easy to understand how a child who is constantly criticized might develop the belief that she can't do anything right. Being criticized for normal childhood behavior, like making messes, can be deeply discouraging. When children understand that mistakes are part of how everyone learns, they can break the power of the perfection myth. The child who pursues this mistaken goal may be pictured wearing a drab-colored ski hat pulled far down over her face. What you will find stitched on the front (if you look closely enough) is "Show me small steps; celebrate my successes."

Responding to the Message

Feeling inadequate and giving up is a lonely place to be. Since their goal is to be left alone, these children are rarely much trouble to others and are often overlooked. There are many things parents can do to meet this child's needs.

ENCOURAGEMENT FOR ASSUMED INADEQUACY

- Have faith in your child and let her do things for herself.
- Take time for training and encourage even the smallest steps.
- Teach that mistakes are wonderful opportunities to learn.

HAVE FAITH IN YOUR CHILD AND LET HER DO THINGS FOR HERSELF

Parents may not realize that doing too much for children (probably in the name of love) is discouraging. A child may adopt the belief "I'm not capable" when adults insist on doing things for her that she could do herself. Another possible belief is "I am loved only when others are doing things for me."

It may be helpful to remember that self-esteem comes from having skills, and that pampering a child actually discourages her. Make room for your child to learn and practice new skills—even when she does things imperfectly. When she says, "I can't," have patience; tell her, "I have faith that you can handle this task." Encouraging a child who believes that she is inadequate requires a great deal of patience, gentle perseverance, and faith in the child's abilities.

TAKE TIME FOR TRAINING AND ENCOURAGE
EVEN THE SMALLEST STEPS

It is not surprising that Jean does not know how to ride a bicycle; no one learns without teaching and practice. Instead of feeling frustrated, Grandma might share a story about her own experiences learning to ride a bike. Perhaps she could tell Jean how she felt the first time she fell and her brothers and sister laughed. When Grandma shares her own story, she is also telling Jean that feeling embarrassed is okay and that everyone has to learn how to do new things. Staying on a pedestal may be good for your image, but it can cripple the growth of closeness and trust.

How you react to your own struggles is important. Your child is watching and may believe you always succeed easily (and feel inadequate because he does not). Or he may watch you try something and meet with repeated failure. *How you react—whether you can laugh at yourself and keep on trying or whether you give up in discouragement—*

will give him clues about his own experiences. Never underestimate the power of role modeling.

Children who have already developed the belief "I'm inadequate" may resist attempts at training. This is why small steps are important. Grandpa might start by letting Jean sit on the bike inside the house. He might be sure the bike has training wheels and show Jean how they work. Before starting her down the block, he can reassure her that he will not let go until she is ready. Teaching her how to pour her own milk (from a small pitcher) would be helpful too.

TEACH THAT MISTAKES ARE WONDERFUL OPPORTUNITIES TO LEARN

What is your attitude toward your own mistakes? Most people learn much more from what they see than what they hear. One of the best ways to help a discouraged child is to stop all criticism, and to focus on learning from the inevitable mistakes. If Jean messes her dress up with paint or mud, Grandma may consider dressing her in more durable clothes. What a great message it would send if Grandma could learn to say, "Wow, you are covered with paint! You must have had a great time painting today."

Family members also can share mistakes on a regular basis. During dinnertime each person can take turns sharing a mistake they made and what they learned from it. This can create a sense of fun and learning—and a more helpful attitude about mistakes.

Be Aware of the Hidden Message

"Whew," you may be saying, "I had no idea there was so much going on in my child's head when he acts that way." It is important to understand that children do not *consciously* decide to pursue one of the mistaken goals; they are rarely aware of their own beliefs and are not out to baffle their parents with a game of "guess my goal." It also takes time to translate awareness of your child's mistaken goal into kind, firm, and encouraging action.

And sometimes we get it right without even realizing it.

Mellie and Ali dreaded mealtimes. One spill would turn into a table-size art project in a nanosecond. Their two daughters seemed to vie for who could make the biggest mess—until Melli and Ali changed their nightly routine.

After picking the girls up at their childcare, both parents quit rushing into the evening's cooking and cleaning. Instead, they started their evenings by gathering on the sofa, reading stories together, and simply reconnecting for a short time. After a few weeks, Ali commented that dinners weren't nearly as messy. It was true. By meeting their daughters' needs for connection with focused and appropriate attention, mealtimes were no longer a constant bid to keep their parents busy with them. When the real need was met, the problem was solved.

The Power of Contribution

Finding ways for even young children to contribute to the family and to learn new skills is another way to create a sense of belonging and significance—and to avoid at least some misbehavior. With patient teaching and practice, children can learn to do many helpful things, learning a sense of self-worth and confidence in the process. Here are some suggestions.

AGE-APPROPRIATE TASKS

AGE	SELF-CARE	FOOD	HOUSEHOLD
3	Undress self Wash hands Take off shoes Put on coat (with some help)	Feed self (with hands and spoon) Pour milk from small pitcher Serve fruit Oil potatoes for baking Peel bananas Stir batter (pancake, etc.) Rinse lettuce and other produce Slice hard-boiled eggs (with a special slicer)	Pick up toys Put own clothes in hamper Dig in garden Harvest berries and other garden produce Set table (napkins and silverware, except knives)
4	Select clothes Dress and undress self (with some help) Put on shoes	Squeeze fruit for juice Grate cheese Butter toast Scrub mushrooms Slice bananas, pickles, etc. (with butter knife) Knead dough Measure water to reconstitute juice Frost cupcakes	Straighten bedcovers Arrange cut flowers Stack newspapers Crush cans for recycling Set table Wash car (with help) Sort laundry
5	Help pack lunch Comb and help brush hair Wash hair Tie shoes (with some help)	Slice soft fruit or vegetables (with sharp knife, under supervision) Roll out dough Put together a cake mix Spread peanut butter and jam on crackers or bread Help plan menus "Smash" cooked potatoes with hand masher	Fold washcloths Care for pet Put away laundry (with some help) Wash windows Help grocery shop Polish shoes

(You can find more ideas in Lynn Lott and Riki Intner's *Chores Without Wars*.)[1]

When parents are aware of the message hidden in their child's behavior and when they can observe their own feelings and reactions, they then can take steps to encourage a discouraged child and to celebrate a child's willingness to take risks and make mistakes. In so doing, parents nurture children who believe they are capable, lovable, and worthwhile.

QUESTIONS TO PONDER

1. Think of a time when you believe your child misbehaved. What were you feeling? Now look at the chart on page 178 and determine which set of feelings in the second column best matches yours. Read across and decide if any of the other descriptions for that row seem to match up. What might your child's mistaken goal be? What is your child's mistaken belief?

2. Using the example you came up with in step 1, look at the list of alternative behaviors in the final column of the mistaken goal you have identified. Choose one or two responses that you are willing to try if this behavior happens again. (Remember, your attitude is an important ingredient in changing behavior.)

3. Think of a mistake that you made recently. What was your self-talk about this mistake? Did you scold yourself? Did you try to figure out what went wrong so you could do it differently? Was your inner dialogue helpful to you? If not, how would you like to change it?

CHAPTER 12

Mistaken Goals in the Preschool

Misbehavior—the coded messages children send us about their beliefs—doesn't happen just at home with parents. Misbehavior happens everywhere young children go. Teachers and caregivers also can learn to decipher children's mistaken goals and respond in ways that teach and encourage.[1]

Undue Attention in the Preschool

It should come as no surprise that where groups of children are gathered, the desire for undue attention appears.

There are 12 five-year-old children in Marcia's classroom at the Tiny Treasures Childcare Center this morning. At about ten o'clock, Johnny finds Marcia; his shoe is untied, and he asks her to tie it for him. Marcia does so, and Johnny goes off to play. Less than five minutes later, he needs help sharpening a pencil. Marcia helps him do that too, but no more than two minutes pass before she notices that Johnny has begun to mess around with Ben's blocks. Marcia reminds him that these are Ben's blocks and Johnny needs to choose something else to do. By ten-fifteen, Johnny's shoe is again untied. . . .

By now, Marcia is longing for her break. In addition to feeling annoyed by Johnny's constant demands, she is also feeling guilty that she doesn't enjoy being around this child very much. These feelings, as you will see in the second column of the Mistaken Goal Chart (page 178), are the first clue that Johnny's behavior is motivated by the mistaken goal of undue attention.

Marcia's reactions to Johnny's behavior are typical, and another clue to decoding his mistaken belief. She does things for Johnny that he could reasonably be expected to do for himself—or that he could learn to do on his own. She also spends a good deal of her time reminding Johnny to stop certain behaviors. A third clue that the mistaken goal is undue attention is that Johnny stops his behavior for a short while, but soon finds other ways to keep Marcia busy with him. Every teacher will recognize a child she knows in Johnny.

What are Johnny and other children like him really saying by their behavior? When a child seeks undue attention, he is acting on the belief that he can belong or count only by being noticed or by keeping adults busy with him. When you learn to decode their mistaken goal messages, you will understand that what children who misbehave are really saying to you is "I'm a child and I just want to belong."

Responding to the Message

Even when his teacher is able to understand that Johnny's behavior is a cry for belonging, it is not always possible to give one-on-one attention in group settings. Still, a number of things can be done routinely with all of the children that will greatly diminish constant bids for attention such as Johnny's.

ENCOURAGEMENT FOR UNDUE ATTENTION IN THE PRESCHOOL

- Help children get attention in useful ways through meaningful involvement.
- Teach nonverbal signals.
- Give special attention before the child seeks undue attention.
- Take time for training.

HELP CHILDREN GET ATTENTION IN USEFUL WAYS THROUGH MEANINGFUL INVOLVEMENT

As you learned in Chapter 10, the message for the mistaken goal of undue attention is "Notice me. Involve me usefully!" *It can be very effective to ignore misbehavior while redirecting a child to get attention in a useful way.* Marcia might involve Johnny by asking him to help her with something—washing out paintbrushes, erasing the board, or ringing a bell to let everyone know it's time to come in from lunch.

TEACH NONVERBAL SIGNALS

Consider teaching children nonverbal signals to let you know that they need your time or attention. Marcia might have taught the children in her class to gently place a hand on her arm to let her know that she is needed. Marcia's signal that she notices that child's request for assistance is to make eye contact with the child, hold up an index finger and nod, then resume what she was doing. This gives attention in a reasonable way, while still allowing a child to feel acknowledged.

GIVE SPECIAL ATTENTION BEFORE THE CHILD
SEEKS UNDUE ATTENTION

Marcia could comment on something that makes each child feel special. She might greet Johnny and tell him she found a spider's egg sac and brought it over to the science table. She knows that spiders fascinate Johnny. Her special attention and recognition of his interests will help him feel included and cared about.

Another way to say "I notice you" is to greet children individually. Some teachers take the time to offer every child a hug or a handshake as they enter the preschool or childcare center. This gesture says, "I care about you and am glad you are here." You can find ways to inject effective doses of special time into a class full of children. Large centers may want to designate one teacher as the morning greeter.

TAKE TIME FOR TRAINING

What about Johnny's shoes, the ones that come untied every ten minutes? Marcia could create a plan to help Johnny learn to tie his own shoes. After taking time for training, Marcia can tell Johnny that she would love to watch him tie his own shoes. Eventually Johnny will be able to tie his shoes and come back to show Marcia when he has been successful.

Just as children often make the mistake of trying to get undue attention, adults often make the mistake of giving inappropriate attention, instead of finding a way to redirect children into feeling a sense of belonging and significance in useful ways. Remember, encouraged children do not need to find mistaken ways to find belonging and significance—at least, not as often!

Power Struggles in the Preschool

It is a lovely, sunny day at the Silverport Preschool. Over by the apple tree three-year-old Sarah and her teacher, Julie, are glaring at each other. Julie says it's time to go inside. Sarah refuses to go. Julie emphasizes that playtime is over: everyone else has gone inside and Sarah must come in right now. Sarah wraps her arms tightly around the tree trunk. Julie's face is turning pink and she begins to threaten her small pupil, "If you don't come in this minute, you won't be allowed to come outside the rest of the day."

Sarah sticks out her tongue. "You can't make me!" she taunts. Julie is angry (and a little embarrassed—after all, this is a three-year-old) and feels that her authority has been challenged. Julie and Sarah continue to glare at each other, but Julie realizes that Sarah is right: she can't make Sarah come inside. She feels utterly defeated.

What is the message behind Sarah's behavior? She may be saying, "I want to be the boss and have some power in my life!" Sarah's way of achieving power is by proving that "you can't make me!"

Identifying Misguided Power

Julie felt angry; she also felt that her legitimate authority had been challenged. These are the typical feelings adults have when they are involved in a power struggle—and these feelings provide the first clue to identifying misguided power.

As we've mentioned before, a power struggle takes two. Sarah needed Julie's reactions to engage in the battle. Julie got hooked and used her strength to overpower Sarah and carry her inside. But did Sarah ever give up her end of the fight?

The child who acts upon the mistaken goal of misguided power will spend a great deal of energy resisting cooperation. Sarah had to clutch the tree trunk fiercely to maintain a hold that her teacher couldn't loosen. In the heat of battle, this ferocity may be described as "stubbornness." (When the same child is learning to do a complicated math problem, however, or running those last few miles of the marathon, this same trait may be seen positively as "tenacity.") The underlying belief of the mistaken goal of misguided power is "I belong only when I am in control. No one can make me do things."

Responding to the Message

How might Sarah's teacher give her power in appropriate ways? There are several possibilities.

ENCOURAGEMENT FOR MISGUIDED POWER SEEKERS IN THE PRESCHOOL

- Ask the child to help.
- Offer limited choices.
- Do the unexpected.
- Withdraw from the conflict.
- Seek win-win solutions.

ASK THE CHILD TO HELP

If there is a pattern of power struggles between Julie and Sarah, Julie could break the cycle by asking for Sarah's help—which invites Sarah to use her power in productive ways. Julie might say, "Sarah, I need your help. Would you please tell the boys in the far corner that it is time to come in?" An opportunity to help often appeals to a child who is seeking misguided power, providing her with an opportunity to have power in a useful way.

Remember that few people—including little ones—enjoy feeling powerless or victimized. Everyone needs opportunities to experience self-control and to learn that personal power can be used in helpful ways. *It is not the need for power that is mistaken; it is the misguided use of power that creates problems.*

OFFER LIMITED CHOICES

One of the best ways to empower a child is to give her limited choices in which all alternatives are acceptable. Asking a child if she is ready to come inside now implies that she doesn't have to come in if she isn't ready. If that is not an acceptable alternative, do not include it in your choices, stated or implied.

Sarah's teacher could ask Sarah whether she would like to lead the class inside at the end of playtime or hold the teacher's hand and follow the others. These are limited choices, both of which are acceptable. Staying outside is not one of the choices. If a child answers by naming an alternative that was not given, such as staying outside, simply respond, "That is not one of the choices."

Another option might be to let Sarah choose which equipment to play on before going inside and to say that the bell will ring in two minutes. This requires planning ahead, which is a wise thing to do when power struggles have become a pattern.

Choices empower a child, meeting the need for power and belonging in acceptable ways. (Remember, your attitude influences how a child perceives your actions.)

DO THE UNEXPECTED

Adults and preschoolers sometimes find that their behavior has become rather predictable. Julie and Sarah probably have enacted this little scene many times before. Instead of responding to Sarah's challenge in her usual way, Julie could do the unexpected. When Sarah refused to come inside, Julie could have said, "I'll bet you can't catch me," and then run away from Sarah. What a surprise that would be for someone who is clinging fiercely to a tree trunk. Sarah just might let go to chase her teacher, and when Sarah caught her, Julie could give her a big hug and walk peacefully inside with her. The standoff evaporates; both are winners.

WITHDRAW FROM THE CONFLICT

Power struggles require at least two participants. When an adult refuses to participate by focusing on what he will do (instead of what he is trying to make a child do), he withdraws from the power struggle. Julie could say to Sarah, "I can't make you come in, and I would really appreciate your help in the classroom. I hope you will come in soon. I can really use your help when you are ready." Julie could then wait, without further engagement. It is our guess that with no one to fight against, Sarah would soon give up her power struggle and come into the classroom to see how she could help.

SEEK WIN-WIN SOLUTIONS

Another secret to dealing with power struggles is to seek win-win solutions. No child (or adult) wants to be the loser. When you invite children to help you solve a problem, they have the opportunity to use their energy and creativity in positive ways.

If Sarah continued to refuse to come in, Julie could offer to hold her hand as they walked inside and to help her place this problem on the class meeting agenda. Julie can also invite Sarah to think about possible solutions.

Revenge in the Preschool

It is a Tuesday morning, and four-year-old Eric has been throwing the toy dinosaurs across the room. His teacher, John, comes over and removes the toy dinosaurs, telling Eric he cannot have them for the rest of the day. Eric is furious. Eric remembers that when Zachary threw the blocks into the corner yesterday, nothing happened to him. This isn't fair! Eric stomps off.

A little while later, John makes the charming discovery that Eric has stuffed the toilet full of toilet paper. John shows Eric the mess he has made and asks, "How could you do such a thing to our school?" Eric doesn't hesitate. "I hate this place," he says, "and I'm glad the toilet is broken." John tells the little boy that he will write a note to Eric's parents about this and that Eric will have to stay in at recess. Before the day is over, Eric has also managed to rip the pages out of several books.

John can't take another day of this child and is already deciding to call in sick tomorrow. Eric's message is "I've been hurt, so I'm going to hurt others back. Life is unfair!" John is undoubtedly feeling pretty discouraged and hurt himself. He feels disgusted and disbelieving, and he is baffled by Eric's disdain for the school's property. We call this a "revenge cycle."

Identifying Revenge

Adults (and children) often cover their hurt feelings with anger. John's reaction to Eric's behavior was to hurt back through reprimands and punishment.

A child who has chosen the mistaken goal of revenge believes that if he can't belong (which hurts a lot), at least he can get even. Unfortunately, it is difficult for most adults to love and enjoy a child who is hurting others and destroying property. By acting upon his belief that he doesn't belong, this child behaves in ways that prove his point.

Responding to the Message

It can be difficult to deal with a child like Eric, but once his teacher realizes that Eric feels he has been treated unfairly and is hurt, he can respond to Eric's real need. Eric wants to feel belonging, to be a real part of the group. How can that be achieved?

ENCOURAGEMENT FOR REVENGE SEEKERS IN THE PRESCHOOL

- Seek connection before correction by validating feelings.
- Teach the difference between feeling and doing.
- Ask if a positive time-out would be helpful.
- Schedule a time (after the conflict) to work on solutions.
- Repair the damage; make amends.
- Work to help the child feel a sense of belonging.

SEEK CONNECTION BEFORE CORRECTION BY VALIDATING FEELINGS

Young children aren't consciously aware that their misbehavior is motivated by hurt feelings. However, when an adult correctly guesses what they are feeling, children feel understood and validated. John could say, "Eric, when you behave that way, I feel hurt. My guess is that you might be feeling hurt too. Can you let me know when you are ready to talk about our hurt feelings?" Eric may need time to cool off before he is ready to discuss his feelings. If Eric still does not want to say anything, the teacher might tell a story about a time that he felt really hurt. By spending this kind of time with Eric, his teacher can gain Eric's trust by showing that he accepts Eric, even when Eric is not feeling likable. When Eric's feelings have been acknowledged, he can begin to feel (and act) better.

TEACH THE DIFFERENCE BETWEEN FEELING AND DOING

Learning to name their feelings gives children a new tool for self-regulation. John told Eric, "What you feel is always okay, but what you *do* is not always okay. Later let's brainstorm some things we can do when we feel hurt that don't hurt others or damage our school." John knows that Eric probably needs time to calm down before he can engage in a helpful discussion, so he adds, "Let me know when you feel calm enough for a brainstorming session. I'll bet we can come up with several ideas."

WHEN A HURTING CHILD HURTS ANOTHER CHILD

Understanding that a child's mistaken goal might be revenge does not make injuring others acceptable. Making amends for physical aggression involves three steps:

1. **Provide damage control.** Separate involved children or place one child out of reach of the offending child until everyone is calm enough to make better choices.

2. **Address hurt feelings.** Take the time to find out what might be causing a child to feel hurt and allow the feelings to surface. When you accept and validate a child's feelings, you encourage his sense of belonging by sending the message that it is safe for him to have all kinds of feelings. Sometimes children come to school with pent-up feelings. You can't do anything to erase the cause of a child's pain. Parents fighting with each other, illness in a family, or other life events are beyond your control. But simply allowing a child a safe place to express his feelings and to feel supported and listened to can help him heal.

3. **Make amends.** Making amends is part of learning to take responsibility for one's actions—an ability all of us need to cultivate and practice. You might ask the aggressor if he can think of ways to help the injured child feel better. You and he might come up with ideas such as offering to provide a service (clearing the other child's place at the table for him, reading a story to him, or drawing a picture for him). A child may also choose to offer an apology, but it isn't helpful to force him to say "I'm sorry." Doing so teaches a child to mouth words without meaning them. If a child initiates a sincere apology, it will have real meaning.

ASK IF A POSITIVE TIME-OUT WOULD BE HELPFUL

If John has already taught his class about positive time-out, he can ask Eric if it would help him to take some time to cool off until he feels better. If Eric wants company and John has a few minutes, he could offer, "Would you like me to go with you or would you like a buddy to go with you?" Children who feel they don't belong usually jump at the chance to have someone go with them—they can cool off and feel a sense of belonging at the same time.

SCHEDULE A TIME (AFTER THE CONFLICT) TO WORK ON SOLUTIONS

Eric can be invited to brainstorm what to do when difficult feelings arise. John can start by suggesting that next time Eric is feeling hurt, he can come to John and practice naming the feeling. John can tell Eric kindly that he will try to be a good listener. Because Eric has been learning about "using his words," he might say, "I could tell someone I don't like it when they hurt my feelings." John might also suggest, "How about putting the problem on the class meeting agenda?"

It is important to remember that this process may need to be repeated many times before Eric will learn to name his feelings, accept them as okay, and find acceptable ways to handle his feelings.

REPAIR THE DAMAGE; MAKE AMENDS

What about Eric's destructive actions? Remember, making a child feel worse is unlikely to encourage that child to act better. Retaliation and punishment are typical adult reactions to destructive behavior, but they often provoke a child to respond with more revenge. Instead, when a child destroys something, it is reasonable to ask him to take responsibility for replacing the damaged item.

When Eric stuffs the toilet with paper and causes it to overflow, he can be encouraged to help clean up the mess. Eric will be more likely to cooperate in the cleanup efforts when his feelings and the belief behind his behavior have been dealt with. *Notice that the focus is on the mess in the bathroom, rather than the mess Eric made. This is a time not for blaming but for working together to find a solution to the problem.* It takes time, but this kind of respectful and caring approach is much more likely to lead to improvements in Eric's behavior.

WORK TO HELP THE CHILD FEEL A SENSE OF BELONGING

In order to make a lasting change in the way Eric sees himself, John must focus on ways to give Eric a sense of belonging in the classroom. During a class meeting or circle time, John could begin a discussion of how good we feel when others want to do things with us. John could then say that he has chosen Eric to pass out the morning snack. He could ask who would like to share this task with Eric. Several hands would go up and a helper would be chosen. By focusing on "sharing the task with Eric," John has sent a different message than if he'd simply asked, "Who else wants to serve the snack?"

Afterward, John could spend a moment with Eric and comment on how many children raised their hands to do something with him. How did Eric feel when so many children raised their hands to pass the snack with him? In this way, John would be helping Eric become a contributing member of his class, as well as helping Eric perceive himself as a likable person. This sort of processing is a crucial part of helping Eric form different beliefs about his experiences and move beyond his need for revenge.

Assumed Inadequacy in the Preschool

Paul is five years old but he is still in the three-year-old group in his swim class. The instructor, Tom, is trying to get everyone to blow bubbles in the water. Paul hates to get his face wet and blows little puffs well above the surface. Tom comes over and suggests that Paul pretend to blow out a birthday candle. Paul only folds his arms around himself, puts his chin into his chest, and gives a tiny shake of his head. After a minute or two, Tom gives up and goes on to the next child.

A little while later, the other children are holding on to the edge of the pool and practicing kicking in the water. Paul sits on the side, refusing to get into the pool. Tom offers to hold Paul while he kicks, but Paul refuses and turns his body away from the pool. Eventually Tom gives up.

Paul has successfully convinced his swimming instructor to leave him alone. Paul believes that he is not "good enough" and acts upon this belief by convincing others to give up on him, demonstrating to perfection the mistaken goal of assumed inadequacy, or giving up.

Identifying Assumed Inadequacy in the Preschool

Tom must stay alert to the needs of all of the children in his swim class—he can't spend all of his time with Paul. He feels hopeless when he can't convince Paul even to try the various activities. Tom cannot force Paul into the water or make him blow bubbles. His only choice seems to be to leave Paul alone, to give up on him. Paul's response is to retreat further. He isn't fighting or being aggressive. In fact, he makes it easy to ignore him and leave him alone.

Where did he acquire his belief in his own inadequacy? As it happens, Paul has athletic parents who excel in most sports. They bike, they ski, and they run marathons. When Paul is with them, it's difficult for his parents to hide their impatience at how much he slows them down. They love Paul very much; they just don't know how to adjust their activities to Paul's level.

Responding to the Message

Paul believes that because he is not as good at sports as his parents are, he might as well not try at all. He can't seem to do anything well enough. They are "perfect" and Paul, obviously, is not. If Paul can convince others that they can't expect much from him, they will leave him alone. What can Tom do besides ignoring Paul?

ENCOURAGEMENT FOR ASSUMED INADEQUACY IN THE PRESCHOOL

- Encourage even the smallest steps.
- Focus on what a child can do.
- Break up the tasks into small steps and celebrate success.

ENCOURAGE EVEN THE SMALLEST STEPS

When Paul is backing away from the pool, Tom might say, "Paul, I know it took a lot of courage for you to get in the pool with us. I really appreciate that."

Tom did not assume that learning to swim was easy; in fact, he acknowledged how hard it is for Paul. Tom took time to notice the small step that Paul had been willing to take. Over time, this kind of gentle encouragement may help Paul take additional risks.

FOCUS ON WHAT A CHILD CAN DO

Adults can learn to focus on what a child can do, to help him to see his own abilities first through others' eyes and eventually through his own. Tom swishes Paul's legs through the water while Paul remains perched on the edge, and when Paul attempts a few kicks on his own, Tom com-

223

ments on how strong his legs are. All too often, teachers are occupied by the attention-seekers or are busy waging power struggles with defiant children. Yet the child whose mistaken goal is assumed inadequacy or giving up is the one who least can afford to be ignored.

BREAK UP THE TASKS INTO SMALL STEPS AND CELEBRATE SUCCESS

Adults who live and work with small children can learn to recognize and encourage small steps toward success and to have realistic expectations. Rudolf Dreikurs said, "Work for improvement, not perfection." An important part of encouraging small steps is to break a task down into small pieces that don't seem so intimidating to a discouraged child. Paul's teacher notices and congratulates him on getting his arms and belly wet today (both big steps for Paul). The key words for a child with this mistaken goal are "Believe in me!" and "Encourage, encourage, encourage!" As difficult as it may seem sometimes, try to have faith in the discouraged child. The energy of your belief in him may be contagious.

Will It Make a Difference?

Teachers and caregivers sometimes feel frustrated by the enormity of the task they face each day. It is no easy matter to teach and manage dozens of small, active people—especially when so much of what they believe about themselves and their world is shaped at home, out of the teacher's control.

Still, each person can only do his or her best. The hours that a child spends with caregivers each day may provide an important opportunity to feel belonging and significance—and strong, caring relationships formed with preschool teachers and caregivers will affect that child for years to come. Better still, when parents and teachers work together to truly understand a child's behavior and deal with it effectively, the results for everyone can be nothing short of miraculous.

1. Imagine a limited choice that you might offer a child when it is time to move from one activity to another. Think of two things you could say if the child answers that she wants a choice that's different from those offered.

2. Ask a local librarian to recommend books dealing with feelings a child might encounter during a typical day at preschool or with peers. Develop a center library with a selection of such resource books. When a child experiences hurt feelings (or other intense emotions), you can read an appropriate book together. Allow time to talk about what the character may be feeling, and to look for ways to feel (and behave) better.

3. Think of a recent frustrating experience with a child in your care. Look at the Mistaken Goal Chart on page 178. Match your own feelings to the ones in the second column of the chart. Read across the chart to determine if your reactions or the child's response also match. (It doesn't have to be a perfect match.) What is the mistaken goal you have identified? What belief does the child with this goal have? What possible solutions does the chart offer? Consider trying this new response next time the situation arises.

CHAPTER 13

Ending Bedtime Battles: Preschoolers and Sleep

It is naptime, and all of the children in the preschool class are asleep—except Margaret. The teacher has read a story and offered back rubs, but Margaret is still awake.

Mary is a different story. Mary's mother worries that Mary sleeps too long at naptime, which makes it difficult to get her to bed at night. The teacher promises to keep Mary awake longer or to wake her up earlier, but despite her best efforts, Mary is usually the first to fall asleep and the last to wake up.

The bottom line is that you can't make a child sleep, and you can't control when he will wake up. During the preschool years, most children give up taking a long, regular nap—if they ever did! Parents often miss those peaceful afternoon hours during which they could get something accomplished or rest a bit themselves. It becomes very tempting to try to coerce a child into taking naps—but unfortunately, making him fall asleep (whether at night or during naptime) is simply beyond adult control.

Most parents have experienced the frustration of a child who is happily wide awake long past bedtime, tumbles out of bed at awkward moments, or refuses to wake even when Mom and Dad have urgent business to attend to. Is there anything parents can do to help children settle into a sleep cycle that works for everyone?

Routines: Everyday Magic

A familiar routine in the morning, at mealtimes, and at bedtime can eliminate the need preschoolers often feel to test their boundaries. Clear expectations and predictable activities can smooth the rough spots out of a youngster's day (and that of his parents and teachers). As children grow older and begin school, familiar routines can eliminate many of the hassles surrounding chores or homework.

Issuing commands usually invites resistance, but when you and your child create routines together, that routine becomes "the boss." Children as young as two and a half can participate in creating routines (and routine charts), with a little help from you, and they can develop a strong sense of self and a willingness to contribute. You have only to ask, "What is next on our routine chart?" and your child will tell you.

Routine and consistency (while occasionally boring for adults) work well with a young child's brain development and encourage cooperation and learning. Children thrive when their lives are clear and predictable, and they enjoy the security of comfortable repetition. In this and the following chapters, you will discover basic guidelines that are helpful when planning any type of routine.

UNEXPECTED BENEFITS OF ROUTINES

Routines create a unique safety net when children and families experience traumatic events. Reestablishing a familiar routine in the midst of change or chaos will help children feel safe and protected. Whether a child has been uprooted by a natural disaster, a political upheaval, or a family change (divorce, death, or a move to a new home), the sooner a routine is back in place, the sooner that child will feel safe and secure.

According to research, children who live in families in which daily life is predictable do better at school and acquire higher levels of self-control.[1] This consistency and self-control contributes to a child's ability to be resilient, even in the face of stress. Taking part in regular daily routines may also lead to lowered risk of substance abuse, as well as fewer school suspensions during later adolescence.

Mapping Tasks: The Routine Chart

The first step in creating a routine chart is to invite your child to brainstorm a list of bedtime tasks. Try to keep the list to three or four (but no more than six) tasks. Remember, a routine chart is not for rewards or stickers; it is simply a "map" to help your child remember what comes next. Children love it when you take pictures of them doing each task so that pictures can be pasted on the chart. Some prefer to draw pictures of themselves doing the task, or create simple symbols. The chart can then be placed where it is easy for your child to see and follow. Remember the magic words "What is next on your bedtime chart?" so she can tell you instead of being told.

Bedtime Routine Possibilities

Having a familiar routine can take the struggle out of bedtime. The following ideas for bedtime routine activities may help you build a routine for your child that helps him (and you) enjoy sweet dreams.

PLAYTIME

A family playtime is a good way to begin your nighttime routine. One family enjoys playing board games, while another likes a rousing game of tag or a pillow fight. It is best to place more active games at the beginning of your routine. The idea is to move steadily toward quiet, calming activities.

TIME FOR CHOICES

Planning ahead can eliminate many a power struggle. For instance, allow your child to choose between two pairs of pajamas *before* getting into the tub. She can lay the chosen pajamas out on her bed so they are ready as soon as bathtime is over.

Power struggles and meltdowns often occur in the morning when your child can't decide what to wear, wants to wear something she can't find, or puts on something you think is inappropriate (such as shorts in the middle of winter). Consider choosing clothes the night before to eliminate at least one potential morning power struggle. (This may sound obvious, but another simple solution is to put winter clothes away in the summer and summer clothes away in the winter. Inappropriate choices for clothing are then less likely.)

BATHTIME

A soak in the tub can be wonderfully soothing—and it can be a time for closeness and play too. There are many wonderful bath toys available (although your kitchen measuring cups and spoons will probably do quite nicely), and the sound and feel of warm water helps relax most children. An evening bathtime should probably follow any active games and begin the "settling down" part of your routine.

TOOTHBRUSHING

Did you know that brushing teeth can be fun? Some families put toothpaste on each other's brushes and all scrub happily away together, not only teaching good oral hygiene but creating connection without daily power struggles.

STORY TIME

Telling or reading stories is a familiar part of bedtime, for good reason. Young children love to hear stories; in fact, some never tire of hearing the same story over and over—and woe to the lazy parent who tries to leave anything out! And story time really helps children learn: a child's earliest "reading" experience may consist of reciting a book to you, even turning the pages at the right spot. Children's poetry and simple rhymes are wonderful too, and help your child learn language.

As your child grows older (or if she often has difficulty falling asleep), you may want to let her look through books as she lies quietly in bed. It is best to choose hardcopy books since screen lighting can affect sleep, as well as the brain's ability to consolidate the day's learning.

Do beware of manipulation: some children beg for "just one more story," and then, "just one more, pleeeeeease." This can be prevented by agreeing together on the number of stories in your bedtime routine. Then, when the begging starts, you can ask, "What does our routine chart say?" Another possibility is to give your child a hug and say "Nice try" (with a warm smile) as you leave the room or move on to the next part of your routine. Simply reflecting this request ("I can tell that you really want to hear another story") followed by reassurance ("Let's put this book beside your bed so we'll remember to read it first thing tomorrow night") demonstrates kindness without allowing manipulation. Children know when you mean it and they know when you don't. Being kind and firm at the same time will let them know that you mean what you say.

SPECIAL ACTIVITIES

Since children often feel cozy and willing to talk just before they fall asleep, bedtime can be one of the best parts of your day together—if you let it be. You may want to pray together or sing a special song. One dad carries his small son around his room to say good night to each stuffed animal and picture. Soothing lullabies, white noise, or soft music can create a relaxing atmosphere.

Some parents enjoy asking their children to share the happiest and saddest moments of their day and then letting their children ask them the same questions. (Because children's grasp of time is a little fuzzy, you may hear about things that happened this afternoon, last week, or even last month.) Such moments go far beyond helping a child sleep; they are filled with shared love, trust, and closeness.

HUGS AND KISSES

Bedtime is the perfect time for hugs, kisses, and gentle reassurances of love. There are families where hugging, kissing, and saying "I love you" happens daily. In other families, these things rarely happen. Not surprisingly, researchers have discovered that a daily ration of hugs encourages emotional health, and if you haven't been dispensing regular hugs and kisses, you might consider giving it a try.

> Every night, Cissy's aunt Elaine loves to sit on the edge of three-year-old Cissy's bed and say, "If we were to line up all of the three-year-old girls in the world, guess which one I'd pick? I would say, 'I want that one!'" Aunt Elaine then points at Cissy, who giggles happily and launches herself into her aunt's arms for a hug.

Set a Consistent Bedtime

Evenings for many families are chaotic, filled with work, errands, sports practices, dance recitals, and an endless list of other activities. Not surprisingly, spending the evening in the car racing from place to place does not contribute to a peaceful, consistent bedtime. While life is never entirely predictable when you live with a preschooler, do your best to begin your bedtime routine at about the same time each evening. Sleep researchers have found that one of the best ways to encourage healthy sleep—for children and for adults—is simply to go to bed at the same time each night.

Practice Your Routine

A bedtime routine does not guarantee that your child will never have difficulty falling asleep. If a child says he "can't sleep," tell him it's okay. He just needs to lie quietly in bed and look through a book or think quiet thoughts. Keep in mind that falling asleep is your child's job. You can only provide him with the opportunity. The hardest part of your job may be to ignore (with kindness and firmness) demands for more drinks and stories after you have completed a loving bedtime routine.

A bedtime routine may make it possible for you and your young child to enjoy sharing a special part of the day together rather than repeating the same nightly battle. The possibilities are endless. Pick out some ideas that appeal to you—or use your own creativity to find a routine that works for you and your child. Whatever you decide on, practice it often enough that it becomes a familiar, predictable part of your day—and a peaceful way to help and encourage your child to fall asleep.

Preschool Routines for Naptime

Teachers can follow a similar procedure to create naptime routines in the preschool or childcare setting. Include soft music, muted lighting, or gentle back rubs. Involve children by allowing them to help set out nap things, take off and line up shoes, and use the toilet before and after lying down to rest. Calm caregivers invite children to enjoy a restful atmosphere.

The Importance of Comfort

Even though we stress the importance of getting children involved, there are many things adults can do on their own to help children sleep cozily. You can make sure children are comfortable in pajamas that fit, in beds or cribs that are secure, and with the appropriate number of blankets. You can also remember to consider your child's temperament. Is the sleeping area warm or cool enough? Does your child need absolute quiet or a steady hum of activity? A nightlight or complete darkness? Like adults, children have different needs regarding light and dark, noise and quiet. There is no right or wrong; finding out what works best for each child will take patience and a bit of trial and error.

If your child spends time in more than one household, special smells and textures can make bedtime much less stressful. A pillow or blankie that travels with your child from home to home or a special cuddly toy at the childcare center can be very helpful. Children have been known to curl up with their jackets tucked under their heads when nothing else was available or the preferred item had been left behind, drawing comfort from the familiar feel and smell.

Although research is inconclusive, avoiding sugary food late in the evening or before naps may prove helpful. (Be sure to read labels; you may be surprised at the sugar content of some so-called healthy foods.) Use trial and error to discover what works best for your child.

Testing Time

How many times have you heard that plaintive cry, "Mommy, I'm thirsty"? Agree with your child on how many drinks of water she may have (and put the allotted number on your routine chart). Whatever your agreement, follow through with kind and firm action. You might say, "I hear you. I'm sure you can make it until morning." (Children often stop testing when they don't get a response.)

If the testing escalates and your child gets out of bed, kind and firm action without any words is usually most effective. It looks like this: Your child gets up. You take her by the hand and lead her back to bed with a kind manner and your mouth shut (lectures are never helpful). Then give her a kiss and leave. If she gets up again, take her by the hand and lead her back to bed with a kind manner and your mouth shut; give her a kiss and leave. If she refuses to walk beside you, you may need to pick her up and carry her. Do this in a calm, matter-of-fact manner, with a firm but loving touch. If you repeat this process as many times as it takes, your child will learn that you mean what you say—and she can count on you to treat her with dignity and respect even when she is testing you. Summon all your patience, and don't get discouraged. When you are consistent, the testing usually does not last longer than three nights, five at the most (although they may feel like five *very* long nights).

One mother shared that on the first night they tried this new plan, her daughter was put back to bed twenty-four times. The second night, it was twelve times. The third night, it took only twice before the daughter knew her mother meant what she *didn't* say. By the fourth night, her daughter was happily following the bedtime routine.

Remember, the only behavior you can control is your own. The magic that occurs is that children usually change their behavior in response to you.

Control Your Own Behavior

Q. *We have a three-year-old daughter who has been having a very difficult time going to bed at night. We have a bedtime routine—we give her a bath with her baby sister, read her a story, get her a glass of water, and say prayers. As soon as it's time for us to leave, she starts acting up. We tell her that if she keeps yelling or crying, we'll have to close her door because she's going to wake up her sister. She doesn't care about this and will call us stupid, stick her tongue out at us, and so on. When we close her door, she goes absolutely crazy—banging on the walls and doors, messing* *up her blinds, dumping her toy box, or yelling by her window, "Somebody help me—I need my mommy and daddy." We wait for three minutes (one minute of time-out for each year of her age) and then open the door and ask her if she's finished being mad and ready to get back in her bed and behave. She'll say no and go through it again for another three minutes. We give her one more chance and then tell her that we'll have to close her door for the remainder of the night. The other night we had to stand by her door until 1:30 a.m. with her going crazy for four hours. We're exhausted, and she is the only one who gets to take naps!*

A. It sounds like no one is getting much rest except your daughter. Four things will help to solve this nighttime dilemma:

- Help her feel sleepy.
- Respect her needs—and yours.
- Stop fighting and work toward cooperation.
- Use kind, firm follow-through.

HELP HER FEEL SLEEPY

Your daughter is able to marshal all her physical and emotional reserves for bedtime. Is she getting enough physical exercise during the day to make her feel tired at night? Try making active play part of your bedtime routine. Consider taking a trip to the park, engaging in some rough-and-tumble play, or even signing up for evening swim classes. Once she is tired, you will have nature on your side. You might also consider helping her give up naps so that she is ready for an earlier bedtime. Although you can't control when she will sleep or not sleep, by eliminating the nap rituals you at least make it less convenient for her to take a nap.

RESPECT HER NEEDS—AND YOURS

Your daughter may be feeling "dethroned" by her baby sister. Babies and toddlers take up lots of adult time and energy. What is left over for the older child? Your three-year-old has discovered an effective way to get her parents' attention—and keep it! You can replace this negative attention with positive attention at other times of the day.

Carve out some special time with her alone. Be sure to point out to her that you are glad to have time alone with her and that you enjoy having an older child with whom you can do special things. Special time can be as simple as drawing together or taking a walk around the block. When her need to feel included, noticed, and special is met in this way, she will have less reason to seek attention through bedtime battles.

You have needs too. Your children will be more likely to respect you if you demonstrate that you respect yourself. Give yourself time to unwind, relax, and focus on the evening together. A late-afternoon shower, a cup of tea, or a short exercise routine might make a real difference in your energy level. Meeting your own needs means you will be better able to respond to the needs of other family members.

STOP FIGHTING AND WORK TOWARD COOPERATION

Where does your daughter get her amazing tenacity? Two parents who are willing to wait at her door for hours must have some genetic connection to the howler on the other side. It is time to start building cooperation, and the only people in this power struggle you can control are yourselves. You may not be able to control your daughter's sleep habits, but you can decide what you will do. Here are some suggestions:

- Ask for her help. (You might be surprised at how well this works.)
- Explain that you do not like to stand by her door at bedtime. Ask her if she has any ideas about ways you could stop doing that.
- Create a bedtime routine (and chart) together.
- Decide what you will do instead of what you will try to make her do. (You may decide to take her back to her bed, give her a kiss, and leave.) Let her know your plan. Some possibilities are to go to bed yourself, read a book, and keep your own door closed rather than stand guard over her door.
- Seek solutions that work for all of you.

USE KIND, FIRM FOLLOW-THROUGH

It may be comforting to know that you are not alone in your bedtime hassles. If you have tried all of the above and your child is still getting out of bed, simply put her back in bed. This is effective when you remember the following:

- Don't say a word. Actions speak louder than words—and they are much harder to argue with.
- Be sure your actions are both kind and firm. This means you eliminate even the nonverbal lectures (i.e., your angry body language).
- Be consistent. If you put your child back in bed five times and then give in, you have taught her that she only has to be more persistent than you are.
- Be sure you are spending special time with your child at other times during the day. (For details about special time, refer to Chapter 10.)

What About Naps?

Young children may resist sleep, not because they don't need it but because they don't want to miss out on anything as they explore their exciting world. Children do not all need the same amount of sleep. Quiet time may work better for some children than naptime.

Whether it is a naptime or quiet time, follow these guidelines:

- Don't tell your child she is tired. Admit that *you* are tired and need some quiet time.
- Get your child involved in planning for his naptime or quiet time. Allow your child to choose a special naptime stuffed animal, or a bed or blanket that is different from what he uses for bedtime.
- Teach your child to use a simple music-playing device. Let her choose from a collection of naptime music. Do not use earphones but allow music to play softly nearby.

- Give her a limited choice: "Do you want to start your nap [or quiet] time at one o'clock or at one-fifteen?"
- Avoid the use of screens to put your child to sleep.

Whose Bed?

There are many people who believe in the family bed. Usually this is a happy period for families who choose it. However, many parents have small children in their bed not by choice but by default. They may have enjoyed snuggling with their little one for a while, but now they want their privacy back.

Parents need to decide what they truly want and be ready to follow through with kind and firm action. The reality is that, as with all habits, breaking this one can be painful for everyone. Children read our unspoken messages quite well.

If you are ambivalent about where he should sleep, the child will recognize your doubts. When you are sure of your decision that he should sleep in his own bed, he will sense that as well.

Marissa and her husband want their bed back. Jonathan had slept with them until he turned three. For the past six months, Jonathan has had his own bed but has refused to use it unless Mom or Dad lies down with him until he falls asleep. Because they often fall asleep before he does, the rest of their evening is lost. When they do wake up and go to their own bed, Jonathan usually wakes up and cries until they take him into their bed.

This issue is a bit more complex than it may seem. Since Jonathan shared his parents' bed for quite a while, it isn't surprising that he wants to continue. Being with his parents at night probably has many meanings for Jonathan. He gets attention, security, and lots of cuddles. On the other hand, being alone in his bed feels lonely and a bit scary at times. Jonathan's feelings may be logical, or they may provide an excuse for him to continue seeking undue attention—a habit his parents have unwittingly reinforced. He may be missing an opportunity to learn self-soothing, an important life skill. Now the real question is what his parents want to do—and what they are willing to do to change their son's habit.

If you have decided that it is time for your child to sleep in his own bed, be prepared to follow through. Please remember to do lots of deep breathing, because this plan requires patience.

Learning to go to sleep on her own will not create lifelong trauma for your child; it is usually more traumatic for parents than for children. *Your attitude is the key. If you feel confident that you are doing the right thing, your child will feel the energy of your confidence. On the other hand, if you feel guilty, angry, or ambivalent, that energy will be communicated and will invite manipulation, helplessness, or power struggles.*

Coddled or Capable and Responsible?

Kindness and firmness at the same time are the keys to effective parenting. Giving in to a child's continual demands may feel loving in the moment, but it is not in a child's long-term best interest. Children are more likely to feel safe and trusting when adults establish clear, respectful boundaries. Allowing a child to learn to fall asleep on her own is a lifetime gift.

The suggestions in this chapter can help parents use bedtime as an opportunity for teaching important life skills instead of manipulation and power struggles. Children can learn thinking skills, problem-solving skills, self-control, responsibility, and trust—that when parents say it, they mean it and will follow through with dignity and respect. They can also learn to trust themselves and to believe "I am capable and responsible." Bedtime truly can become an opportunity for connection and peace.

1. Make a routine chart for a time of day when you and your child experience challenges. Tell your child kindly that you would like to stop arguing with him, and ask if he would be willing to help you create a plan. List three or four tasks (but no more than six) that are needed. Include your partner, if possible. Invite your child to help you decide in what order these tasks should be done. Then design and create the chart together, using stickers, photographs, markers, or other art supplies. Display the finished chart at your child's eye level. When it is time, ask your child to tell you what needs to happen next by consulting the chart.

2. Identify a daily struggle that you have with your child. Instead of trying to make your child do something, focus on what you will do ("I will read stories when you are quiet in bed"). Tell your child your plan, then follow through with kindness and firmness.

3. If you are struggling with bedtime, take a moment to list the positive skills or outcomes that you want to foster, such as learning healthy sleep habits and allowing family members to get enough sleep. List the steps you are willing to take to achieve these goals. (This can be the hardest part.) Once you have decided what you are willing to do (or not do), explain the plan to your child—then follow through with confidence.

CHAPTER 14

"I Don't Like That!": Preschoolers and Eating

Imagine you've invited Maria, her husband, Marcus, and your neighbor Sam over for a meal. As you pass around your favorite lasagna and a bowl of broccoli, the conversation goes something like this:

YOU: "I'm so glad you're all here for dinner. I'll pass around the lasagna."

MARCUS: "Just a small serving for me, please. I'm not very hungry tonight."

YOU: "Oh, nonsense! A big man like you needs lots to eat. Here—I'll give you a proper serving. Sam, have some broccoli."

SAM: "No, thanks. I'm not much of a broccoli eater."

YOU: "Sam, broccoli is good for you. You have to try a little bit or there will be no dessert for you! Now, Maria, I expect to see your plate all clean; there are still some yummy veggies there."

How do you think Marcus, Maria, and Sam would feel? Does this sound a little bit like the conversation around your own dinner table?

All too often, the dinner table becomes a battleground for parents of young children. Parents worry about what their children eat—or refuse to eat. Have they had enough? Did they get enough vitamin C? Too much sugar? Enough calcium and protein?

Eating under surveillance is not relaxing, and children don't enjoy it any more than adults do. Listen to your own mealtime comments and ask yourself, "Would I say this to an adult guest?"

Children treated with respect learn to treat others the same way— eventually. Just because they are small people doesn't mean they aren't entitled to opinions and preferences about food. It may help to remember, though, that those opinions often change as they grow and mature.

During the mid-twentieth century, university early childhood programs conducted studies to see what foods young children would eat when a balanced selection of healthy foods was made available. The children were allowed to eat whatever they wanted. Sometimes children would eat dessert first. Sometimes they would eat vegetables first. And the results were always similar: when children were left to follow their own instincts, over time they chose a balanced diet.

How might these studies look today if the choices were fast-food hamburgers, french fries, and soda pop? *In order for children to make nutritious choices, they need to be given healthy options.* Processed foods and chemical additives can alter taste preferences. The flavor of a real orange can seem less appealing if a child has become accustomed to the overly sweetened or chemically enhanced flavorings used in juice drinks and snack products.

Health Problems and Your Kids

The rate of obesity among children has been an ongoing public health challenge for decades, due largely to too much sugar, fat, and salt in diets and not enough exercise. Many children spend a great deal of time sitting (and snacking) in front of screens. According to the Centers for Disease

Control, as of 2015–16 one in five school-age children in the United States suffered from obesity. That number is even higher for Latinx and African American children. Obese children are being diagnosed with health problems that used to be seen only in adults, such as diabetes, high blood pressure, and unhealthy cholesterol levels—problems that may impact a growing child for the rest of his life. There are also social risks associated with obesity, as overweight children are often stigmatized, bullied, and excluded from activities.

Sometimes obesity is genetically linked and requires connection, empathy, and a doctor's care. Obesity prevention involves a focus on energy balance—calories consumed versus calories expended—so taking action against childhood obesity must address both eating and physical activity. Research confirms that social pressure can affect one's food choices, so what you model through your own eating habits is as crucial as the foods you provide to your children.

Picky Eating

It is helpful to offer children a wide selection of nutritious food, remembering that special menus only reinforce finicky eating. To increase the odds that your child will eat the food you serve, be sure that at least one food on the table for each meal is familiar and something your child enjoys; then serve whatever else you wish. *Remember, the more often a child is exposed to a food, the sooner it too will become familiar.* But no matter how hard you try, you can't force your child to eat something he or she doesn't want to eat; that will only invite a power struggle, a sure-fire recipe for many miserable meals.

Nancy and Karen worried that their three-year-old son, Leo, wasn't getting enough to eat. They found that by hand-feeding him small bits of different foods, they could coax him to eat more. Leo soon figured out that by getting up often and running around the room or only nibbling at his food, he could prolong his parents' focused attention indefinitely. Meals were getting longer and longer, and Nancy and Karen were becoming more and more worried that Leo wasn't getting enough food or showing any interest in eating on his own.

What do you think Leo is learning? He is certainly an expert at keeping people busy with him. Do you think he is learning to make healthy eating choices? Is he learning to tune in to his body's hunger signals? Probably not.

Hand-feeding a child capable of feeding himself deprives him of the opportunity to experience feelings of capability, not to mention increasing the frustration the adults providing this time-consuming service will feel.

There are a number of things parents can keep in mind to encourage healthy eating habits in their children and to make mealtimes together pleasant for the entire family.

TIMING

Young children see no reason to get hungry on anyone's schedule but their own. Infants nurse on demand, toddlers want food when they're hungry, and preschoolers often just can't make it from one meal to the next without something in between. These are normal variations; try to be flexible. The key is to be certain that the choices available to your child are healthy ones. If your child isn't eating full meals, her snacks should provide her with the nutrients she needs. A pile of carrot sticks or even a baked potato, for instance, is much better than chips or a soda.

A child who doesn't eat his entire lunch at the childcare center can snack out of his lunch box on the way home. *When children eat is not as important as what they eat.* Nutritious lunch food is just as good eaten at five o'clock as it would have been at noon.

SIMPLICITY

Your church group may have raved about your prawns in Cajun sauce, but your preschooler is unlikely to be equally impressed. Children are often suspicious of unfamiliar foods or unusual mixtures. A cheese sandwich with lettuce and tomato may be spurned, while a piece of cheese, some tomato slices, and a few crackers will be consumed quite happily. If your little one looks askance at the pasta and vegetable salad, try serving the ingredients to him separately. You certainly don't need to provide a separate menu, nor should you, but being aware of your child's natural preferences will help you find ways to encourage cooperation and experimentation.

CHOICES

Allowing children to develop their own eating habits requires mutual trust. Children will eat foods their bodies need, and if you provide a variety of healthy and appetizing foods, as well as access to clean drinking water, they will be more likely to choose foods and beverages that are nourishing.

Remember, though, that even adults need a splurge now and then; thousands of children have been raised on occasional doses of fast food, pizza, and hot dogs without suffering permanent damage. The key, as always, is balance. Providing a regular diet of nutritious foods will help you feel better about the Easter jelly beans, chocolate Santas, and Halloween tummyaches that seem to be an inevitable part of childhood. However, if you have jelly beans, potato chips, cookies, cupcakes, and soft drinks around the house all the time, you are inviting poor eating habits and food battles.

Try not to become the food police. Families committed to special diets often defeat themselves by creating a vigilante atmosphere around food. If you want your child to avoid foods with sugar, do not become frantic when a stray cookie passes his lips. Your overreaction is likely to invite food-related power struggles, now and later.

PORTION SIZE AND HUNGER

When children are served extra-large food portions, studies show they eat larger bites of food and cumulatively more food than if portions were smaller. Preschoolers are capable of dishing up their own food (with training). An important part of this training is to teach them to take appropriately sized helpings. (They can always take more if they want it.) It is not helpful to make your child eat everything on her plate when she makes a mistake and takes too much. It is helpful to help her explore, through curiosity questions, what happens when she takes too much and how she can solve the problem.

When you insist that a child eat everything on her plate or eat only at specified times, you teach her to ignore her body's cues. This is why snacks play an important role in these preschool years. Little tummies need frequent fueling, so snack choices are important.

Choose Your Battles

It may seem absolutely imperative to you that your four-year-old eat her lima beans. Or you may feel comfortable watching your child eat a steady diet of salami slices, raisins, and crackers. But be aware that if you *in*sist, your child may feel compelled to *re*sist—and it's doubtful that staring at a plate of cold lima beans after everyone else has left the table has ever persuaded a child to love veggies.

Some parents claim that making their children sit at the table until they finish their dinner "works." If you talk to the children, you get a different story. They either figure out how to feed most of the food to the dog or hide it in their napkin. (Aren't parents suspicious when their children offer to clean up the table?) Or they develop eating problems as adults. *Someone will always lose in battles over food, whether in the short term or in the long term.*

HELP FOR PICKY EATERS

- **Avoid becoming a short-order cook.** Teach children older than four how to make their own peanut butter sandwiches or pour a bowl of whole-grain cereal.

- **Offer choices.** When a child complains about a food, say, "You can eat what is on the table or fix your own sandwich (or serving of cereal). What is your choice?"

- **Invite solutions.** If a child complains about the food served, ask, "What do you need to do about that?" This invites children to use their thinking and problem-solving skills, and to feel capable.

- **Invite your child to help plan menus during family meetings.** Kids are more cooperative when they have been included. Get your child involved in creating the shopping list.

- **Share tasks.** Let your child help with shopping. Many grocery stores now have small carts that can be pushed around by preschoolers. Let your child find items on the shopping list to put in his cart. When he wants something that isn't on the list, kindly and firmly say, "That isn't on our list."

- **Invite your child to help in the kitchen.** Even young children can help rinse lettuce, stir cake batter, or put cheese slices on burger buns. Again, children are more likely to eat what they help cook and to be more cooperative if they have been involved in the preparation of the meal.

- **Respond without rescuing.** Simply avoid the sparks (bids for undue attention) that become bonfires when you add fuel to them. Use active listening ("I guess you don't like that.") and avoid engaging in debates. And have faith in your child to handle the problem ("You don't have to eat it. I'm sure you can make it until our next meal").

- **Ease your own anxiety about nutrition.** Give your child a good multiple vitamin. One simple rule of thumb is to serve food in many different colors, which often indicates a healthy blend of fruits, vegetables, and protein. Then relax. She'll eat when she's hungry.

Mealtime Routines

Yes, routines work for eating too. Mealtimes in busy families often become hectic, rushed, and stressful occasions that no one truly enjoys. Parents arrive home tired after a long day's work; children are often both hungry and cranky. Comfortable routines can make mealtimes proceed far more smoothly. Here are some suggestions that may help you create routines for your own family.

Take Time to Relax

If dinnertime is often rushed in your home, try beginning the process differently.

> Tom always packs an extra-large lunch for his four-year-old daughter, Katie. During the drive home after work and preschool, Katie opens her lunch box and enjoys whatever is left over from lunch. When they arrive home, Katie is not urgently hungry and her dad doesn't feel pressured to serve dinner immediately. Instead, they usually manage time for a cuddle and story before Tom tackles the dinner preparations.

Taking time to wind down at the end of the day is worth the investment. You may want to spend a few minutes curled up on the sofa with your child, reconnecting and sharing moments from your day. A warm bath or shower might refresh you for the evening ahead, or you may want to take time for a walk or a quick game together. Slices of fruit or a bag of crackers may satisfy the hunger pangs long enough for the entire family to catch its breath. "But I don't have time," you may be saying. "I simply have too much to do!" Regardless of how busy your lives may be, taking time to relax and reenter your family's world will eliminate the hassles and bids for undue attention that often consume even more time.

Prepare the Meal Together

Nothing wins a finicky eater over better than helping plan and prepare the meal. And most parents fail to recognize the wonderful helpers they have right there beside them. Get a big apron, pull up a stool to the sink, and invite your child to scrub vegetables or rinse lettuce.

James, a preschool teacher, invited a group of children to help prepare a smoothie made with kale and pineapple. Now, most adults would cringe at this particular flavor combination, yet every one of the children who helped wash and tear up the kale and took part in the preparation process not only tasted this concoction but pronounced it delicious and went back for more. Then James filled a tray with samples of the smoothie and brought it out to share with the children in another classroom. Guess what? Not one of them would so much as try it. It would be difficult to find more persuasive evidence of the value of including children in food preparation.

Giving your child a way to contribute encourages the growth of her sense of initiative, teaches her life skills, invites her to see herself as a contributing member of the family or community, and builds her sense of belonging.

Create Moments That Draw You Together

Lunch at the Roundtree Childcare Center is a special time. The children join hands around the table, one child is invited to share something she feels grateful for, and then they take turns squeezing the hand of the person on their right, so the "squeeze" goes all around the circle before the children begin their meal. Aaron is from a traditional Jewish family, and before each meal in his household, he recites special Hebrew prayers. In Jenny's family, each person stands at his or her place at the table, and when all have gathered, they sing grace together. At Emmy's home, the whole family meditates in silence for several minutes before beginning each meal.

In our busy families, meals are often eaten on the run. Everyone has somewhere to go, and the moments of communication and togetherness can be lost if we're not careful. Rituals—religious or not—can be wonderful ways to preserve a sense of family and teach your children to value it, and to create warm and loving moments with your children. The National Center on Addiction and Substance Abuse at Columbia University has linked regular family dinnertime to such diverse issues as a reduced risk for alcohol and drug abuse, lower suicide rates, and improved school performance. Those are pretty compelling reasons for making time for family meals—and for making mealtimes with our families pleasant. These times spent gathered around the table offer priceless opportunities for connection and closeness, times to create memories that feed our souls as much as Grandma's home-baked bread feeds our bodies.

Set Guidelines for Finishing Up

Should children be expected to sit quietly until everyone has finished eating? Or should they be allowed to leave the table to play quietly? There is no "right" answer, but it may be wise to decide the matter beforehand rather than arguing over the cold mashed potatoes.

Even young children can be involved in some aspect of cleaning up after a meal. If your child can walk well on his own, he probably can clear his plate, scrape away uneaten food, or load his utensils into the dishwasher. Many childcare programs set out small basins for mealtime leftovers and provide different bins where children can sort their dishes, cutlery, and cups. Some centers go a step further and allow children to take turns bringing the food scraps to a worm bin or the center's compost container, thus adding a new level of learning as children come to appreciate the relationship between food and the environment.

Allergies, Medications, and Special Diets

Many a battle is being fought to make children take their medications or to make them avoid foods that create serious problems. It is amazing what children are willing to suffer to avoid being controlled. We want to emphasize how important it is to engage children in the problem-solving process so they develop thinking skills and feel both empowered and capable. Here are some suggestions.

- **Avoid lectures.** Instead, engage children in self-exploration by asking "what," "why," and "how" questions: "What happens when you don't take your medication (or when you eat this food)?" "How do you feel when that happens?" "What ideas do you have to solve this problem?" This will not be effective if children sense even a hint of a lecture instead of true curiosity about their thinking and ability to learn and solve problems.

- **Involve children in creating a medication routine.** Decide together on a time of day that works best for both of you. Work together on creating a reminder chart and on reminder methods (such as an alarm watch that goes off at the same time every day).

- **Take your child to the library to explore food allergies.** Find books that explain these issues in simple terms. (Be sure your goal is education, not fear.)

- **Decide what *you* will do.** This could mean that you are willing to take responsibility for kindly reminding your child every day at medication time, or that you will allow him to remind you when the medication alarm goes off.

- **Recognize that you may not always be around to supervise your child's diet.** In age-appropriate ways (and with kind, firm supervision), allow your child to take responsibility for selecting special snacks, packing appropriate lunches, or helping to measure medication doses. Remember that confidence and competence come from practice.

CHILDREN, MARKETING, AND FOOD

In 2006, the Institute of Medicine released a summary of 120 studies on children and food marketing.[1] They found that advertising scattered throughout children's commercial television programming was saturated with plugs for fat-, salt-, or sugar-laden treats with little nutritional value. This advertising heavily influences what children younger than twelve pester their parents to buy. The institute found that children younger than four cannot distinguish between an advertisement and entertainment programming and do not understand that advertisements are intended to sell products—yet another reason to pay careful attention to what your child watches on television.

Exercise

Growth and healthy weight involve both calories consumed and calories expended. Sedentary activities like watching television and playing video games are not healthy for brain development, nor do they strengthen the rest of the body. It is easy to enjoy the peace and quiet while your child watches TV or plays with your iPad, but it will be healthier for all of you if you go outside and play ball.

Make your home movement-friendly. Designate spaces where running or tossing soft balls is allowed, such as a long hallway or a playroom with minimal (and unbreakable) furnishings. Try to get your apartment complex to sanction an area for active (supervised) play.

Go for walks, which are both fun and practical, especially if the family pet needs exercise too. Cap off an evening with a family swim night once each week. Turn technology into part of the solution with family dance or exercise programs that can be engaged in together. Play music and dance around the house, or have a basket of bells, tambourines, and other noisemakers to make your own music. Have fun, and everyone will reap the benefits.

If the school your child attends is eliminating recess and physical education (and many are), become an advocate for reinstating it. Research has shown that adding recess and outdoor time to the school day improves both academic achievement and behavior.[2] Share the statistics about childhood obesity and how important regular exercise is for a child's brain and body.

Bon Appétit!

Remember that allowing children to be involved, encouraging mutual trust and respect, and having realistic expectations will take much of the struggle out of eating and may make mealtimes together an event the entire family looks forward to.

No matter how tempting the foods, your child must choose to eat them. Remember: you can't make 'em do it!

QUESTIONS TO PONDER

1. If you are worried that your child is not getting adequate nutrition, first gather information. Make a list of everything he eats daily for three to five days. Include all beverages and snacks. Now ask yourself whether he has eaten vegetables, grains, fruit, and protein during this period. If something is missing, ask yourself why. Were those foods offered? When? If not, why not? Use this information to understand your child's eating habits and preferences. Do you need to provide healthier snacks or food items? How can you invite your child's help in this process?

2. If providing healthy meals is a challenge for you, consider one of the following ideas:
   • Use a crockpot. Gather and prepare the ingredients the night before, then assemble them in the pot before leaving for work. You will enjoy coming home to a hot meal that is ready to eat.

- Make more than you need for one meal. When preparing soup, stew, or muffins, make enough to freeze for another meal.
- Consider taking a cooking class if you are not skilled at cooking (or never learned how). Ask friends and family members for simple, quick recipes, or search food websites for recipes your family might enjoy. Don't be afraid to experiment; your child will enjoy making messes in the kitchen with you.
- Create instant variety. Whenever you make a sauce (such as spicy peanut sauce, pesto, or meat gravy), freeze extra portions in ice cube trays. The same bowl of pasta or rice will taste different with the addition of these sauces. Add different vegetables, beans, or meat and you have a quick and tasty meal.

3. Make a list of nutritious foods your child likes. Include one of these at each mealtime, along with the other foods you prepare. Continue to offer new foods until they too become familiar.

CHAPTER 15

Preschoolers and Potties: The Ongoing Saga of Toilet Training

You may be thinking, "Surely preschoolers have mastered toilet training. Aren't kids supposed to be trained by the age of three?" Not necessarily. Bathroom habits and hygiene remain issues of concern for young children and their parents well beyond the age of three—or even four. And few topics arouse such strong emotions (and as much parental frustration) as potty training.

Let's say your child is still in diapers, while more and more of the neighbors' kids are potty trained. What should you do? Do you love your child just as he is? Do you avoid power struggles? Do you engage your child in joint problem-solving to figure out what will work for him—and how to clean up messes when he make mistakes? Or do you feel embarrassed and competitive, and try to make him do what he is "supposed" to do?

If you answered yes to the last question, it is likely that you are engaged in a power struggle. (It might be helpful to review the section on power struggles on page 192.) Toileting is one of the areas where a child can be most stubborn as he proves to you that "you can't make me."

Q. *I have a son who needs to be potty-trained. He turned three a couple of months ago. He does not like to use the potty. He does not show me signs* *when he has to go, but he will tell me when to change him. I feel so discouraged. Please, I need some advice!*

A. Parents often feel desperate when they find themselves changing diapers as children grow older, especially when younger siblings come along. Your son's delay in using the toilet is magnified by your own discouragement. He will succeed eventually, but it may take more patience than you knew you had. Children develop on their own schedules where toileting is involved.

Difficult as it may be, try to deemphasize the whole issue. Your son can read your nonverbal messages and knows that his toilet habits are extremely important to you—which is an invitation to a power struggle. If you invest less energy in this issue, he may be more willing to try something new. Meanwhile, when he needs to be changed, show him ways to help. He can wash or wipe himself off, help empty the stool from his potty into the toilet bowl, and wash his own hands afterward. In the

meantime, enjoy him and his other life successes. Express your confidence that he will use the potty successfully one day. He too needs encouragement.

You will be amazed at how quickly time passes when you detach emotionally from the potty-training issue. *Children are much more likely to become interested in potty training when allowed to do so according to their own timetable—and when there is nothing to rebel against.* A big part of detaching and relaxing is to know that a number of things can cause a temporary setback.

WHAT TIME IS THE RIGHT TIME?

Children acquire toilet skills more readily when their parents choose the right time to begin training. In one study, when children began toilet training before twenty-seven months, the process took a year or more; when children began training between twenty-seven and thirty-six months, training took five to ten months. According to this study, the optimal time for speedy toilet training is when a child is just shy of his third birthday. It takes approximately five months to toilet-train a child when he begins between the ages of thirty-three and thirty-six months. If your child wants to try the toilet earlier, help her do so, but don't push if her interest doesn't continue.

INVITING COOPERATION

Not surprisingly, potty training is just that: training. And there are many things parents can do to make it easier. The first involves your attitude. Knowing your child's temperament and abilities will help you keep your expectations reasonable. If you are relaxed and comfortable, your child is likely to feel the same way.

Pressure to succeed will only frustrate both of you. If accidents happen—and they will—be patient. If your child is wet, change her. If she is old enough, buy pull-up diapers so she can change herself (which often encourages a child to be more aware of her body's signals). Be sure, however, that you never humiliate or shame a child about toileting setbacks. Always be available to help. Dry pants aren't worth a damaged sense of self-worth.

Do your best to make the process easy for your child. Provide clothing that is easily pulled down and up; elastic waistbands are perfect. If the weather is warm, wearing underpants alone (or nothing at all) may simplify the process.

Having predictable toilet times may encourage youngsters to develop the habit of using the bathroom regularly. When leaving for an outing, even a short one, it is wise to invite a young child to use the toilet beforehand. (Most parents quickly learn where the restrooms at the neighborhood grocery store are located.)

Elaine decided to take her preschool class on a field trip to pick blue-berries. They blithely sailed out of the preschool together and into a nearby field. Trouble soon arose, however: Elaine had forgotten to remind the children to use the toilet before leaving, and now the only option was a well-used outhouse. Elaine spent most of the field trip holding one child after another over the outhouse toilet, and she never forgot pre-outing reminders again!

Pull-ups and diapers are now available for children as old as five years old. Unfortunately, diapers marketed as being extra-absorbent may actually discourage toilet training because children remain comfortable and never feel wet. It may be wise to consider using less effective diapers, or those specially designed for training.

How Can You Set Your Child Up for Success?

There are six important factors that can help parents set the stage for this important developmental milestone: physical readiness, ease of wakefulness, understanding your child's perspective, logic versus power struggles, cooperation, and detachment.

IMPORTANT FACTORS AND ATTITUDES TO END TOILET BATTLES

- Physical readiness
- Ease of wakefulness
- Understanding your child's perspective
- Logic versus power struggles
- Inviting cooperation
- Detach, relax, and enjoy

PHYSICAL READINESS

Many children become potty-trained before they reach the preschool years. This fact adds to the frustration of parents whose preschoolers have not yet accomplished this goal. Some children are not yet physically ready to perceive and respond to the signals sent by their bodies. A child must have a bladder large enough to allow him to wait for increasingly long periods of time before urinating, especially for overnight control. The reality is that some children simply don't develop bladder control as soon as others.

Mariana was very familiar with the level of bladder control of her three children. This knowledge helped her know how quickly they needed to stop the car when their children requested a bathroom stop on long trips. In response to seven-year-old Kenny's request, Mariana would remind her husband, "We can keep driving for about twenty minutes." When three-year-old Lori would ask for a bathroom, Mariana would say, "Well, we have about ten minutes to find a good stopping place." However, when five-year-old Jacob said, "I have to go," Mariana would say, "Pull over immediately. If we can't find a bush, Jacob will just have to settle for the side of the road."

EASE OF WAKEFULNESS

Another important factor in toilet training is ease of wakefulness. Many children who remain bed-wetters during and even beyond their preschool years are the same children who have difficulty waking up. Even bed alarms that go off when urination begins sometimes do not wake these children. When parents try getting their heavy sleepers up in the night to take them to the toilet, the children are like limp rags who cannot stand or sit. They simply cannot wake up. Lighter sleepers may fuss and complain when awakened for a night trip to the toilet, but boys can still stand up, though seemingly half asleep, and girls can sit on the toilet without falling off. Some children cannot wake enough to do either.

Children should always be treated with dignity and respect, but it is especially discouraging to use punishment with children who don't have the physical capacity to do what you are asking of them. Understanding inspires patience.

UNDERSTANDING YOUR CHILD'S PERSPECTIVE

Imagine for a moment that you are a preschooler. You know that Mom and Dad are eager for you to learn to use the potty, to be a "big boy" and wear "big boy pants." Suddenly you feel that strange tingly feeling that you are beginning to recognize as meaning that you have to go. So you head toward the bathroom, becoming aware as you trot down the hall that there may not be a lot of time. You know you have to get your pants down, but the buckles on your overalls are stiff and your fingers are small. Then you glance at the toilet, which looks very tall from your perspective. Maybe, you think, a little assistance is called for. But by the time you alert your parents or the teacher, it's too late.

No wonder children often decide that it's easier just to stay in diapers! Understanding the occasionally overwhelming nature of the task can help parents set the stage for their child's success. Remember, toilet training is vitally important to diaper-weary adults—but rarely does it matter that much to a child. *As with eating and sleeping, creating a toileting-friendly environment with easy-off clothing and accessible facilities is a parent's job; deciding when (and where) to go is a child's.*

LOGIC VERSUS POWER STRUGGLES

Parents often rely on logic in their attempts to resolve problems, but issues such as potty training are usually based on illogical power struggles. The more determined parents become to have urination and defecation take place in the toilet, the more determined many preschoolers become to have it take place somewhere else—usually in their pants.

Remember, your child is still developing a sense of autonomy and initiative and probably has an "I can do it" attitude. When parents try taking control of a child's bodily functions, they often meet with resistance. It could be that the child is deciding (at a subconscious level), "I prefer to walk around in urine-soaked pants rather than to give up my sense of power."

In other words, when parents insist on winning power struggles, the only option for the child is to become the loser—and children will fight diligently to avoid being the loser. Since parents are the "mature" ones, it is up to you to end the power struggles and find ways to invite cooperation.

Q. *I'm at my wits' end. I have a four-year-old boy who, after a playdate with an older cousin, learned the joys of peeing off a bridge. Now he is peeing everywhere: the carpet, trashcan, off the porch, and so on. It seems to be an act of rebellion, often happening after I tell him to do something he doesn't want to do (like get dressed). We've tried time-out (which only precipitates a tantrum) and taking away privileges (TV, computer time, or dessert). I have to admit I spanked him in frustration when I caught him in the act last time. I've tried talking to him about this problem but I get nowhere. I'm at a loss. Help!*

A. The best thing to do is try to redirect these power struggles into useful power. Four-year-olds are ready to use their personal power in ways that contribute to the family. When parents use controlling methods and punishment, children resort to destructive power instead.

Our crystal ball suggests that when you say "I've tried talking with him," what you really mean is "I talked and talked and lectured and lectured." "Talking" often means "telling"—over and over again. One suggestion is for you to stop telling and start asking, using curiosity questions. You might ask, "What happened? How do you feel about what happened? How does this create a problem for you or for others? What ideas do you have to solve this problem?" You can also share your own feelings, with kindness and respect: "It's frustrating for me to have to clean up these messes. How can we solve this problem?"

It is essential that these questions be asked in a calm and friendly tone of voice and with sincere curiosity about your child's point of view. You may have to wait a while between finding a puddle and talking to your son so that you can calm down first. Inviting discussion (rather than lecturing) will help your child develop thinking skills, awareness of the consequences of his choices, and problem-solving skills. "Telling" invites your child to become defensive or even more rebellious.

Another possibility is to get him involved by teaching him to use his power to problem-solve in all areas of his life, not just where toilet habits are involved. This can take many forms:

- Ask him what he needs to do in a given situation. If it is morning and time to get dressed, ask what he needs to do when he finishes eating.
- Work together to create routine charts. You might be surprised by how well this invites cooperation instead of rebellion.
- Stop using any form of punishment, including enforced punitive time-outs.
- Start having regular family meetings so your child can learn respect and problem-solving skills. If your son has many opportunities to use his power in useful ways, he is less likely to be rebellious.
- Teach him to help clean up any mess he makes, not as punishment  but as a part of learning responsibility. (Be patient and kind about toileting messes; your child is unlikely to enjoy them any more than you do.) With a kind and firm tone of voice say, "You'll need to clean that up. Would you like my help or do you want to do it by yourself?" If he resists, say, "Would a hug help you feel better? I know you will want to take care of this problem when you feel better." (When doing this, always be sure to help a child wash his hands with soap and water afterward.)

All of these methods create positive long-term results. Ask yourself, "Do I want to make my child pay for what he did, or do I want to help him learn to do better in the future?"

Be sure to train your child to wash his hands thoroughly. Have a stool available so he can reach the sink, and have soap and a towel for drying within easy reach. One preschool teaches children to sing this song (to the tune of "Skip to My Lou") while they wash their hands (when repeated twice, the song lasts about twenty seconds, just the time it takes to kill *E. coli* bacteria).

Wash, wash, wash your hands	Scrub, scrub, scrub your hands,
Wash your hands together.	Till they're clean and sparkly.

Setbacks: "Whoops!"

When a child is experiencing new things—a new preschool, a new house, or a new sibling—it's common for potty training to suffer a setback. A new environment or an especially exciting activity can cause a child not to pay attention to his body's signals; other major life events, such as death, divorce, illness, or travel can interfere with toileting. All of these events represent major adjustments in a child's life, and toilet issues often take second place to coping with change.

Your attitude will make all the difference in how your child handles accidents. Imagine how confused and discouraged a child might feel when she not only loses control of her body but faces an adult's anger and disappointment as well.

Ann was four years old when she was asked to be flower girl in her aunt's wedding. She wore a white gown made especially for her, with a lacy veil and a tiny pearl necklace. People smiled and nodded at her as she walked down the aisle scattering rose petals, and Ann glowed with the attention and excitement.

The reception was beautiful, and Ann was thrilled by the celebration. She had crawled under a table and was listening to the adults talking when she became aware of something she'd been ignoring all afternoon. Before she could get up, it happened: she wet herself, soaking her lovely white dress.

When Ann's mother discovered her, she was horrified. "I can't imagine what got into Ann," she told the assembled aunts and grandmothers. "She never does this anymore." Turning to her crying daughter, she said coldly, "You should be ashamed of yourself." Ann was changed into her old play clothes and spent the rest of the day hiding from everyone.

When children have toileting accidents, the last thing they need is a disapproving audience. Ann's mother could have taken her quietly aside, helped her to change, and explained to her daughter that excitement can sometimes make people forget to do the things they should.

It is wise to keep a change of clothing nearby when your child is learning to use the toilet. It is also immeasurably helpful to be patient and to offer your child unconditional love and acceptance. Once you have taken into account your child's personal time clock, provided him with appropriate clothing and accessible facilities, and taken time to train him in the skills he needs, it is time to relax, celebrate his successes, and sympathize with his disappointments.

Constipation

Bowel control is another issue where a parent's desire to speed training may cause complications. Some children will not release their stool, even to the point of physical damage.

Quentin's grandma had a lot to say on the issue of toilet training, most of it to his mother. "My children were all trained by the time they were two," she said disapprovingly, glaring at four-year-old Quentin while his diaper was being changed.

So Quentin's mom embarked on a full-scale assault. Quentin was placed on the toilet several times each day while his mom knelt nearby and urged him on. Quentin grew to hate the bathroom, and so did his mom. She would encourage, threaten, and scold; he responded by refusing to produce the desired result—anywhere or anytime. Before long, Quentin lost the ability to respond to his body's signals and could no longer tell when he needed to have a bowel movement.

One day at his regular checkup, his pediatrician gave Quentin and his mom the news that he had a severely impacted bowel, with stool backed up well into his intestines. Daily doses of mineral oil and enemas were prescribed to relieve the problem, and both mother and son shed many a tear until the problem—which need never have existed—was resolved.

It is never helpful to force toileting issues. If your child is resistant, first look for natural or environmental causes. Does your child eat sufficient fiber to produce soft, regular bowel movements? If not, switch to juices containing fiber, such as peach or apricot nectar. A spoonful of prune juice mixed in with other foods might help. Serve kiwi fruit daily, and your child's stools should improve quickly. Children may reject cereals such as raisin bran or other high-fiber choices unless they are baked in muffins. Serve fewer dairy products and apple juice, which tend to be constipating. But do be careful: don't set up a new power struggle trying to get him to eat these foods!

Sometimes children simply need a more gradual approach to mastery. As soon as he begins to have a bowel movement in the diaper, accompany your child to the bathroom (but leave his diaper on). This creates a positive, comfortable association with being near a toilet while pooping. Children with other problems, such as some medical issues, may have a high likelihood of associated bowel control problems. Whatever the reason, a child who is having difficulty defecating may loosen up and relax his muscles with simple tricks, such as blowing bubbles or playing a harmonica or small flute while sitting on the toilet—it is difficult to squeeze and blow at the same time!

Expectations beyond a child's emotional ability can also create problems.

The Mackey family deferred all kinds of decisions to their three-year-old. "Where should we eat dinner?" they asked. "Should Mommy and Daddy go out tonight?" "Do you want to go to preschool this morning?" The list went on and on.

This child experienced severe constipation because she felt overwhelmed by all the decisions placed on her shoulders. Her parents worried that setting limits would restrict her too much. They went so far in the other direction that she experienced enormous distress.

As you can see, control issues of all kinds may play a role in stool retention problems. Avoiding power struggles, empowering your child in positive ways, and encouraging cooperation are as effective in solving bowel problems as they are in other areas of family life.

Other Challenges

Major life changes affect all family members, and sometimes a child's toilet issues are a response to stress. One parent, concerned over her own father's terminal illness, did not make the connection between her struggle to face this crisis and the toileting problems her son experienced. Although he had been potty-trained, he began having daily accidents. When setbacks occur, consider whether external circumstances may be having an effect.

Pushing a child to master too many tasks by signing him up for an endless string of classes may create stress too. Similarly, expecting perfection from your child invites anxiety. Though some children may show interest in learning new skills early on, *forcing* them to do so takes an emotional toll. If your child appears anxious about the toilet itself or is frightened by the loudness of the flushing sound or a fear of falling in, find opportunities to talk gently about his fears. Wait to flush the toilet until after he leaves the bathroom and help him to see that his body is bigger than the toilet opening (or provide a potty chair if that feels safer). By tuning in to your child's feelings, you may promote and improve potty success without creating power struggles or inviting him to feel shame and discouragement. Toileting can be harder for some children to master than it is for others. Simply knowing that your child is not the only one experiencing such difficulties may help you cope.

DETACH, RELAX, AND ENJOY!

When readiness and training have been taken into account, trust that successful toileting will result in due time. Perhaps the best advice is simply this: relax. After all, children rarely go off to kindergarten in diapers. When he's ready, he'll do it—and probably not a moment sooner. You may not be able to make 'em do it, but there is much you can do to set the stage for success.

QUESTIONS TO PONDER

1. Look over the bathroom your child is expected to use. Is the toilet seat hard to climb onto? Would a small step stool help? Can she reach the sink easily? Would a faucet attachment that brings the water flow closer to a child's shorter arms be helpful? Consider kneeling so you can view the bathroom from your child's point of view. What do you notice?

2. Think of a song or nursery rhyme your child likes to sing or recite. Time it to make sure it lasts about twenty seconds. Practice

singing or reciting it together while your child washes his hands after toileting.

3. Consider ways in which you may be trying to "make" your child eat, sleep, or use the toilet. What is one change you are willing to make to let go of your part in this power struggle?

PART FOUR

The World Outside Your Home

CHAPTER 16

Selecting (and Living with) Childcare

Jim has two children. The oldest is four and the youngest is eighteen months old. His marriage has just ended in divorce; he has sole custody of his children and cannot afford to give up a career that provides him with a way to support his family.

Bethany is director of research, midway through a ten-year project. If her research produces the results she expects, it may provide treatment for a type of cancer that has been considered hopeless. Bethany just turned thirty-four; she and her husband have decided that they can wait no longer to begin their own family. Bethany knows that continuing her research and having a baby will mean using childcare or employing a nanny.

Elena's three-year-old daughter, Mitra, is lonely and wants playmates, but there are no other children in their neighborhood. Elena does not want her daughter to watch television all day. A preschool has opened on the next block, but Elena's not sure if it's the best thing for Mitra and worries that placing Mitra in preschool while she stays home will make her seem like a neglectful mom.

Keiko was such a devoted parent that she didn't leave her first baby until he was six months old. Then she left him with a sitter for only two hours and called at least once an hour to make sure everything was all right. The baby slept soundly the entire time, but she was still not comfortable leaving him.

Childcare: A Modern Necessity

These days, childcare is a fact of life for most families. In fact, many young parents were themselves enrolled in a childcare program or had a "helper," grandparent, or nanny as part of the family. Indeed, early childhood education offers children wonderful opportunities to experience their world, to play (and learn), and to develop social emotional skills. While parents may still agonize over leaving their child in someone else's care, the real question for many parents is this: "How will I know if a childcare program is high-quality?"

Roslyn tells this story:

For decades the Montessori childcare we run, the Learning Tree, has been a safe refuge for families. Countless times over the years, parents related to us how important it was to them that their child was in a safe place. This was great to hear, but because either my husband or I was always present when our own children attended, I don't think I truly comprehended how much those statements meant.

Then I had to place my mother in assisted living. One day, while thanking the director and telling her how much it meant to me to know that my mom was in a safe place, a lightbulb went off. I finally got it. It means everything.

Childcare today may replace the extended family of aunts, uncles, grandparents, and cousins that past generations grew up with. There may not be a sister or cousin to compare notes with when Belinda pulls a neighbor's hair or Jeff wakes up with a fever in the middle of the night.

Today's childcare center can be a place to meet other parents, share concerns, and find support.

This knowledge may help you feel confident about your decision to find quality childcare, whether you need it for a night out, a special event, or for full-time work. Remember, children absorb the energy of your attitudes and react to it. If you feel fearful, so will your child. If you feel guilty, your child may sense an opportunity to manipulate you. It is ironic, but both working parents and stay-at-home parents seem to feel some degree of guilt and regret about their choice, whatever it is. Guilt rarely does anyone any good. The key is to make the best decision you can in your own situation, and then to relax. You will find this easier to do when you know how to recognize quality childcare.

What Is the Best Way to Prepare Your Child to Learn?

There is a growing tendency for parents to seek childcare centers that offer academics, such as reading, writing, and computer skills. This concerns most early childhood experts, and you need to know why.

Many research studies have demonstrated that children who attend academic preschools do know more numbers and letters than children who attend play-oriented preschools. However, by age five, the kids from the play-oriented preschools have caught up, while those attending academic preschools often feel less positive about school. In addition, as you have already learned, play is how preschoolers learn. Adults may believe that pushing children to acquire academic skills early will benefit them, but the research (and a child's own development) say otherwise. When preschoolers are pushed to excel in academics, they may miss out on more developmentally appropriate and effective ways to learn.

Take a moment to get into the world of your preschooler. How would you feel if you were pushed to learn something, and you knew

273

learning it would make your parents proud? How would you feel if learning these tasks was difficult (even though you could do it)? Might you have feelings of inadequacy? Might you feel only conditionally loved? On the other hand, how would you feel if your parents allowed you to explore and experiment in a nurturing environment filled with enticing equipment that allowed you to feel capable with every accomplishment? How would you feel if you were learning to be creative and mastering social and problem-solving skills instead of regurgitating facts and figures?

Does this mean academics should be eliminated entirely during the first three years? No. The key is to follow the interests of the children. (Maria Montessori knew this over 100 years ago.) Some three-year-olds want to read and feel excited rather than pressured to learn. Some enjoy learning to sing the alphabet song (even though they don't have a clue what it means). Be aware of what your child is learning and how he feels about it. Your child may not have the words to tell you he is feeling pressured, but if you are paying attention, you will know.

Selecting Childcare

Perhaps the most important question of all is "What is quality childcare and how do I find it?" It is extremely important not to bargain-hunt when it comes to childcare. As most parents have discovered, childcare can be breathtakingly expensive. Although cost must be considered, it should not be the most important factor in your decision. Many extremely important hours of your child's life will be spent in the childcare setting that you choose.

Simply put, find the best care possible. If quality care is unavailable, make what you find into quality care by providing the caregivers with information, such as books and training in Positive Discipline.[1] Work to bring early childhood training to your area if it is lacking.

Don't be in a rush to choose; be sure to visit several different childcare programs. Take notes on what you see.

- Are the children happy?
- Do they move around the center confidently?
- Do the teachers get down on the children's eye level to talk with them?
- Is the artwork displayed low enough for children to see, or is it only at adult eye level?
- Is the building clean?
- Are there visible safety hazards?
- Do the teachers look cheerful or frazzled? (Of course, do remember that even the best teachers can have tough days!)
- Does the equipment provided allow children to play freely, to dress up, to learn, and to be active?
- Are children expected to be quiet, sit still, and "be good"? (This may sound desirable, but it does not fit with typical child development and learning.)

Parents sometimes look at lists of qualities and requirements for good childcare and feel overwhelmed. You may be wondering how you will ever know if the facility you are considering meets these standards. There is a relatively simple solution: ask. Childcare is an important decision, and your confidence as a parent will influence your child's comfort with and response to her new setting.

Don't hesitate to ask for all of the information you need to make an educated decision. If a center or provider seems reluctant to answer your questions or to allow you to observe them in action, it's probably wise to look elsewhere. *One of the most important criteria is to find a licensed center or home that welcomes parents anytime. These centers have nothing to hide and will treat you as a respected partner in your child's care.* If you feel like an intruder when you visit your child's preschool, childcare center, or home care, find another where you feel welcome. Childcare centers should be safe, nurturing places for children to be.

HOW TO SELECT QUALITY CHILDCARE

Identify quality childcare using the following indicators on this checklist.

1. The center or home has:
   - Licenses displayed and current
   - Low rate of staff turnover
   - Local, state, and/or national accreditation
   - Loving, child-centered environment
2. The staff is:
   - Well trained in early childhood development and care
   - Working as a team
   - Staying up-to-date through training programs
   - Adequately paid
3. Discipline is:
   - Positive and respectful rather than punitive
   - Kind and firm at the same time
   - Designed to help children learn important life skills
4. Consistency shows:
   - In the curriculum
   - In the way problems are handled
   - In day-to-day center management
5. Safety is demonstrated by the:
   - Physical setting
   - Program health policies
   - Preparedness for emergencies
6. Curriculum, equipment, and activities are:
   - Varied and age-appropriate
   - Well maintained, planned, and supervised
   - Child-size and accessible to all

THE CHILDCARE CENTER OR HOME

Most states or cities require centers and homes to meet a variety of licensing requirements. Seeing licenses posted tells you the requirements were met. Check dates to be sure that licenses are current (although many states are so backlogged that long intervals between licensing are common).

A low staff turnover indicates that the center's staff are well treated, receive fair compensation, enjoy their work, and feel supported by the center's administration. When staff do not receive decent wages, they go elsewhere, often leaving the childcare field.

Look for special accreditation. The best known is NAEYC (National Association for the Education of Young Children), which takes a multifaceted approach. Centers spend several months doing self-assessments and correcting any weak areas; they then are visited by independent accreditors, usually on several occasions. This accreditation is only valid for two years, then must be repeated. Programs displaying this type of accreditation truly have earned it. (Look for local and state accreditation as well, if these exist in your community.)

THE STAFF

Training and experience make it more likely that caregivers will truly understand the needs of young children, provide activities that meet those needs, and have developmentally appropriate expectations.

Look for the types of training staff receive. Are there special training requirements? Montessori, Waldorf, High/Scope, Creative Curriculum, and many other programs have specialized training curricula for their teachers. Community college, undergraduate, and master's degree programs in early childhood studies exist in every state.

It is also helpful to examine consistency in the center's management. Are expectations (both of staff and of parents) made clear? Are events well organized? Are finances handled in a businesslike, respectful manner?

Do staff at the center you're considering attend workshops? Are there in-house training programs, or are employees encouraged to take part in additional educational programs? Do staff stay current by taking part in seminars, workshops, and special-topic trainings such as Positive Discipline? Teachers learn about new research, get inspired by and reminded of basic concepts, or feel encouraged when they hear others share solutions to common dilemmas.

Look for harmony. When there is discord at a center, the children feel it. Remember, young children can "read" the energy of the adults around them, and they respond to what they sense. Centers that encourage cooperation, both among children and among staff members, model the value of teamwork. Look for regularly scheduled staff meetings, in-house communication tools, and an atmosphere of camaraderie.

DISCIPLINE

Is there a written discipline policy? In what manner are problems handled? Are there texts on discipline recommended by the center? Ask what teachers do about a child who hits, bites, or grabs toys. Find out if teachers receive any training in how to deal with problems that arise. Does the center condone spanking? Is the attitude at the center positive or punitive?

Notice how teachers interact with children. Do they speak to children in a respectful way? Does the teacher get down to the child's eye level when talking to him, or do teachers yell instructions across the room? One-to-one communication indicates more appropriate and effective caregiving.

Are boundaries made clear, or does a teacher giggle uncomfortably when children run up and slam into her? Is there follow-through? Do teachers do what they say? Does the teacher call out to a child to "Put down that stick!" and then proceed to chat with a coworker while the child brandishes the stick overhead? Or does the teacher walk over and calmly remove the stick after giving the child a moment or two to do so himself? Are children being taught what *to* do, rather than being reprimanded about what *not* to do?

What lessons do children learn about their own abilities? Do the teachers put on everyone's coats, socks, and shoes or do they help children do so themselves? Are children encouraged to wash their own hands before lunch? Look for programs where skills are being taught and children are not simply objects to be fed, dressed, and carted around.

What type of atmosphere do you sense when you visit? Happy, peaceful children are a good sign. (Please note: This doesn't necessarily mean quiet children!) The level of activity should indicate that the children are involved in and enjoying whatever they are doing.

CONSISTENCY

Consistency in the curriculum means that certain activities are provided regularly. Circle time, art projects, and singing are examples. Children thrive on routine at their care facility as well as at home. Consistency also means that learning objectives exist and are implemented. Contrast a well-defined program to a place where children are given some old egg cartons to cut up, plopped down in front of the same container of blocks every morning, or left to watch endless videos and television programs. (In the context of a clear curriculum, some of these activities may be fine.) Be sure that your caregiver values hands-on learning, healthy activity, and developmental growth—not just silence and obedience.

Centers with consistent programs encourage children to develop trust, autonomy, and a healthy sense of initiative. These traits are important at home, and they are also important where your child will spend so much of his time.

SAFETY

Safety includes the physical setting, the program health policies, and the emergency preparedness of the center. A facility with exposed electrical cords, unimpeded access to a laundry cupboard, or broken-down play equipment does not provide an environment that is safe for little ones.

Look for everyday preparedness.
- How are emergencies handled?
- Are there regular fire or other emergency preparedness drills?
- Do teachers have CPR, HIV/AIDS, and first-aid training?
- How are medications stored and administered?
- Are meals and snacks healthy (including fresh fruits and vegetables, whole grains, and unprocessed foods)?
- What about allergies? (Many centers are now nut-free due to an increase in severe nut allergies.)
- What is the center's policy on illness and exclusion?
- Ask how injuries are handled.

If you are in an earthquake-, flood-, or tornado-prone area, what provisions have been made in case of such an emergency?
- Are food, water, and clothing set aside?
- Are out-of-area emergency contact numbers listed in case local services become unavailable?
- What evacuation site or route is designated?

Reassure yourself that the staff knows how to care for your child under a variety of circumstances. The more satisfied you are that these details have been addressed, the more comfortable you can feel about leaving your child at this center.

CURRICULUM, EQUIPMENT, AND ACTIVITIES

What curriculum guidelines does this program follow? Are there posted themes or a daily schedule of activities or learning objectives? Most learning takes place during play. Setting out toy kangaroos and Aboriginal art designs while learning about Australia; including woven African cloth, batiks, and child-size tunics to promote multicultural appreciation; or providing a variety of sponges, brushes, and textures for painting will enhance the type and quality of children's play and exploration.

Outdoor access and equipment such as climbers that encourage large-muscle development should be available for use. Be sure these areas are maintained and are safe and clean. Be sure there is regular outdoor time daily and that supervision is always provided. On outings, high adult-to-child ratios must be met.

Any equipment that children have access to should be scaled to their use, such as low-level sinks, easy-access shelves, and displays at a child's eye level. Whenever possible, there should be child-size equipment. Small pitchers, drinking cups, and child-size tables and chairs are helpful for young children. If child-size items aren't available, then some adaptation of adult-size equipment will help. An example would be to make sinks or toilets more accessible by providing sturdy step stools.

Look for puzzles that have all of their pieces; a varied and changing supply of blocks and art supplies; and music, singing, or rhythm experiences. If all you see are stacks of paper and pencils and children sitting at desks or tables for long periods, beware. A program that engages all of the senses as well as encourages active play and movement promises the most appropriate learning balance.

Living with Your Childcare Decision

Once you have made your decision, you still may have feelings of sadness and anxiety about leaving your child. Several things may help. The first step is to recognize that this is a necessary choice for you and your child. *When a parent can accept the need for (or see the value of) childcare in the life of the family, concerns begin to diminish.*

The next step is to deal with the many questions you may have about handling the details of daily life when childcare is part of your family's routine: "How can I handle leaving my child in the morning?" "How do our home routines change when we are away from our child all day?" "What about my child's friends?" "Will my child feel a sense of belonging?" Many of these questions will be resolved once you feel confident that you have selected a quality childcare situation.

Separation

Parents often feel a bit guilty when they leave their child. Many children cry in the morning at drop-off, or in the evening when a parent goes out with friends. How parents react to this influences a child's ability to be content in childcare. The parent who, though sad, believes that her child will be well cared for and secure while she is absent communicates that confidence to her child.

The other side of separation is connection. While you and your child are apart, whom will your child connect with? Take time to help your child begin a relationship with his new caregiver(s). Both he and you need to know that he can trust that person to be there for him when you cannot be.

Provide tangible ways for him to feel connected to you and his more familiar world by supplying a nap blanket or cuddly toy from home. Set up playdates with the other children in his class to broaden and strengthen the connection he feels with his new friends. The more connections he feels, the better he will handle his time away from you.[2]

The Childcare Day

Your daily routines will be influenced and altered by the schedule, commute, and details of your child's care. Some families have to include food preparation time if they bring in all or part of their child's food. Getting dressed and out of the house, coping with naptime, establishing departure routines, and keeping up with your child's budding and shifting friendships are common issues that may overtake the whole family.

It can be difficult to remember in the midst of rushing out the door, but even though two-year-old Nick insists on wearing one purple sock and one orange sock and five-year-old Susan drops the jar of honey on the kitchen floor, do take a moment to rejoice in the fact that Nick dresses himself at all and that Susan is helping set out breakfast things without being asked. There will always be imperfections. Use your energy to focus on the daily victories—no matter how small they may sometimes seem.

Morning Hassles

Routines are critical for getting out of the house in the morning. We've explored children's differing perceptions about time and the "process versus product" thinking that prevails in early childhood (see Chapters 2 and 3). These traits sometimes work against a smoothly flowing morning. Remember that young children thrive on routines and predictability. Establishing clear routines for getting your little one to childcare can be the difference between a calm morning and a hectic one.

There are four busy people in the Jasper family. Dad has to be at work by eight-thirty, Mom begins work at nine, and their four-year-old twin daughters, Angie and Amy, must be taken to childcare. Since they have only one car, the family commutes together.

Each evening the twins help pick out the clothes they will wear the next day. Because Amy wasn't always happy having to take off her warm nightgown, she and her mom agreed that Amy could sleep in the shirt she would wear the next morning. Either Mom or Dad would pack lunches the night before, with occasional "help" from the twins. Whoever packed the lunches also helped the twins make sure that all coats and shoes were laid out near the door so there would be no last-minute panic over missing items.

The twins knew that they had to be dressed before they could have breakfast. Mom or Dad was available to help with difficult buttons or shoe tying, but the girls did a good job of getting their clothes on. Mom and Dad had begun training and encouraging their daughters' efforts to dress themselves when the twins were toddlers. Amy liked to pour her milk, and her parents kept a small pitcher in the refrigerator that she could manage. There was a sponge by the sink that the girls could use when the occasional spill occurred.

Both Angie and Amy had tasks each morning to help with breakfast: setting out napkins, putting salt and pepper on the table, mixing the juice, and so on. Angie and Amy felt good about the contributions they made each day. While the twins helped one parent clear up the breakfast things, the other parent got the car out and everyone's gear loaded up. Then, relaxed and smiling, out the door they went.

Does this sound like a fairy tale? Yes and no. It is possible to set up careful routines and achieve this kind of morning harmony, but it does not happen overnight. First Mom and Dad had to agree on their own morning responsibilities. Then Amy and Angie had to conduct a few tests to see if their parents really meant what they said. Once or twice, Amy and Angie did not have time to eat before leaving in the morning because they had delayed getting dressed. (Their parents knew that they could survive an hour or two until morning snack.) Amy and Angie's parents did not mistreat their daughters; they gave them the opportunity to become responsible in ways that were respectful by learning from the results of their own choices. Angie and Amy soon believed that their parents meant what they said.

Usually the result was a hassle-free morning routine. Notice the word "usually." The day did not always begin smoothly. Sometimes a parent overslept and got a late start or was just plain grouchy in the morning. Other times, no amount of routine would get Amy into her clothes. They learned to celebrate improvement instead of looking for perfection.

Arrival

Eventually the moment comes when you and your child arrive at the childcare center. Here are some things that will help both of you feel better about the day ahead:

- Arrive early enough to create a smooth transition.
- Take a moment to look around the center with your child.
- Find out what the teacher is planning for the day.
- Prepare your child if you find out there is a substitute; meet the substitute and make sure you introduce your child to any new person she will be with that day.
- Notice any changes in the environment. If a new toy or easel is out, explore it with your child.

You may have time to read a story or do a puzzle with your child before you leave. If time does not allow that, ask him what he will play with when you leave. This will allow you to feel more connected, and you and your child can visualize what he will be doing after you have gone.

When it is time to leave, go quickly (dragging out the farewell leaves you, your child, and the caregiver emotionally drained), but never just disappear. Tell your child that you are leaving. Tears may follow your announcement, but if you are respectful and honest, your child will learn that she can trust you. If your child clings to you, gently hand her into the caregiver's arms so that she can be held and comforted as you leave. It may help to have a place for children to wave to parents as they leave.

Remember that your child will learn that she can trust the adults in her life—and that she can trust herself. This is reaffirmed every day by the fact that you do, in fact, return (and that she does survive these separations).

Even when parents leave in a respectful and loving way, children still may cry. Eventually the tears will lessen and the routine of morning departure for parents and children will be easier. (If you feel the need, call the center midmorning to reassure yourself that the tears were brief and all is going smoothly. Your peace of mind will be worth it.)

Pickup Time

When you arrive to take your child home, allow time for a friendly greeting and a bit of reentry. You are both about to begin a new segment of your day.

When Madelyn arrives to take her three-year-old daughter, Anna, home, she finds her playing with some dress-up clothes. Madelyn gives Anna a hug and admires the orange wig and flowered purse that Anna has chosen. Madelyn then tells Anna that she may play for five more minutes.

During that time Madelyn reads the notes about Anna's day that have been left by the morning teacher. She also signs up to bring a casserole to next week's potluck. When she returns to the dress-up area, Anna is still wearing the orange wig. Madelyn comments on how much Anna must enjoy that wig; perhaps she will be able to wear it again tomorrow. She then tells Anna that it is time to leave. Anna pouts a bit but puts on her coat and takes her mother's hand. Together they hunt down Anna's missing shoe. Madelyn signs Anna out for the day and mother and daughter leave the center together.

Madelyn feels comforted that her daughter is so happy at her preschool that she doesn't want to leave. By taking time to reconnect with her daughter and giving Anna time to conclude her play, Madelyn has set the stage for a calm departure. Anna may fuss anyway—after all, she was having a lot of fun—but she is likely to fuss less than a child who is dragged away from her play.

The school staff has contributed to a smooth departure by taking time half an hour before departure to have the children find everything they need to go home (coats, lunch boxes, art projects, notices for parents about the upcoming potluck). In spite of all this preparation, some children may not be as cooperative as Anna when their parents arrive to pick them up.

There is a good reason children are fussy at the end of their day. An important element of childcare is that young children must cope with a highly social and stimulating environment. This means that tension and stress may build up in your child. When a child falls apart at her parent's arrival, it may be her way of saying that you are the person she can trust to love and accept her, no matter what side of herself she shows to you. Social expectations can be relaxed in the warmth of a parent's arrival.

Family Support

Whatever a family's configuration, resources, or location, all need support from time to time. Parents of young children need other parents with whom to share concerns, ideas, and stories. Children need other children and adults in their lives to learn about the variety of people that populate their world.

Parenting classes, books such as this one, and other resources provide valuable tools for parents today. Many communities boast parents' groups where parents can gather to share ideas and allow their children to play. In addition, the Internet has opened a vast world of information, including sites with forums for conversation, advice, and even opportunities to ask questions of recognized experts in a variety of fields. Caregivers also have access to an array of resources. One of the comments heard most often in parenting classes is how relieved parents feel to know that other families are having similar issues. All parents need reassurance that they aren't alone in their struggles.

Nannies and Sitters as Caregivers

Q. *I have a wonderful sitter who is great with my two-year-old girl and four-year-old boy. She has a three-and-a-half-year-old of her own, and my one concern is that she does not discipline her child. Consequently, her child is a tyrant and my two-year-old is starting to behave like the sitter's* *daughter. This child screams, hits her mother, and tells her mother "no" or "shut up." My daughter is starting to act this way at home, and it takes at least an hour to settle her down to our rules. I don't want my children to become tyrants as well. In all other aspects this sitter is wonderful. What do I do?*

A. Your sitter's daughter did not develop such behavior in a vacuum. Although you feel satisfied with her treatment of your children, we suspect she is not very effective at setting limits. The behavior of her daughter is a big clue. Does her daughter act this way all of the time? It could also be true that her daughter is jealous of sharing her mom's attention and so devotes her energy to misbehaving in order to keep her mom busy with her. Talk over your concerns; ask the sitter how she feels about her daughter's behavior and see if the two of you can come up with a win-win solution. If this does not resolve the problem, you may face a decision about whether to change your childcare arrangements.

Choosing a sitter or a nanny requires careful consideration. Always check references, interview candidates (without children present), and set up a trial visit where you, the caregiver, and your child can get acquainted. Conduct transactions in a businesslike manner; provide sitters with emergency, medical, and health-related information; and honor agreements paying for a sitter's time in the event of a last-minute cancellation.

The advantages of employing a sitter or nanny include not having to take your child out of the home for care. Children sleep, eat, and play in a familiar and consistent environment. There is often more flexibility if parents must work varied schedules or if jobs include traveling. On the other hand, a child at home with a nanny misses opportunities to develop social skills unless she plays regularly with nearby friends and relatives or attends a part-time preschool program. Most parents worry about the danger of abusive or neglectful care; some install camera systems in order to observe what happens when they are not present. Careful screening and a thorough checking of credentials are essential, as is developing a relationship of mutual respect and trust.

No matter whom you select to watch your children while you're away, be sure you've talked with him or her enough to feel comfortable—and to be sure that person shares your philosophy of raising children. It may be helpful to take a parenting class together. If your child is old enough to communicate easily with you, check her perceptions occasionally to be sure everything is going well. And always listen to your heart; your instincts will help you know when changes are required.

Grandparents and Other Relatives

Many children spend their time with grandparents or other relatives while parents work. Being cared for by relatives gives children opportunities to forge strong family bonds, and many of us have fond memories of times spent with our extended families. There may also be problems, disagreements, and clashes between the generations.

Q. *How can I raise a well-mannered four-year-old if his grandmother lets him get away with murder and spoils him rotten? He stays with her while I work part-time in a nearby office. I feel like I always have to be the bad guy since she won't discipline him. I'm even afraid that he loves her more than me. I need help.*

A. Parenting disagreements with grandparents usually have more to do with the relationship between a child's parents and the grandparents than with the child himself. Your own parents may continue to see you as that adorable chubby-cheeked darling they dandled on their knee—or as the "problem child" who hasn't learned anything in the years since childhood. Some grandparents are convinced they know more about raising a child than that child's parents, and genuinely intend to be helpful.

It sounds a bit as though you and your child's grandmother are using your child as a way to prove superiority over each other. Children love their parents. They also love their grandparents. It is possible to love both without diminishing the love for either. Children can learn what behavior is acceptable in different circumstances. If your child whines, "Grandma lets me do it," just smile and remind him that your rules are different.

Unfortunately, when child-rearing philosophies, expectations, and rules clash, tolerance may not be enough. If parents make a sincere attempt to achieve a healthy relationship with grandparents or other family members and differences cannot be resolved, childcare arrangements may need to change.

If you ever believe your child is at risk, do not hesitate to remove him from the environment. Then find a caregiver you can trust and feel comfortable with.

What If I Have Doubts?

Whenever a parent feels truly uncomfortable with a caregiver, related or not, the situation must be addressed. Suspicions of abusive treatment, exposure to harmful conditions, widely differing philosophies regarding discipline, or concerns about children falling behind developmentally merit immediate attention.

If the concerns are not threatening to your child's safety or health, work toward solutions. Communicate your concerns and voice ideas, wishes, and requests in a respectful fashion. Listen respectfully to your caregiver's ideas. Work on solving problems together. As with any care setting, when adults work together, children benefit.

Your child will, in all likelihood, spend at least part of these important preschool years in the care of someone other than her parents. The time and energy you invest now in making childcare arrangements that work for all of you will be repaid many times over in peace of mind, enjoyment, and your child's healthy development.

QUESTIONS TO PONDER

1. Think of the tasks or decisions needed on a typical morning before leaving home, such as clothing and meal choices or supplies. Can any of these be done the night before? How can you make this part of your evening routine?

2. Reread the "Pickup Time" section (page 286). Are you following as many of those suggestions as possible? If not, decide on one more action that might make this transition time smoother.

3. Evaluate your own support systems. Are you feeling overwhelmed or isolated? If so, look for at least one way that you can begin to connect with other parents on a regular basis.

CHAPTER 17

Class Meetings for Preschoolers (and Families)

It is class meeting time at the ABC Preschool. After the youngsters have exchanged compliments, Mr. Scott, the teacher, consults the agenda. "It sounds like we've had a problem on the playground with kids throwing wood chips at one another. Does anyone have something to say about this problem, or can someone offer a suggestion of how we might solve it?"

Five-year-old Girard raises his hand. "Whoever throws wood chips could take a cool-off!" Four-year-old Natalie waves her hand, and when called upon, offers, "We could not have wood chips anymore and have grass instead."

The teacher looks toward three-year-old Cristina, whose little hand has been patiently held aloft, and calls on her. "Guess what?" Cristina says with a bright smile.

"What, Cristina?" Mr. Scott asks.

"I had bananas in my cereal today."

"Mmmm, that must have tasted good." Mr. Scott smiles and thanks Cristina for her comment, then asks for more suggestions about the wood chip problem. Although Cristina clearly is not thinking about wood chips, she is still a valued member of the group.

Class meetings are a wonderful way to help children develop a strong sense of capability through contribution and problem-solving skills. This class agreed that they wouldn't throw wood chips anymore—a suggestion that had never worked when teachers pleaded, but was very effective when suggested by a child and agreed upon by the whole class.

What Is a Class Meeting?

Class meetings are far more than group problem-solving sessions. In a class meeting, children gather on a regular basis to help each other, encourage each other, learn communication skills, focus on solutions, and develop their judgment and wisdom. By far the most powerful effect of class meetings, though, whatever the age of the child, is to create a sense of belonging. Because the need for belonging lies at the heart of all mistaken goal behavior (see Chapters 10, 11, and 12), it makes sense that addressing this need, along with understanding development and social emotional growth, will have the greatest long-range effect on the behavior of the children.

Class meetings also aid in the acquisition of social skills and promote language development. The meetings foster a sense of both group and individual responsibility and empower young children with positive attitudes about their own capabilities and significance—attitudes that not only help shape their behavior but also build their self-esteem.

How Young Is Too Young?

"I can see the value of class meetings for elementary school children," you may be saying, "but aren't preschoolers a bit young?" The answer really is no—children can begin learning the basic skills for class meetings when they are around the age of three and can sit together for circle time. Even the youngest members of your preschool group can begin to cultivate the attitudes nurtured by the class meeting process. In a mixed-age group, the younger children can learn from their older role models, and the older children can learn to consider and include the needs of the younger ones. Three-year-olds like Cristina will certainly have different contributions to make than will older children. Still, there is real value in including the little ones, the greatest being that their sense of belonging to the group is established.

Even if your entire class consists of two- or three-year-olds, you can still enjoy class meetings together. The teacher becomes the role model when there are no older children; he may need to generate most of the suggestions and help the children learn to make choices. Taking into consideration the social and language skills of the children you work with will help you know how much you can expect to accomplish.[1]

One of the most important elements of Positive Discipline class meetings is that the agenda is generated mostly by the children. Teachers can also add items to the agenda, but children's ideas are encouraged. Another important point is that the teacher does not use class meetings as a platform for lectures. Instead, children are encouraged to express their ideas about the problems and to share ideas for solutions.

By the time children reach the age of four, they learn the elements of class meetings by jumping right in and participating. For example, the concept of "helping others" can be taught whenever the children are made aware of a need. Even young children warm quickly to the idea of solving problems—and are surprisingly good at it when taught the skills and given the opportunity to practice.

Elements of Success for Preschool Class Meetings

There are four main goals for class meetings with preschoolers. Listing these elements on a brightly colored chart can provide a stable agenda for every meeting and help focus children's attention on the project at hand. Once you have established the routine, preschoolers can take turns running the meeting. They love to call the meeting to order, invite compliments and appreciations, call on people who have their names on the agenda (sometimes with a little prompting from the teacher), ask for suggestions to solve problems or make fun plans, and close the meeting.

THE FOUR ELEMENTS OF CLASS MEETINGS FOR PRESCHOOLERS

- To give compliments and appreciations
- To empower children to help each other
- To solve problems that affect the group
- To plan future activities

COMPLIMENTS AND APPRECIATIONS

Compliments and appreciations are an opportunity for young children to find the good in other people, and are clearly influenced by the age of the children offering them. Four- and five-year-olds may say things like "I appreciate Jane for being my friend" or "I appreciate Eddie because he played dress-up with me." You may even hear an occasional "She pushed me off the swing!" (Well, they don't have it perfected yet.)

Two- and three-year-olds don't always understand the concept of compliments. They are more likely to say, "I love my mommy," "I like my sparkly shoes," or "I get to have pizza for dinner." Teachers can smile and thank them for their contributions. The feeling of belonging and significance is no less because the "compliment" was a bit off target.

It helps to ask questions that guide children in learning how to give encouraging compliments and appreciations: "What is something that you like about our school?," for instance, or "Is there someone who helped you feel good today?"

Teachers can also model giving appreciations. "I want to compliment all of you on the delicious cake you made yesterday. And thank you for washing the tables after we mixed the batter." "Leah, I want to thank you for letting us help you with the problem you were having about not liking your lunch. I appreciated the ideas that I heard because I can use some of them too." (A sincere "thank you" is often the best compliment of all.)

"I Love You, But . . ."

You've heard it before: the compliment that simply sets up criticism. "You did a good job, but . . ." "Thanks for picking up your toys, but . . ." Children will do this too, especially when they're just learning: "I appreciate Maggie for playing with me instead of pushing me like she did last time." It's usually best to offer a sincere compliment without conditions. If a child's behavior needs a bit of work or a task remains undone, consider making a respectful request later, instead of adding it to the compliment.

Keep in mind that compliments can easily become empty praise when we're not paying attention. Do your best to focus on encouragement, especially of skills and growth, rather than handing out compliments as rewards for obedience. Remember, it will take young children time and practice to understand how to give meaningful compliments and appreciations—but practicing this skill creates an atmosphere of belonging and contribution that is worth the effort.

KID OF THE WEEK

A special variation on appreciations at one childcare center is called "Kid of the Week." Each week there is a special Kid of the Week circle time, and every child in the class will be selected at least once during each year.

The teacher brings a large sheet of paper and an assortment of colored pens to the circle. At the top of the page she writes the child's name. Then each of the children take turns saying what it is they like or appreciate about the child while the teacher writes their comments on the sheet of paper. "I like her because she's my friend." "She plays with me." "She has a sparkle in her eye." (Wow!) "She jumps like Tigger."

If the children seem to be a bit stuck about what to say, the teacher can offer some guidance by asking questions. "Who remembers a game you played in the dress-up area with Maureen this week?" The teacher can also add comments to show appreciation for the child and to model the skill of appreciating others. If some of the children still have trouble thinking of something to say (or are just a bit shy), the teacher can ask, "Who would like to have his name written on the paper as one of Maureen's friends?"

When all who want a turn have finished, the teacher rolls up the paper and ties it with a bright ribbon. Another child is chosen to present the scroll to Maureen, and the circle finishes with another song, perhaps a variation on "For He's (or She's) a Jolly Good Fellow." Not a bad way to start a child's day, is it? Being Kid of the Week can be a special treat for every child—but remember to focus on creating belonging. (It is easy to slip over the line of encouragement into praise, which teaches children to depend on the evaluation of others.)

One teacher who had seen Kid of the Week demonstrated during an internship at an American school brought the concept back to her home classroom in Asia, renaming it "Star of the Week." In her culture, families were not involved in the school's activities except for fundraising events, but they responded with interest and curiosity when she proposed her Star of the Week idea.

One week, a father who was poorly educated and whom the teachers had tended to look down upon took part in his son's Star of the Week event. Together he and his son had constructed an elaborate representation of their small home, creating this model entirely out of toothpicks and plastic straws. The resulting product was a true work of art. Watching this man's obvious pride and love for his son, the teachers felt humbled by his talent and the amount of time and labor he had devoted on his son's behalf. A new sense of respect between the teachers and all the children's families began to develop, and the beautiful sculpture was kept on display for the rest of the term. Sometimes simple ideas can result in extraordinary transformations. Class (and family) meetings invite such connections by inviting children and adults alike to honor the contributions of each member of the group.

HELPING EACH OTHER

Next up at the class meeting is "helping each other." This time in your class meeting is an opportunity for children to ask for help with something that is a problem for them.

It is Tuesday morning at the Hill Harbor Childcare Center. The class of three- and four-year-olds is just beginning their class meeting with Miss Karina, their teacher. She asks if anyone needs help from the group today.

Matthias raises his hand and announces, "I can't wake up in the morning." Many of the other children agree that it's hard for them too. Karina asks if anyone has a suggestion for Matthias. The children offer all sorts of helpful ideas: "Go to bed earlier." "Just get up anyway." "Come to school in pajamas." Karina turns to Matthias and asks, "Do you think any of these ideas will help you, or should the group think of some more?" Matthias pauses to consider, then says he is going to "get up anyway."

Next, Julian raises his hand and says he needs help because "my mom doesn't have enough money." After sympathizing with Julian, other children volunteer that they have that problem too. Julian's friends are eager to help. Some of the children offer to bring in money. Bobby suggests that Julian could do some jobs to get money. Katie says, "My mom will give you money."

It is unlikely that Julian's mom will have more money as a result of this discussion. But Julian was genuinely concerned about money and his concern was treated respectfully. He has also learned that his classmates care about his needs, and that some of them share similar worries. "Helping each other" can become a very powerful part of class meetings.

Parents may be invited to place items on the agenda too and to visit and join in the class meeting. Seeing firsthand the experience their child is enjoying may encourage them to try similar meetings at home.

"PUT IT ON THE AGENDA!"

An agenda is a list of topics written in a class meeting agenda notebook or posted on the wall where everyone can reach it. Children and adults can use the agenda to list things they wish to discuss at the next meeting. In addition to providing a list of things to discuss, an agenda can serve as a cool-off device as well.

When Jon comes stomping over in a rage to tell the teacher, "Ben just killed a beetle," the teacher can share his concern and suggest that "How insects should be treated" would make a very good topic for their class meeting. She asks Jon if he would like to put it on the agenda. He readily agrees and together they write "bugs" on the agenda. The teacher sounds out the word "bugs" with Jon and he writes his name next to it. If Jon is too young to write, the teacher may write down Jon's name and topic for him. Or she may encourage Jon to draw a picture of a bug and either trace over his own name or make his own mark. Involving Jon in some way is respectful and creates a sense of responsibility and influence.

When it's time for problem-solving, the teacher will look at the agenda and ask Jon to explain the problem of bugs to the others. Jon's teacher will watch to see that the group focuses on the treatment of insects—not on who killed the beetle or how he should be punished.

SOLVING PROBLEMS

It may come as a surprise, but young children can be remarkably creative when it comes to solving problems. One afternoon, the following note appeared near the sign-out sheet at the Mountain View Preschool: "We are having a small bake sale this Thursday afternoon. We are learning to be responsible by replacing a ripped-up library book. We will bake cookies at school and sell them for twenty-five cents each. The children would also like to earn twenty-five cents at home by doing a special job. The bake sale idea came out of our class meeting discussion about a damaged book. We also discussed and demonstrated how to carry books and how to turn pages at the edge."

Over the course of the next week, the children prepared several batches of cookies during class time, learning new skills (and having a great time) in the process. On Thursday, the sale took place and was so successful that even after subtracting the cost of the cookie ingredients, the children had raised enough to replace the damaged book and buy another new one as well. They spent time at the next class meeting discussing what type of new book they wanted for their classroom.

Imagine if the teacher had scolded the children and taken away their book corner privileges. The opportunity to learn and practice these vital life skills would have been missed.

Class meetings can also provide valuable opportunities to learn social skills.

One morning at meeting time, Candace, who is four, said that another child had called her friend Eric a bad name. The teacher asked Eric if this was a problem he would like the group to address. It was. (It is important that children learn to be responsible for their own needs.) After Eric had told his story, the teacher asked whether anyone else had ever been called names. "How does it make you feel?" she asked. A lively discussion followed, and the children agreed that it hurt to be called names. They then came up with a list of possible solutions: "Maybe the name-calling person could control himself." "Walk away." "Say 'Don't say that!'" "Get a teacher to help." "Tell them you don't like it." "Ask them to take a cool-off." "Say 'Stop!'"

The suggestions may have sounded similar, but all were honored and written down. Eric and his classmates could now talk about the possible results of each choice (with some gentle help from their teacher) and decide on ways they might respond to name-calling in the future. Remember, preschoolers are still refining their social skills; suggestions like "Call him a worse name" or "Punch his lights out" would provide opportunities to learn about more appropriate responses.

PLANNING FUTURE ACTIVITIES

When young children are asked about fun activities they might do as a group, not all of the suggestions will be practical: "We could all go to Disneyland." "I suggest we go to the beach." (Never mind the snow outside.) "We can go on an airplane trip. My daddy will take us with him." Once children start offering improbable suggestions, they tend to get on a roll, so it is helpful for the teacher to guide them by offering some practical, fun ideas for activities and outings.

There are dozens of practical ideas. Visits to the police station, fire station, zoo, and park may be possible field trips, depending on your program. A field trip can also be a wonderful opportunity to invite children to solve problems in advance. Ask them what problems they had on their last field trip or what they think some good rules for the group would be. If the children can't think of anything, the teacher can ask about expectations for crossing streets, or if pushing and shoving, running around, or not listening respectfully when the fire chief talks would be acceptable.

More immediate activities can also be planned. Classroom treats such as ice cream or popcorn are fun and easy to provide. If an expenditure of money is involved, the children can work out plans to raise the needed funds. One bunch of enterprising youngsters decided to sell baked potatoes at the end of the day to tired and hungry parents. The aroma as parents entered the school was wonderful, and needless to say, this fundraiser was a rousing success.

The group may set a goal, such as throwing a pizza party when all of the shelves and toys have been washed. The teacher can provide buckets and sponges, and the children can pitch in. One program has an occasional floor-scrubbing day during which the furniture is cleared away and there are buckets of water (without soap or cleaning products) and scrub brushes for all. The children love the water play, skills training, and social interest, all rolled up into one activity.

The goal is not a perfectly clean floor or spotless shelves, but rather time to practice behavior that contributes to the classroom community.

Remember that involving children in planning an activity, whether in art or cooking or play, will make that activity more successful. When children are invited to feel capable, creative, and involved, they almost always respond with enthusiasm.

Special Tips for Effective Class Meetings

Keeping a few ideas in mind will ensure the success of your class meetings.

BE AWARE OF TIMING

Class meetings for preschoolers require that you be flexible. Depending on your children's age, mood, abilities, and attention span, you may need to keep meetings short or focus on only one element each time. Many preschools find that one meeting each week is ample. Others like to have a short meeting every day so that children can practice giving and receiving compliments and appreciations, listening with empathy, and focusing on solutions regularly. Trial and error will help you find just the right balance.

USE SPECIAL SIGNALS

Young children love special signals, such as the same song being sung each day to signal cleanup time or a ringing bell that means "freeze and listen." It also works well to develop a special signal to open and close class meetings. In one classroom, the kids sit on the floor in a circle and place their arms together with the elbows bent. To begin the meeting they slowly move their arms apart, like opening a book, and announce, "Class meeting is open!" At the end of the meeting, they reverse the process while saying, "Class meeting is closed!"

INCLUDE VOTING (WHEN APPROPRIATE)

In preschool, children can vote when the choice involves everyone. They can learn that people think and want different things, and they can learn to give and take, and to demonstrate empathy and compassion. (It is not appropriate to allow children to vote on a "solution" for another person. The person with the problem should be allowed to choose the solution she thinks will be most helpful for her.)

The concept of only one vote per child can be challenging. Try giving each child a piece of paper or a small marker. To vote, each child places her marker into the cup representing that choice. Add to the experience by emptying the cup and counting out the votes as a group project.

TAKE NOTES

Keeping track of what happens in a meeting can be helpful, especially when your class needs to remember just what it was they decided. Because most preschoolers can't write, an adult probably will need to take these notes. At the beginning of each meeting, you can review the previous meeting's notes and see how your plans and decisions are working out. Evaluate what did not work about the solution that was tried. If a problem persists, it is important to encourage a child to put it back on the agenda and discuss it again.

USE A "TALKING STICK"

A decorated stick, a magic wand, or a small toy can be passed around the circle. Whoever holds the object has permission to speak. (You might want to avoid stuffed animals since they are hard to wash and may spread germs.) A physical symbol can help young children learn to listen respectfully and speak in turn, and may encourage shy children to contribute to the group discussion when they have the object in their hands.

Family Meetings with Preschoolers

If you have older children, you may have already discovered the many benefits of having family meetings. If your children are all preschoolers, the concept may be new; you may even question the value of having family meetings with young children.

It is simple to adapt the material in this chapter to family meetings, and the benefits and blessings are well worth the time and energy. Family meetings teach children that they are valuable, capable members of the family, and demonstrate that spending time with them is a priority for you. You may be amazed at your preschooler's resourcefulness and creativity.

Preschoolers can offer compliments, help solve problems, plan family fun, and learn to express their needs and get help in positive (and surprisingly enjoyable) ways. Regular family meetings will help you and your children build a sense of mutual respect, trust, understanding, and love—and that can lay the foundation for the many years that lie ahead.

FAMILY MEETING STRATEGIES

- Be realistic.
- Prioritize time to meet.
- Begin (or end) with compliments or appreciations.
- Post an agenda.
- Have fun.

Here are a few ideas to keep in mind when beginning family meetings with preschoolers:

- **Be realistic.** You can have worthwhile, entertaining family meetings with children as young as three years old, but remember that the younger the child, the shorter the attention span is likely to be.

Keep your meetings short and to the point; that way, no one will get tired of them.

- **Make family meetings a priority.** Our busy lives have a tendency to get in the way of even our best intentions. If you want your family meetings to work, set a regular time to get together, and stick to it. As children grow older, they often have commitments such as sports or music lessons, the timing for which cannot be controlled. If a regular day and time doesn't work, create a family calendar that shows each member's upcoming activities, and use it to plan future meetings. Remember, it is easier for everyone to practice the skills when meetings happen consistently. Don't allow chores or other distractions to get in the way, and be sure all screens are turned off.

- **Begin each meeting with compliments and appreciations.** This can feel awkward at first, especially if you have siblings who are more comfortable teasing than complimenting each other, but looking for and commenting on the positive will encourage everyone and will get your meeting off to a friendly start. A variation some families prefer is to end the meeting with appreciations instead of beginning with them. When difficult issues are dealt with or strong emotions emerge, ending with appreciations can set a healing tone.

- **Post an agenda board in a handy place and help your preschoolers use it.** Even young children can "write" their problems and concerns in an agenda notebook or make a mark to indicate they have something to talk about. Taking these concerns seriously (and being careful not to immediately squelch your little one's sometimes unrealistic ideas) will show your children that you value them. The mere act of writing down a problem can be the first step toward finding a peaceful, effective solution.

- **Leave time for fun.** Make sure part of your meeting is devoted to just enjoying each other, perhaps by playing a game, watching a video together, planning a family activity, sharing a special dessert, or reading a favorite story.

However you decide to do them, family meetings are one of the best habits you and your children can get into and will help you stay tuned in throughout the increasingly busy years ahead.[2]

A Learning Opportunity

Class and family meetings are astonishingly productive, teaching many life skills while helping children develop a strong sense of belonging. Adults sometimes underestimate the ability of young children to be creative and responsible, and class and family meetings allow this learning opportunity for everyone.

QUESTIONS TO PONDER

1. Decide upon a day and time that will work best for a family meeting. Consider the steps listed in this chapter. Which do you want to include for your family, and how will you begin? For example, will you begin by teaching the skills, or by inviting family members to participate?

2. Consider adding a special activity to your weekly family meeting. While you are all gathered, what is something fun or helpful that you can do as a family? (Examples might include making a special dessert together, assembling puzzles, or making a family art project.)

3. If you want to initiate class meetings in your program, consider using the information in this chapter to have a staff meeting or professional development day. Share the elements of successful class meetings with your colleagues. In which classrooms will you begin? What skills must be taught? When will you hold your meetings? At a future meeting, evaluate everyone's experiences. What has been a benefit? What are the challenges?

4. Another way to introduce class meetings is to model compliments and appreciations. During the week, jot down kind or helpful things you notice each child (and teacher) doing. Do your best to find at least one positive action for each child. Then, at circle time, offer these appreciations to each person in the class.

CHAPTER 18

When Your Child Needs Special Help

All young children have both assets and liabilities, and all occasionally need extra encouragement or support. But some preschoolers have needs that go beyond everyday parenting. They are born with physical, emotional, or cognitive differences, and their parents and teachers must learn to provide kind, firm discipline, connection, encouragement, *and* special help for their unique needs.

These children may struggle in school, may have trouble making friends, or can't seem to learn basic skills. Others never stop moving, are constantly bouncing off the walls, or struggle to connect with adults and peers. These children (and their families) may need more than just good parenting skills. Attention deficit disorder (with or without hyperactivity), fetal alcohol or drug syndrome, autism spectrum disorders, sensory integration disorder, metabolic disorders, dyspraxia, and other developmental delays are among the conditions preschoolers, their families, and their caregivers may encounter. How can you tell when your child needs special help?

Taking a Closer Look

For some families, a child's preschool years are burdened by stress and anxiety.

Karen will never forget those panicked midnight trips to the hospital as baby Sandy's small face took on a bluish tint. Asthma threatened to steal Sandy from Karen throughout her infancy and toddlerhood. Now, as she watches her four-year-old daughter race across the playground and take a tumble in the dust, Karen must learn to give her daughter room to explore and grow while continuing to care for her health.

Carol and Brad have their own worries: they agonize over their son's stuttering. No matter how many people advise them to ignore Jacob's tortured language, both parents feel fiercely protective when other adults and children hear him struggling to speak. Their pain only makes Jacob more anxious. Is his problem somehow their fault?

Most parents are quick to blame themselves when their children encounter repeated problems. Special needs that involve behavior or development create anxiety, guilt, and confusion for families, and may require time-consuming and expensive treatments. *Guilt will not help you or your child. Accurate information and support will help you let go of guilt and replace it with beneficial action.* The first step, of course, should be a physical or neurological evaluation from a doctor who specializes in the area of your concern.

If it is your child's behavior that troubles you, usually it's best to start at the beginning. Take a moment to think about the information already presented in this book. Consider the following:

- Your child's age and developmental progress
- Your child's social emotional skills
- Your parenting style and expectations

- Your child's temperament
- The possibility of mistaken goal behavior

It may be wise to write down your observations to share with a professional. Most parents will find clues to understanding their child's behavior somewhere in this information. But if you've carefully considered these things and you find that your child still seems to need more help than you can provide, it may be time to look deeper.

The Reality of Special Needs

Carl was a difficult baby from the start. He never stopped moving, overreacted to every noise, and had difficulty nursing because everything distracted him.

Richard, four years old, darts all over his preschool classroom and seems startled by the sound of the gerbil moving in its cage, even when he's sitting across the room coloring.

Kim just can't sit still or pay attention for more than five minutes, no matter how hard she tries.

These children may not be misbehaving; they may be struggling with things that are genuinely difficult for them. The set of symptoms known as ADHD (attention deficit disorder without or with hyperactivity) is a chronic lifelong cluster of behaviors. It does not appear overnight, nor is it limited to children.

Be careful in trying to diagnose your child yourself, though. According to some estimates, 5 to 10 percent of all people experience symptoms such as difficulty sitting still and paying attention or acting impulsively, and not all of these people will have ADHD. Remember too that these characteristics may be indicators of different temperaments and normal development; in fact, many medical professionals will not diagnose a condition such as ADHD until a child is at least of school age. Hyperactivity, difficulty with controlling impulses, and inability to self-regulate can also indicate childhood trauma or sensory dysfunction. These symptoms bring many desperate parents to counselors' offices and parenting classes.

It is generally acknowledged that ADHD is overdiagnosed. Many children are being medicated because they can't sit still at an age when they aren't *supposed* to sit still. Sometimes parents and teachers invite power struggles by being too demanding and controlling. *Often children calm down when parents and teachers learn age-appropriate expectations and discipline methods.*

There are children for whom ADHD is a real problem. Whatever special needs a child has, knowing that those needs are real and not the result of poor parenting, inadequate teaching, or a child's deliberate misbehavior brings a great deal of relief. Determining whether a child has a special need is a sifting process that begins with looking at all of the variables discussed throughout this book. *In truth, even if a child is given a formal diagnosis, all of the Positive Discipline tools and skills will be helpful, in addition to whatever extra support a child may require.*

Is My Child Okay?

Pediatricians have learned that parents are often the best judge of a child's development. Because early intervention is essential in the treatment of many developmental delays and disorders, your instincts—and concerns—about your child are always worth paying attention to. Early behavioral signs may appear as early as six months, but diagnosis can seldom be clearly made before eighteen months and may happen at any time during the preschool years, as symptoms become more pronounced. The incidence of autism and autism-related disorders has risen dramatically in recent years, now occurring in approximately one out of every sixty-eight births.[1] While only a trained specialist can diagnose autism, you might look into getting a specialist's opinion if you answer no to many of the following questions.

- Does your child recognize and respond to familiar faces?
- Does he use his finger to point or show you something?
- Does your child turn his head toward you when you say his name?
- Does he imitate your actions, gestures, and facial expressions?
- Does he make eye contact with you?
- Is your child interested in other children, people, or objects?
- Does he respond to your smiles, cuddles, and gestures?
- Does your child try to attract your attention to his own activities?
- Is your child acquiring language and learning to communicate with you?

Other things to watch for include rocking, bouncing, spending long periods of time staring into space, and being unusually insistent on routines, predictability, or specific objects. Of course, symptoms do not necessarily indicate a problem. However, early intervention is critical for many developmental disorders. If you suspect that your child is not developing on schedule, do not hesitate to talk to your pediatrician or to ask for an evaluation.

All children, whether or not they have special needs, need to feel belonging and unconditional acceptance and will benefit from teaching, encouragement, and understanding. Parents of children with virtually any chronic condition experience a sense of frustration, sadness, and grief, as well as anxiety. They may also need to develop specialized skills. Knowing that you're not alone works wonders; so does information about finding help and support.[2]

KEEPING THE BALANCE

Q. I have twin boys. One of them was born profoundly deaf. Because of the special classes, doctor's appointments, and treatments this child needs, the one with hearing must put up with lots of waiting. He used to be help-

ful, patient, and "easy." Since their third birthday, though, things have changed—he's become defiant, whines all the time when he doesn't get his way, and is withdrawn. This is the opposite of his personality just a few months ago. I have racked my brain trying to find out what is different now in our lives, daily routines, or family situation. Do you have any suggestions, or is this just a phase and it too shall pass?

A. It takes a great deal of patience and sensitivity to raise children with special needs. Children are wonderful perceivers but not very good interpreters, and your son may believe that the special therapies, doctor's appointments, and treatment that his sibling receives indicate more parental attention and thus (or so he mistakenly believes) more parental love.

It's wise to remember that while children develop at different paces emotionally as well as physically, three-year-olds are often experimenting with what we call "initiative"—forming their own plans, wanting to do things their own way, and (occasionally) practicing that by becoming defiant, whiny, and generally less compliant.

You're probably right that some of this will pass, but be sure to include regular special time with each of your children. This doesn't mean spending money or huge chunks of time: fifteen minutes to go for a walk, throw the ball, or read a story is usually all it takes. The key to each child's behavior lies in what he believes about himself and his place in his family.

Labels: Self-Fulfilling Prophecies?

Labels such as "clever," "clumsy," "shy," or "cute" all define who a child is in others' eyes, creating an image that may prevent that child from being appreciated and experienced for who she really is. On the other hand, some labels simply describe what is obvious. Labeling a child who wears glasses as "the little girl with glasses" doesn't necessarily cause people to prejudge her behavior. Diagnosing a child as having autism or sensory integration disorder can actually be helpful when that diagnosis is provided by a professional. Most parents and teachers find it easier to encourage and support a child who has a diagnosed condition than one who has been labeled "disruptive," "squirmy," or "a troublemaker."

Adults often must struggle with their own attitudes and expectations about children who are different or special.

When Veronica was told that her four-year-old daughter was going to need glasses, she went home and cried, grieving that her "poor" little girl was going to be "disfigured." Abruptly she stopped and listened to what she had just told herself. She had described her daughter as "poor" and the glasses as "disfiguring." Veronica asked herself whose problem this was. Her four-year-old would want and need her mother's support and acceptance. In fact, the glasses would help her to see better and would enable her to grow and develop normally.

Veronica realized that the real problem was her own attitude. If she wanted to provide her daughter with the help she needed, Veronica had to recognize the value of that help. From that moment on, she chose to support her daughter and obtain whatever care she might need, including glasses. Her daughter's "disability" had existed only in her mother's mind.

The diagnosis of any special need or condition does not define who a child is. It is simply a way to understand that child's abilities. If your child is diagnosed with a special need, you may feel some distress and will need to find ways to deal with any associated problems. But it is equally important (if not more so) to look at the assets and attributes your child possesses. Children who have dyslexia, for example, are often highly intelligent and creative: their brains simply process information differently. Understanding those differences can be helpful rather than hurtful.

When a child lacks one ability, growth is likely to occur in other areas.

A person who cannot see often develops acute hearing. What are your child's special gifts? A gentle spirit, a lively sense of humor, or a tender heart often will outweigh the liabilities that accompany differentness—if you choose to let them.

Denial and Grief

Denying a child's special needs, even if it's because you fear labeling your child, is not helpful. It requires a brave heart to accept and parent your children as they really are, to give them what they really need.

At age four, Raleigh was diagnosed with autism. His parents were filled with anxiety about Raleigh's future, as well as discouraged by their many daily conflicts with him.

One ongoing struggle involved Raleigh's reaction to touch. Because they lived in a sunny environment and his mother had a family history of melanoma, applying sunscreen to Raleigh was extremely important. But the touch and feel of the lotion was so unpleasant for Raleigh that he ran away whenever his parents tried to put it on him.

One day Raleigh's mother decided that Raleigh was who he was, and it was her job to accept that. After some brainstorming, his parents asked Raleigh if he would rather wear a sun hat and play clothes made of high-SPF fabric when he went outside instead of sunscreen. Raleigh tested the feel of the new hat and clothing and decided it was okay. That helped everyone relax. This sort of solution-seeking became a regular part of their lives, as Raleigh's parents learned to accept his unique needs and to stop insisting that he meet expectations he could not manage.

Parents of special needs children may also feel a deep sense of grief. After all, a child with developmental differences or disabilities is rarely what they dreamed of when they were planning the birth of their baby. Remember, you will do a more effective job of parenting your child when you are able to deal honestly and gently with your own needs and feelings. You may find a support group or a therapist helpful as you learn to parent your child.

Learning to Accept

It is often easier for adults to respond to children who have a highly visible disorder or who behave in extreme ways rather than children whose disorder may be less obvious. If Sally, whose limbs are contorted with cerebral palsy, accidentally bumps into a classmate while struggling to maneuver the stairs on her crutches, a teacher probably will not tell Sally that she must stay in during recess for pushing her classmate. Nor will Sally's mother be called in for a conference and told that if she would just improve her parenting skills, Sally would be able to feed herself and walk unassisted. Unfair as it seems, parents of children with ADHD, fetal alcohol syndrome, sensory integration disorder, and dyspraxia often receive such criticisms because these conditions are not as obvious, clearly defined, or well understood as physical disabilities.

Learning Positive Discipline parenting skills will help both you and your child, but parenting is not the cause of your child's special need. Parents and caregivers are, however, all too human, and it is sometimes easy to scapegoat a child whose behavior or appearance is different. Adults and other children need to learn and practice the art of offering respect, rather than blame, to those who are different. Tolerance, patience, and encouragement will go a long way toward helping all people (including children) live together peacefully.

Misbehavior or Special Need?

Q. *My daughter, now four years old, has had an ongoing problem with getting dressed. She complains that her clothes "hurt." She takes about fifteen minutes to put on socks, pulling them on and off, often dissolving into a tantrum because she claims they are painful. I have tried buying all different types of socks, as well as allowing her to pick them out in the store and make her own choices in the morning. She asks me to cut all the tags out of her clothes because the tags hurt. I have tried ignoring her as she throws a fit over her socks, but what else can I do?*

A. Some children struggle with the way their bodies process sensory information. While your daughter's complaints seem trivial or imagined to you, they may be quite real; her socks really may be hurting her. There is a condition known as sensory integration dysfunction that might be affecting your child. Consult an occupational therapist or a pediatric neurologist for further information. You may also find useful support on the Internet.

Most important, accept that your child really does feel pain, and resist the temptation to engage in power struggles with her. Treating her behavior as a parenting problem will not be helpful; accepting the validity of her complaints and finding help and support will.

"Getting Away with" Misbehavior

Dee has two daughters. The younger daughter, Megan, is six years old and has been diagnosed with ADHD by her pediatrician. Sheila, her older sister, is nine and does not have ADHD. Before they go shopping, Dee takes the time to discuss her expectations with her two daughters. She has found this especially helpful for Megan, who has difficulty with transitions (a common characteristic of children with ADHD and children with a slow-to-adapt temperament).

Late one Friday afternoon, Dee follows the usual pre-shopping routine with her daughters. Megan remembers their agreement that this is not the day they will get ice cream cones, and she proudly reminds her mother of this fact. At the store, however, Megan sees a child happily licking an ice cream cone. In Megan's mind, seeing another child with an ice cream cone means she wants one too—now! Soon a tantrum is under way. What happened to Megan's agreement that there would be no ice cream today?

The characteristic impulsiveness of attention deficit disorder translates "wants" almost immediately into "needs," but it is important to remember that this is also developmentally typical behavior for preschoolers. All young children behave impulsively at times, and most occasionally show other traits symptomatic of ADHD.

> Dee asks Megan if she can calm herself down. The tantrum continues, so mother and daughters leave the store, with Megan hitting and screaming. The tantrum rages on in the car; when they arrive home, Megan runs into her room and slams the door. By now Dee is struggling to maintain her own control. She is angry, discouraged, and exhausted. Sheila, hurt and disappointed, is thinking, "I didn't do anything to spoil the shopping trip. Why did I have to miss out on the fun?" It's hard not to resent a little sister who behaves this way.

It's important to note that Dee does not spoil either of her daughters. She does not respond to unreasonable or demanding behavior by abandoning agreements she has made.

"Well," some parents might say, "if my child acted that way in a public place, I'd sure let her know how I felt about it. That mother should have spanked her daughter, or refused to let her have ice cream for a month!" But think for a moment. Has Megan "gotten away with" misbehavior? Will punishment or humiliation help her to change her behavior in the future? Did she intend to misbehave?

It may be hard for her mother, who is experiencing a seething (and very human) mixture of anger, guilt, and blame, to keep this in mind, but Megan likely has not consciously chosen to defy her mother. She was proud of remembering her agreement with her mother and she knows that her mother follows through on those agreements. Dealing effectively with Megan's behavior means recognizing her special needs.

What can Dee do? When she and Megan have calmed down, they can discuss what happened in the store. They might also discuss ways Megan could help her sister feel better. Maybe Megan could offer to do one of Sheila's chores or play a game with her. Sheila too has needs that should not be ignored.

It would be easy to allow Megan to feel that she is "bad" or "difficult," and because her mother is human, she will sometimes make mistakes and say or do things she later regrets. But as we've seen before, mistakes aren't fatal. And Megan's behavior may not change anytime soon. Facing reality, learning coping skills, and getting support will help both mother and daughter survive the difficult times.

Despair or Pride

Finding out that your child does not fit the ideal you've had in your head may come as an emotional blow. But once adults move beyond denial and their fear of labels, they can see the wonderful gifts their child has, not in spite of learning or behavioral differences but sometimes even because of them. People with asthma and diabetes have competed in the Olympics and become professional athletes; Temple Grandin, autistic herself, shed new light on autism and became famous for designing new systems of animal management; and Thomas Edison (along with scores of other famous people) is believed to have had ADHD.

What About Treatment?

Robert had struggled with his son, Charles, to the point of desperation. When Charles was five years old, his teacher suspected Charles might have some borderline ADHD characteristics. Robert was horrified and not a little offended by this suggestion. He signed up for parenting classes, bought piles of books, and did his best to be a better father.

But Charles's problems continued. By the age of seven, he was having trouble with schoolwork and friendships, and his difficulties were affecting the entire family. This time, Charles's doctor made a clear diagnosis of ADHD. After several months of counseling without improvement, Robert agreed to try medication.

Within a week, Charles's behavior was much improved. It was

difficult for Robert to believe that those tiny pills could have such an influence on behavior—and equally difficult to admit that his son might need this kind of help. But whenever Charles missed his medication over the next few months, his behavior deteriorated dramatically. Robert began to see his son in a different light and began to enjoy the calm, interesting child he was becoming. Charles too was changing; finally he could be himself.

Medication can be part of a comprehensive and loving approach to helping a child with ADHD or other special needs. However, research and practice are not always conclusive about the need for medication. It is important to do your own research and decide for yourself what works best for you and your child.

Listen to your inner wisdom; trust your knowledge of and love for your child. Be sure he understands his special need as well as his age and development allow. *Research has shown that the more a child understands about the conditions affecting him, the better he will handle them.* Positive attitudes and open discussion are encouraging. Secrecy promotes shame, confusion, and misunderstanding.

Be willing to change what doesn't work for your family. Build a supportive team of family, friends, and helping professionals who can give you and your child the help you need. And learn all you can about encouragement, kind and firm discipline, and other Positive Discipline tools. Confidence in your parenting skills will help you and your child immensely.

Teaching Children to Care for Themselves

Eventually, most children with special needs will leave home and embark on life as independent adults. Just as you teach your child to set the table and do other age-appropriate tasks, you can allow him to understand and learn to maintain his own body.

A few weeks before his fifth birthday, Marshall was diagnosed with celiac disease (a disorder that prevents his body from digesting anything containing gluten, such as wheat, rye, or barley) and his life changed dramatically. His parents, desperate to protect him, began to scrutinize everything he ate. They packed special foods for his lunches, brought in boxes of crackers that were to be served to him at snack time, and turned down birthday invitations to avoid exposing him to cake or cookies at his friends' homes.

It didn't take long for Marshall to rebel. He would trade his classmates orange segments for their cookies. He snuck pretzels from the snack table when his teachers weren't looking. And when he heard he couldn't go to a friend's party, there would be hours of tantrums and tears.

The doctor suggested to his distraught parents that they needed to educate Marshall and involve him in his own care. Although they were afraid of scaring him, they explained to Marshall what gluten is, and helped him understand that gluten made his body sick. Marshall listened to every word. Soon they realized that not educating Marshall had been more about their fear than about how Marshall would feel. In fact, once he understood his disease, he wanted to feel better. He cooperated in monitoring his eating choices and stopped eating things that made him sick.

Marshall and his parents also made a plan about how to manage friends' parties so he would not be left out. Marshall would help prepare special cakes and cookies and enjoyed bringing them to share with his classmates. He explained that he had celiac disease and that these snacks were healthy for him. It was with joy that his parents overheard him say while trick-or-treating, "Do you have anything gluten-free, please?" Marshall had become his own best advocate.

Preschoolers should never be left to handle or take medications without supervision. But they can learn to recognize the signals their bodies and emotions send them. Even young children with asthma or other

conditions can be aware of their body's needs, accept the special treatment they require, and help maintain their own health. When parents allow children to become involved and responsible (in age-appropriate ways, of course), they not only help ensure their child's future health and well-being but also build self-confidence and a sense of capability.

Look for the Positive

Whatever the physical, behavioral, or emotional challenges you and your child face, focusing on your inadequacies as parents or caregivers will not help. Find support for yourself, take care of your own needs, and accept and learn from your mistakes. Educate yourself, your child, and your caregivers about the condition affecting her, practice applying both humor and hope to each day's struggles, and get help for any child who needs it. Above all, make every effort to discover and celebrate the qualities that make each child special, unique, wonderful. Those qualities are always there—you only have to look.

QUESTIONS TO PONDER

1. Think of a time you did something you later regretted, such as losing your temper or eating too much dessert. How did you feel afterward? What self-talk did you hear inside your head? Now imagine that you are a child with limited capacity to control your behavior. What might this child's self-talk sound like after pushing a classmate in anger; yelling at a parent or teacher; or breaking crayons when he was told to put them away? Might he begin to believe he is a "bad person"?

2. How can a misbehaving, discouraged child receive encouragement while still learning different behavior? In what ways can he be helped to make amends for his behavior (and feel better about himself) in contributing (rather than punitive) ways?

Tip: Out-of-control behavior does not feel good to anyone, the child included.

3. Labels on canned goods and warning signs give us information. When labels are applied to children, do they give information or set up limiting expectations? As an example, consider three labels: "clumsy," "left-handed," and "hearing-impaired." One of these labels sets up limited expectations, while the other two offer information that can help to shape our behavior in appropriate and positive ways. Can you identify which each is? Now consider how labels affect the way parents, teachers, and others think of special-needs children. Are these labels limiting or beneficial? Could the same label be both?

CHAPTER 19

Technology Today and Tomorrow

Technology is changing the world we all share, and we feel it inside and outside of our homes. Parents (and preschoolers) walk into the house, look at a slim plastic column, and say, "Alexa, turn on the music"—and Alexa does. Toddlers love sitting on their iPad potty chairs, and not so they can learn to use the toilet. Parents who don't know the dangers of early screen use put their babies in infant seats with screens attached for easy viewing. So many toddlers and preschoolers are watching YouTube videos of children "unboxing" toys that toy manufacturers have reduced advertising on television, despite the fact that YouTube clearly says no one younger than thirteen should view their site. And all of this change has happened in just a decade or two.

Nothing else in our lives has grown so rapidly. New medicines and vaccines undergo years of intensive testing and scrutiny before being distributed for general use. The Apple iPad, however, was in the hands of tens of millions of people just two months after its release. Unfortunately, the exposure of young children to technology has no waiting period. Testing and research are happening after the fact. It should come as no surprise that among the most pressing questions that parents of preschoolers ask are:

- How do we handle technology in our family?
- Should we set limits on our child's screen time?
- What impact will this technology have on our child's learning and development?

There is little doubt that by the time you read this chapter, it will already be at least partly out of date. There is also little doubt that technology is becoming an increasingly essential part of our lives. It is important to thoughtfully consider the real impact these powerful tools will have on your family.

TECHNOLOGY BLUEPRINT

- Can brains keep up?
- Is technology use active or passive?
- What does technology replace?
- What does technology enhance?

"First, Do No Harm": Can Brains Keep Up?

Dr. Dimitri Christakis, director of the Center for Child Health, Behavior and Development at Seattle Children's Research Institute, offers the medical precept of "first, do no harm" as a guiding principle for technology use in early childhood.[1] He explains that a child's brain develops in real time. When experiences or information speed up, the brain cannot keep up. The rush of content overwhelms the brain—already busy with development and learning—and concentration suffers.

Watching or engaging in fast-paced, overly stimulating screen content diminishes the ability to focus on the next task.

Is Technology Use Active or Passive?

Preschoolers engage with technology in many different ways—just like adults. The impact differs depending on whether use is active or passive.

- **Passive use requires no interaction.** The viewer simply consumes content. Sitting in front of a screen to be entertained or distracted is essentially passive.
- **Active use engages a child in learning and deep cognitive processing.** Using a screen to create a story, record an event through photos, play an interactive game with others, or take part in a dance or yoga routine with a parent are examples of active use.

The National Association for the Education of Young Children (NAEYC) and the Fred Rogers Center have issued a joint statement discouraging passive use of media for preschoolers.[2] One way to turn passive viewing into active engagement is for adults to interact and watch *with* children, actively helping to connect what is seen to real-life experiences:

It was kind of the little raccoon in the story to save birthday cake for his baby brother. What could you share with baby Sam?

What Does Technology Replace?

Every hour a child spends using a screen is one hour less doing something else that may very well be more important to that child's growth and development.

Children need:

- Nurturing relationships
- Physical activity
- Unstructured play

None of these things can be found on a screen.

These early years are the training ground for developing relationships and learning how to get along with others. Face-to-face time with adults and peers is needed to hone these skills and to build connection and attachment.

What about physical activity? Research shows some worrisome trends. A child using a screen device is not moving many muscles. In fact, less dexterity and hand strength (necessary for writing skills to develop) have been noted in children who used screens extensively before entering elementary school. Passive viewing can also increase a child's body mass index (BMI); children often snack while watching, and they are simply getting less physical exercise.

Finally, the work of childhood is play. As you have already learned, active play is a cornerstone of healthy development. *A key question is, "Does the use of this technology replace active playtime?"* Unfortunately, screens are often used as babysitters, robbing children of the time and opportunity for the full-body, engaged play they need to develop and learn.

> One mom said, "Well, those who talk about less screen time are clearly not stay-at-home moms. Cartoon time is the only time I get a break."

The initial recommendation of the American Association of Pediatrics was no screen time before the age of two. (Yes, you read that right: none at all!) The AAP has since softened its recommendation to encourage limiting screen time for young children. "No screen time" may be an unreasonable expectation, but even tired parents can get a respite without relying on screen use. Children can and should learn to entertain and calm themselves. A little boredom isn't always a bad thing: it often invites creativity and imagination. By having hands-on supplies available, from blocks to crayons to books, children can find ways to play and create at the same time, without logging more screen hours.

How and when we use technology is also significant. One mom wrote:

I gradually realized that the screen had become my daughter's way to calm herself down. If I didn't give it to her, she didn't know how to calm herself. Then I tried cuddling with her and doing deep breathing together. It really transformed our experience. She became calm and happy and ready for the next activity.

Children learn self-regulation and emotional skills through patient, connected, face-to-face relationships with adults. Screens may appear to be an easy way to stop a child from crying, but the long-term results are not encouraging. We wish we could convince parents to follow the guidelines of the NAEYC and AAP and avoid screens for young children for at least two years, and seriously limit time spent on screens throughout childhood. Many parents, however, do not want to follow these recommendations because screen use makes life with a preschooler so much easier—for now.

Many experts believe that the impact of screens is even greater on infants, toddlers, and preschoolers than it is on older children and adolescents. Not everyone agrees that young children can become physically addicted to screens, but there is no question that these powerful devices can have a serious and lasting impact on a child's social emotional development and learning, and that dependence on screens for entertainment can lead to daily power struggles.[3]

We know that screens are here to stay, and that your child will use them. We hope you will choose quality programs and apps, especially ones that offer interaction. And public television remains a valuable resource for preschoolers because there is no advertising in children's programming. Educate yourself on the issues, then decide what you will do.

What Does Technology Enhance?

There are good reasons to be cautious about technology use with young children. But there are also ways to use screens to strengthen relationships. Young children who live far from other family members or who have a parent who is away because of work, a military deployment, or a divorce can connect through video chats. Getting to see a child's latest accomplishment or hear a favorite song has brightened the day of many a parent and grandparent.

Technology can also provide access to other cultures or lifestyles. Expanding a child's worldview encourages tolerance and empathy. One program that brings technology to developing countries, Technology and Information for All (TINFA), provides opportunities for teachers and students to interact across continents. Children from Guatemala sing a song in Spanish to their counterparts in an American classroom. The children in America draw pictures to hold up and share with their friends in Guatemala during online chats. Teachers also can share resources with one another.[4]

Some technology programs enhance movement and play. Interactive dance programs, musical performances that children can join in using tambourines or rattles, and games that parents and children engage in together are fun and enriching. Technology-enhanced assistive devices are helpful to those with disabilities, allowing interaction, communication, and expression that may otherwise not have been possible.

Q. *My four-year-old twins watch television most afternoons. They also love to play video games with their older cousins. We try to make sure they aren't exposed to really violent things, but it seems harder than ever to screen out the images that are scary or that model aggressive behavior. Yesterday one of the twins jumped onto his brother's back and aimed a karate-like chop at his neck. I was horrified. I feel I have lost control over the harmful influences that my boys are being exposed to, but I can't simply lock them away from the world. What can I do?*

A. Television and video game violence may have a stronger effect on young children than previously thought. A forty-year longitudinal study funded by the National Institute of Mental Health and conducted by the Institute for Social Research at the University of Michigan found compelling evidence linking a child's exposure to media violence to a tendency for violent and aggressive behavior later in life.

Children learn a great deal about behavior and attitudes by imitating others. Remember, young children cannot tell the difference between reality and fantasy in the way older children and adults can. They also may be more likely to imitate aggressive behavior, especially aggression that goes unpunished or is performed in the service of "good" (as in superhero cartoons or movies). Children who see screen violence are less likely to develop empathy for others; after all, if people on the screen get shot and kicked and punched and are still okay (and they usually are), what's the problem? As one young child explained to his dad, "I was only killing him."

The best ways to deal with the effect of video and television violence on your child is to limit his exposure and to do lots of teaching. Watch programs or games *with* him and be sure you teach him the values you want him to adopt. Television viewing encourages passivity. Critical thinking and learning occur only when dialogue takes place. Let your child know kindly but firmly that kicking, punching, or hitting is not acceptable in your family and that real people suffer pain and harm when they are kicked or punched. Most important, put a limit on the time they spend in front of the screen—any screen—and substitute active play and conversation.

CURRENT GUIDELINES

Here is a summary of guidelines for screen use based upon recommendations from the American Academy of Pediatrics,[5] the United States Department of Education,[6] and the National Association for the Education of Young Children.[7]

- Limit use: for children ages two to five, allow no more than one hour per day.
- Designate media-free areas and media-free times.
- Watch or use technology together. Help your child interpret media content.
- Be intentional. Never use technology for technology's sake.
- Support relationships.

Limit Use: Quantity and Quality

Although the recommendation to limit screen time is important, it is equally important to be sure that screen use is developmentally appropriate and of quality content. Make sure you know what your child is exposed to. Watch apps and play games before allowing a child to do so. Organizations such as Common Sense and Common Sense Media curate various apps and programs, including reviews, for children of different ages.[8] When you calculate the hours your child uses screens, be sure to include use both at home and school, and be sure other caregivers are aware of your limits.

Media-Free Times and Zones

Everyone needs sanctuary from the demands and distractions of the world out there. One of the best ways to avoid serious problems is to schedule plenty of screen-free time and to do your best to be sure art supplies, books, and active play materials are easily available. It's also helpful to create media-free times and zones in your home.

- Make bedrooms technology-free zones. Locate televisions, computers, and other technologies your child will be using in common areas so you are aware of what is being viewed.
- Have a "parking garage" where cellphones and tablets can be parked during screen-free times—and especially at night.
- Make mealtimes for eating and face-to-face time. No screens are invited—including adults' screens.
- Make a personal plan for where and when screens are allowed—or not. Consider using a guide like the one provided by the American Academy of Pediatrics.[9]

Watch or Use Technology Together

Research repeatedly shows that best results occur when adults watch and use programming *with* children. There is no better way to monitor the content of programs or videos (and to observe their effect on your child) than to watch or play with him. Invite your little one to teach you his favorite videogame or settle down next to him to watch his special cartoon. You can ask curiosity questions to learn more and to engage your child in exercising thinking skills. Curiosity is a great parenting tool and may help you understand your child's fascination with what he sees.

You can ask your child what she thinks will happen today, or how she feels about what she has seen. You can also plan activities (such as gardening or cooking) that link to something you have viewed together. And sometimes it helps to simply turn off the screen and go outside to run and play.

Ebooks straddle two worlds. An ebook may be a simple digital reproduction of a hard-copy book, or it may include enhanced features such as sounds, movement, and interactive possibilities. These enhancements tend to distract young children and may change the focus away from story content, vocabulary development, and opportunities for adult-child connection. We recommend using ebooks like hard-copy books as much as possible, being sure to read them *with* your child rather than using them as distractions or babysitters.

Be Intentional: Make a Plan

Technology is a tool, not an end in itself. Be aware of why and when you are using screens or other technologies. One mother of a four-year-old shared the following:

We try to teach our son manners and politeness. He is learning to pause the program to greet people, answer when spoken to (to not be a zombie), sit with good posture, make decisions with others about what to watch, and respect our decisions when content is inappropriate.

You can use a family meeting to develop a media plan with your child. It also helps to be aware of your own media use. How often do you use your smartphone and tablet? It is difficult to forbid a child to use screens when she sees parents constantly using theirs. This goes for caregivers too. Children in care should always be the focus. Personal screens do not belong in a preschool teacher's workplace.

Support Relationships

Your child craves real connection with you; when he has it, he is less likely to look for stimulation and company elsewhere. (And he is less likely to misbehave.) As your child grows, his peers and the culture will become increasingly important, and relationship skills can only be learned through practice with real people. Make time to be present, and to provide your child with opportunities to practice social and emotional skills in the real world.

BE A MEDIA MENTOR: SAFETY FIRST

Children must be protected when they use media. Be sure you know:
- Do privacy policies require broad access? (Advocate for apps that have "opt in" clauses that allow you to choose to allow access, rather than "opt out," which places the burden on a consumer's vigilance.)
- Does the app expose your child to advertising? (Many free apps do.) Are the ads safe for a child to view?
- Are purchasing options promoted? (Never use apps that allow purchases within the app for greater access to content or other promotions.)

Finally, protect personal information:
- Use passwords or otherwise protect your own important records and files.
- Activate settings that limit a child's access to content.

Special Considerations: Consumer Kids

Children's media characters jump off the screen and onto lunch boxes, cuddly plush animals, and T-shirts. Children clamor for products (often junk food, candy, or sugary beverages) bearing the image of their favorite characters. Where is the demarcation line between marketing to kids and entertaining them? Unfortunately, the program itself often becomes the advertisement.

Children's programming often creates a desire to imitate behaviors and to want the things a child sees on the screen. Whether you have to deal with a meltdown at the mall over a princess doll or find yourself separating two children on the playground who are reenacting a cartoon battle, media's messages have powerful effects.

It is no accident that advertisers target children for their products. Young children may not have much spending money, but they certainly know people who do—and children are often able to whine, beg, and manipulate adults into buying the product of the moment. In addition to other safeguards, consider becoming proactive by letting advertisers know when you object to their marketing. Your voice and your buying decisions do count.

Balance

There will be plenty of time in the years ahead for your child to master technology. For now, strive for balance. At its best, technology provides tools that help us learn, connect with the outside world, and enhance creativity. At its worst—well, the list is long, including growing concerns about screen addiction. Make your screen use choices with care, and always beware of letting your child become a science experiment for untested technology.

QUICK TIPS

- **Sleep.** Children should not view screens for at least one hour before bedtime. Both the stimulation and the blue light can interrupt healthy sleep.
- **Quiet.** Turn off TVs and other screens when not in active use.
- **Enjoy.** Parents don't take part in media activities they don't enjoy. (Sesame Street intentionally writes adult humor into its shows to encourage adults to watch with their children.) Instead of giving a child a game to play, play together. And if you and your child aren't actively enjoying something, turn it off.
- **Prepare.** Always preview an app or learn about programming (including potential advertisements) before allowing children's use.

QUESTIONS TO PONDER

1. What types of technology or screen time does your child use? Have you set limits on this use? Consider creating a media plan for your household, and involving your child in the process.

2. Watch a program, play a game, or use an app with your child. Name two ways that you helped (or could have helped) your child to relate the content of this activity to something in her world.

3. Designate technology-free areas in your home. Be sure to invite your child to help in this process.

CHAPTER 20

Mother Nature Meets Human Nature

Many adults can remember long, wonderful days spent outdoors, riding bikes, collecting insects, or just watching the clouds go by. These days, though, getting outside may seem like more trouble than it's worth, especially to anxious parents worried about what might happen.

One summer, Jane and her husband took their children on a week-long camping trip to Sequoia National Park. For the first day and a half, the children sat in the camper and complained about how boring it was. They missed their familiar toys, their friends, and their TV. Jane and her husband wondered if they had made a huge mistake. However, after that day and a half of complaining, the kids poked their heads out the door and then decided to explore a bit. It wasn't long before they were climbing trees, making forts with logs and sticks, swimming and skipping pebbles in the lake, and gathering wood for cooking over the open fire. When it was time to leave, the complaining started again. They had been introduced to nature and now they didn't want to go.

Approximately 80 percent of all people in the United States today live in urban areas, many with little or no access to natural environments.

In many parts of the world, there are children whose feet have never touched anything other than pavement. Why does this matter in a book on raising or caring for children? Human beings need clean air, water, and sunshine, along with food that grows in the soil of Mother Earth, but the natural world offers us so much more than just survival. Children—and adults—can become more nurturing, and more connected to one another and the earth itself, when they spend time outdoors.

In his book *Unseen City*, Nathanael Johnson writes, "To pass a tree and simply register it as 'tree' is to never really see it . . . When we connect to nature, we widen the meaning of connectedness."[1]

Emotional Connection and Attachment

Time together in natural settings makes connection simpler, especially when we turn off our devices and allow for true togetherness. Research shows that even a few minutes in nature can reduce stress levels, lower heart rates, strengthen our immune systems, and restore our ability to focus—a win-win situation for children and adults.

In Chapter 4, you learned about the importance of attachment in the early years. You may know that connection is important, but there are so many distractions. For most of us, daily life is busy, complex, and often stressful.

One mother tells the story of working at her computer while her three-year-old sang a song she had learned at preschool that morning. Partway through her song, the child reached up, put her hands on her mother's cheeks, and turned her mother's face toward her. Then she resumed singing.

This little one wanted not just to sing her song but to make an emotional connection to her mother while she did so. Thankfully, Mom got the message, switched off the screen, and soon was singing the refrain along with her daughter.

ENTER MOTHER NATURE

Time spent in nature opens three wonderful pathways to connection and attachment:

- You can become more present and emotionally connected.
- You can share sensory experiences that connect you with your child and the world around you.
- You can follow your child's lead and connect to his interests.

Unfortunately, these experiences rarely happen without planning. You will need to intentionally seek out time to spend in nature.

Follow Your Child's Lead

Grandma may have time for make-believe tea parties or to build a fairy house in her backyard, but most parents are so busy worrying about whether their child has eaten enough or how to get him to go to bed on time that there isn't much energy left to join in his games.

Again, nature makes connection easier. When you're wandering along a beach, it is much simpler to join in building a fort of pebbles. When you explore a trail through the forest, exclaiming together over a snail your child spots, examining a mushroom he spies under decaying leaves, or startling at the splendor of a jumping frog can allow you to join in his exploration of his world. This shared sense of wonder will help your child connect to the world around him, and to those he shares it with.

It is far easier to spend time in nature when you live in a place where access to the outdoors is easy. For many families, "nature" requires a long drive, a train ride, or expensive travel. It may help to know that a walk around the block together, taking time to examine the neighbors' flowers or the ants on the sidewalk, counts as time spent in nature too. So does a trip to the neighborhood park. What matters is fresh air, sunlight, and the opportunity to explore and move—and to do so together.

Shared Sensory Experiences

Nature can be smelly or fragrant, noisy or silent, bright with color or impenetrably dark. All of these experiences enter through the senses, creating connections that actually help to wire your child's brain.

When you show your child a tree, take time to really explore it. You can:

- Touch its bark
- Crinkle a leaf and smell it
- Look closely at the different colors in a single flower on its branches
- Listen to the wind pass through it, or the sound of rain dripping from leaf to leaf

Children who grow up experiencing the wonders of the natural world will be more likely to care about what happens to that world—and the world will need their creativity and passion.

Restoration Benefits

Whenever you or your child feels stressed out or worn down, nature is a ready restorative. Even looking out a window at greenery can provide benefits. Time spent outdoors—even if it's only five or ten minutes—can alleviate a surprising number of the behavior issues parents complain about. Children with ADHD often become calmer and more focused after time spent in nature. All preschoolers have enormous amounts of physical energy, and many spend most of their days cooped up indoors. Getting your child outside to run, jump, and climb will improve mental focus and self-regulation, and may actually prevent the misbehavior that comes from having to sit still too often.

Being in natural settings allows our senses to open without being overwhelmed. Attention softens. Water bubbling over rocks, wind rustling through leaves, and birds calling overhead are soothing sounds that ground us in the present moment. This calmness becomes internalized, providing a resource children (and adults) can draw upon in other settings. There is a growing body of research showing that simple mindfulness techniques aid in brain integration and mental health, and there may be no easier way to introduce mindfulness than by moving through the natural world.

Nature truly is everywhere, if you learn to look closely. Birds, insects, and butterflies may be just outside your door. Learning to "see" is often the problem. Nathanael Johnson tells of tiring of saying "tree" every time his young daughter pointed to one. He challenged himself to say something different each time: "bark," "leaf," and so on. By doing this, he began to see more than a tree too. (When Kevin Matteson, an ecologist from Fordham University in the Bronx, simply stopped to observe each flower as he walked through New York City, he identified 227 different species of bees.)[2]

There is always something new to see, hear, and feel outdoors. You can listen to a bird's call and identify what type of bird it is. The raucous cawing of crows invites attention, and if you and your child look up when you hear that sound, you may notice a hawk being chased away by these intelligent birds. As you learn to observe the world around you, you will develop an appreciation for how intertwined human life is with the natural world.

Tip: Enhance your observations of the living things all around you, wherever you live. Observing connections leads to feeling connected— both to the natural world and to other living creatures.

Lessons Learned

The term "natural consequences" is rooted in nature itself. Time spent outdoors provides a wonderful opportunity for your child to learn to self-regulate and develop healthy coping strategies. As Claire Warden, a consultant with the International Association of Nature Pedagogy, explains, nature provides "feedback or consequential loops." Wise parents can use these moments as opportunities to teach. For example, when it is cold outside, hands get cold. Ask your child, "What can you do to keep your fingers warm?" When a child discovers for herself the value of gloves, she will understand naturally why she has to put gloves on to play outside in the winter.

Nature provides the experiences and children learn to respond with healthy choices. The landscape itself can teach valuable lessons.

- An uneven or rocky surface teaches us to slow down and plan steps with care.
- Crashing waves remind us to stay alert and pay attention.
- A wide-open field both invites us to run and teaches us that the world is much bigger than we are.

These lessons are effortlessly learned but hugely important in how your child will approach life.

Safety and Risk

If you listen carefully to the conversations at a typical playground, you're likely to hear lots of commands and directives: "Don't climb so high—you might fall!" "Look where you're going!" "Don't touch that—it's dirty."

Children need to learn to assess risk and make healthy decisions, but being constantly told what to do and how to do it does not help them learn. Time in nature actually offers many opportunities to make safe decisions and still enjoy a variety of experiences.

Being outdoors gives children the opportunity to use tools—lots of tools: shovels to dig in a garden or beach sand, small hammers to pound tent stakes into the ground, or blunt-nosed clippers for gathering flowers and garden produce. "Wait," you may be thinking. "Tools are sharp and dangerous. My child might hurt himself."

Yes, using tools can have risks. Claire Warden offers three simple "what" and "how" questions to help children assess risk and develop safety plans while learning to appreciate the value (and fun) of each tool.

1. Begin with positives:
   What is brilliant about this tool?
   What great things can it do?

2. Then determine risks:
   What is or may be hazardous about using this tool?
   What are the possible dangers?

3. Finally, plan for safety:
   How can you keep safe?

This is a simple process that can be repeated in many settings, from planning for an outing in the woods to how to treat ducks or other birds encountered at a nearby pond.

Invite your child to enjoy new experiences, to recognize dangers, and to plan safe precautions and responses.

Going Out

Here are some ways to get outdoors with your child more often:
- Do it outside. From story time to dancing to drawing, bring the activity outdoors.
- Visit local parks and walk the pathways instead of only going to the playground equipment.

- Walk through a zoo, making the surrounding area as much a part of the outing as the animals.
- Plant a garden (in your yard, playground, or in small pots) and tend it together.
- Go on a walk after dark (or turn off the lights) and look at the stars.
- Track the changing shape of the moon every night before bedtime.
- Find a good place to view sunrise or sunset.
- Go on a "silence" walk and listen to the sound of birds, wind in the trees, falling rain, or the crunch of snow.
- Run around catching leaves on a blustery fall day.
- Identify small things: the grass growing in cracks of the driveway; tiny flowers on plants we usually call "weeds"; the different colors of beach sand from one location to another.
- Go to the same place each week, month, or season and notice what is different.
- Find a place to sit quietly and do nothing. Give your mind a rest.
- Make a collection of leaves, pine cones, or shells; notice their differences or learn their names.
- Invite wildlife to your school or yard by stocking bird feeders, building a bat house, or planting bee-friendly flowers.

Each of these activities provides time to be together, share experiences, and make connections, with each other and the natural world.

TIPS FOR EXPLORING THE NATURAL WORLD

Here are some helpful things to bring along as you explore:
- A magnifying glass
- Binoculars
- Change of clothing
- Snacks and water

- Layered clothing (layers can be added or removed depending upon weather and comfort)
- Small bags to hold collected items
- A camera (to record what is seen and leave the environment untouched)

Bringing Nature In

Nature provides the materials for wonderful learning experiences, whether you are at home or in a classroom. How can you bring nature inside?

- Use natural objects, such as shells, pine cones, and circles cut from fallen tree branches, instead of plastic toys. (These make great counting objects too.)
- Replace plastic blocks with wooden ones.
- Place colorful leaves in a bowl and provide paints, markers, or crayons that match the leaves' colors.
- Designate a place to display found treasures, such as rocks, a feather, or flower petals.
- Make meals with produce harvested from a garden.
- When trying a new fruit or vegetable, look at it before preparation. Use your senses to explore a carrot with greenery attached, an unpeeled onion, or bananas still connected in a bunch.
- Fill indoor and outdoor play spaces with plants; they provide oxygen as well as beauty.
- Use beeswax candles for a birthday celebration and enjoy their special fragrance.

Your child will enjoy finding and exploring these natural treasures—and they cost far less (and are far more beneficial) than many of the plastic toys and screens in her toy box.

Belonging: Seventh Generation

The term "seventh generation" comes from Native American tribes and describes the belief that all decisions need to be measured by their effect on the world and its people seven generations into the future. Think back to the list of life skills and characteristics you created in Chapter 2. All human beings need to feel a sense of belonging and significance, and all need the opportunity to make meaningful contributions. As a parent raising a young child, you want her to make healthy choices and to grow into a happy and contributing adult. The "seventh generation" principle helps us understand that what we do matters.

As young children grow and expand their understanding of the world around them, they begin to relate to the natural world and ask questions about what they see and experience. For instance, where does food come from? The experience of growing something that can be eaten is exciting to a young child. Something as simple as sprouting alfalfa seeds in a jar can give children this opportunity. In many cities, nearby farms or local fairs make it possible for children to harvest carrots, snip mint leaves, or watch cows being milked. Experiences like these give children an understanding that they are part of a larger system of connection, one that provides the food they eat every day.

What about water? A trip to a river, stream, or ocean (or even watching raindrops fall or puddles fill) invites conversation about water on our planet—where it comes from and how to keep it clean. And watching bits of ash rise above a campfire makes it easy for children to understand that when something burns, dirt can get into the air and make it harmful to breathe. Children have the opportunity to learn how their own actions can impact the larger system, and that they can be effective stewards of the earth.

Nurturing Nature

Nature is complex, but it can be learned about in small, simple ways. Looking at a plant in a pot provides a nice moment. But touching the dirt, placing a seed into the soil, and watering the plant as it grows offers much more. The experience of nurturing a plant's growth supports the development of empathy and provides a new understanding of connection.

As Kathy Wolf, at the University of Washington's Center for Urban Horticulture, says, it also provides an authentic nature experience: "Our ecological system is dynamic and layered, having a ground, middle, and canopy. There are lots of symbiotic relationships, and these give us insight into our own connectedness and mutual need for each other and all life forms. We develop a sense of gratitude to nature when we start to take care of nature as it takes care of us."

Empowerment

Children are always making decisions about their world. The more they experience nature, the more questions will arise: "Why does this tree look all brown?" "Why does this stream have a funny smell?" "If bees sting, why don't we kill them?"

The natural world is currently facing many challenges. Preschoolers love to be helpful, so whenever possible, help them discover tools for positive action:

- Perhaps the brown or black spots on the tree are from air pollution. Explain that riding bikes or walking instead of taking a car might help the trees.
- The funny smell in the stream could be from lawn chemicals. Discuss ways to stop using chemicals.
- Bees are important because they pollinate the plants we eat and make delicious honey. Make plans to grow bee-friendly flowers

or set out wood drilled with holes to provide homes for orchard mason bees.

Making nature a part of a child's world has lifelong benefits. From health to emotional connection to meaningful action and life skills, children need nature and nature needs them. *Mother Nature is a parenting partner extraordinaire.*

QUESTIONS TO PONDER

1. Take a walk around your neighborhood with your child. Find one plant, insect, or type of animal you have never noticed before. Use your senses to experience it. What do you notice? If it is one you have seen before, how is this one different?

2. Commit to going outside with your child, with all electronic devices turned off, two or more times each week. If the weather is cold, wet, or very hot, use this as a teachable moment. What type of clothing will you need? What else will you need to take with you?

3. Identify a time of the day when you or your child seems to be most stressed. Is there a way of connecting with nature at that time that might help you both? Give it a try.

CHAPTER 21

Growing as a Family: Finding Support, Resources, and Sanity

No matter how charming your preschooler is and no matter how delighted you are to be a parent, these early years can be lonely, exhausting, and challenging. Parents staying at home with a young child often find that the job is tougher than they expected. It's not unusual for stay-at-home parents to find themselves longing for adult conversation and entertainment, while working parents quickly grow weary of the daily hassle of getting everyone off to childcare and work. Sleep can be hard to come by, and the battles prompted by energetic little ones who are exercising their initiative can test even the most devoted mom or dad. Your partner may find blow-by-blow descriptions of your child's new achievements and adorable moments enthralling, but many people will not. Most parents have occasional moments when they wistfully remember their pre-child days and long for a moment of quiet and solitude.

During a parenting class, one dad admitted that there are times he thinks about how wonderful it would be to simply skip dinner, have a glass of wine, and watch a movie in peace—something he had enjoyed in his pre-parent days.

Parents of preschoolers need support, encouragement, and nurturing during these important early years of parenting.

Learning from the Wisdom of Others

While people seldom agree on every detail of raising children, building a support network, a circle of friends who've been there, provides an invaluable source of information about raising and living with children. Make an effort to build relationships with folks who have children the same age as yours—or who have recently survived the stage you're going through.

Options for support networks include church- or community-based parenting groups, community college parent-child classes, Positive Discipline parenting classes, friendships with neighborhood moms or dads, or online chat groups. Perhaps your parenting group, with dinner out beforehand, can be part of a night out with your partner. Other parents meet at the park and discuss parenting challenges and successes while keeping a watchful eye as their children play. And some parents have started book study groups where they get together (in person or online) to discuss Positive Discipline books and learn together how to use Positive Discipline tools. Some moms have even attended the two-day Teaching Parenting the Positive Discipline Way workshop so they could learn to facilitate parenting classes, knowing that teaching (and having the courage to be imperfect) is one of the best ways to learn.[1]

As one mom put it, "The meltdowns still happen (both my daughter's and mine), but now I have all of the Positive Discipline tools to help me cope."

PEPS AND MOPS

One successful model of a parenting support group is PEPS (the Program for Early Parent Support), a community-based program in the Northwest. PEPS groups form right after a baby's birth and consist of people whose children are born within days or weeks of one another. These families meet regularly in each other's homes or in family centers. The goal is to reduce isolation and create a network of resources and encouragement. PEPS can be contacted at www .pepsgroup.org.

Another popular group is Mothers of Preschoolers (www.mops.org), which offers get-togethers and parenting support. Look for similar programs in your area, or consider initiating one of your own.

Whether you live in an isolated area or a busy metropolis, the magic of the Internet offers a wealth of information. If you do not have Internet access at home, you can ask a librarian or computer-literate friend to help you search for parenting resources; you'll be astonished at what you discover.

No matter where you find support, however, remember that in the end you must decide what feels right for you and your child. Gather all the wisdom and advice you can, then listen to your heart and choose what will work best for you.

Relationships: Single or with a Partner

Many parents of preschoolers are single parents who face both the challenges and blessings (yes, there are many) of raising a child alone. Making time to spend with other adults without your child will recharge you, making the time you do spend with your child more rewarding for both of you.

If you are parenting with a partner, your relationship with each other is the foundation for your family and sets the tone for your home. There are a number of studies that show just how much young children learn by watching the relationship their parents have with each other. It is well worth your while to make sure your partner doesn't get lost in the chaos of raising an active preschooler and that your relationship remains vital and enjoyable.

Parents sometimes believe that once they have a child, that child should become the center of the family universe. But as you have learned, pampering a child is not healthy or effective. You and your partner should have time on a regular basis to spend together, whether you go out for dinner and dancing, take a walk together, or simply curl up to watch a good movie. You will also need "couple time" to explore and resolve the many issues raising a child together will present.

MAKE ROOM FOR DADDY

Q. *My husband and I have a four-year-old son who is the joy of our lives. I am a stay-at-home mom, but I want my husband to be actively involved in raising our son. At first he got up with me to feed him at night, changed his diapers, and gave him baths. Lately, however, he has been "too busy" to help me. When I asked him about this, he told me he tries but he never does things "right." He says I insist that he do things my way. I feel bad (because I think he's probably right), but I do believe the way I discipline and care for our son is the best way. What should I do?*

A. Many husbands and fathers feel edged out by the close bond between a mother and her child, especially in the early years. It may help you make room for your husband to know that children benefit from the active involvement of *both* parents in their lives, even when those parents don't do things the same way. Studies have shown that fathers and mothers have different styles of play and interaction with children—and that children are clever about learning to change their behavior to fit what works with each parent.

Your son needs a close and loving connection with both his parents. Take some time to sit down with your husband and discuss (not dictate) ways to handle discipline, daily routines, food, and other issues. It may be helpful to take a parenting class together, or to read this book together and discuss what you have learned. Then relax and allow him to do things his own way. You can use the time when he is in charge to take care of yourself or spend time with friends. Whether yours is a same-sex partnership or a traditional mom-and-pop family, children need loving time spent with both parents.

And Baby Makes . . . Four

If you have a preschooler and are planning to have another child, you should know that the arrival of an infant can throw even the most delightful and confident preschooler into something of a tailspin. Most preschoolers claim with disarming honesty to love their new baby brother or sister; they offer to help fetch diapers and "binkies," want to cuddle their new sibling, and gaze with utter fascination into the crib. So why does that same preschooler often resort to tantrums, insist on a pacifier herself, seem to forget her toilet training, or whine for attention?

Well, take a look at the world through the eyes of a dethroned preschooler. Let's say you're almost four years old when your parents come home from the hospital with a noisy, squirming bundle in a blanket. Suddenly, *nothing* is the same. Your parents tell you that you shouldn't cry or whine because you're a "big girl now." Visitors come to the house and walk right past you to coo at the new baby; they bring interesting gifts and toys (which you can't remember having received yourself) for the baby. Worst of all, your parents are completely enthralled by this noisy, messy little person. They tell you to play quietly because "the baby is sleeping," and they're constantly carrying the baby around. They're always "too tired" and don't have time to play the old familiar games you enjoy. It's no wonder that after a week or two, even the most patient big sister is ready to send the intruder back to the hospital.

There are ways to smooth out the process of adding a baby to your family. Here are some suggestions:

- Begin early to prepare your child for a baby's arrival. You can explain in simple terms the process of pregnancy and let your child know when the baby will arrive. A wall calendar can be used to check off the days until the baby's birth. Talk honestly about what life is like with a new baby; it can be helpful (and fun) to get out photos of your child's own infancy and talk together about what those days were like.

- If a child will be joining the family through adoption, ask your local librarian to help you find books to read with your preschooler that will open discussions and help you all to prepare for the coming changes.

- Invite your child to help prepare your home for the baby. You can allow her to make suggestions about colors and designs for the baby's room; she can go with you to purchase items for the baby's layette. She may even want to put some of her own toys in the baby's room as a welcome gift.

- Show her pictures of what you did to prepare for her birth, such as fixing up her room and buying tiny baby clothes for her. Let her know that many people brought her presents and fussed over her, just as they will do with the new baby. Ask if she would like to be in charge of receiving and unwrapping gifts for the new baby, and then thanking the givers (since the baby can't talk). The more she is included, the less she will feel left out.

- When the baby comes home, be sure your older child is included in making the baby welcome. Set safety rules and supervise carefully, and then let your child hand you diapers and wipes at the changing table, sing songs or "read" stories to the baby, and bring you things as you nurse. Remember, self-esteem comes from having skills and making a contribution; your preschooler can be a tremendous asset at this busy time in your family's life.

- Recognize that your preschooler's perception of how and where she belongs in her family will have to change—and her behavior may change too. It may be helpful for you to review the information on birth order in Chapter 3.

In spite of everything you do, your preschooler may still feel dethroned by the new baby. She will have many feelings that she can't name and doesn't understand herself. It's not unusual for an older child to mimic baby behavior in a mistaken effort to gain the same sort of attention the baby receives. Don't be alarmed; instead, focus on restoring your child's sense of connection and belonging. Spending special time one-on-one with her will help.

Grant and Margo waited for just the right time to tell their four-year-old twins, Jason and Joshua, that there was going to be an addition to their family. Still, the twins weren't thrilled with the news.

"You're going to have a baby?" Jason said. "Why? Aren't Joshua and I enough?"

"We don't need any babies around here," Joshua chimed in.

Margo took a deep breath and smiled at her sons. "Come here, guys," she said. "I want to tell you a story about our family."

Joshua and Jason reluctantly sat down next to their mother on the sofa and watched as she lit a tall blue candle. "This candle is me," she said, "and this flame represents my love." Then Margo picked up a tall green candle. "This candle is your dad," Margo said, with a warm smile for Grant. "When I married him, I gave him all my love, but I still had all my love left," she said, using the blue candle to light the green one.

"Then, five years ago I got news just like this—except that time, boys, it was you coming to live with us." Margo lit two smaller candles, one purple and one red, with her tall blue one. "When you were born, I gave both of you all my love, but your dad still had all my love, and I still had all my love left," she said gesturing to all the lit candles. Joshua and Jason gazed, fascinated, at the flickering candle flames.

Then Margo reached into her pocket and pulled out a tiny birthday candle. "Guess what this candle is?" she asked her boys.

"The baby?" they answered.

"That's right. And when this baby is born, I'll give it all my love. Your dad will have all my love, and Jason will have all my love—"

"And I will have all your love!" Joshua shouted out with a grin.

"That's right," Margo laughed as they looked at the tiny, newly lit candle. "And we'll all still have all our love left, because that's how love is—the more we share, the more we have. See how much bright love we're going to have in this family?"

They sat in silence for a moment. Then Jason tugged at his mother's elbow. "Mom, can I light the baby's candle with my candle? I want to share my love."

Margo nodded and blew out the birthday candle, and Jason carefully picked up his candle and lit the tiny one. Joshua took a turn lighting the candle, as did Grant.

Margo looked at her two boys and put her arm around her husband. "This will be our baby," she said, "and your dad and I will need your help to take care of him or her. Will you help us, guys?"

The next months passed quickly. Both Joshua and Jason enjoyed shopping for baby things, helping their parents prepare the baby's room, and thinking about names for boys and girls. They were thrilled when they got to hear the baby's heartbeat at the doctor's office. Jason provided the crowning touch when he placed the tiny birthday candle on the baby's new dresser.

"We're a family," he said proudly, "and there's lots of love to go around."

Having a new baby in the house is both joyous and challenging. Remember, though, that children can be dethroned at any age. One doesn't need to be a firstborn to know the dismay of feeling replaced by a newcomer. This experience also occurs when families blend and stepsiblings are added to the family, or even when a niece or nephew arrives and the former baby of the family is faced with a challenge to his claim to cuteness. *Remembering to get into your child's world to experience life from her perspective will help all of you adjust and grow together.*

Refilling the Pitcher

Q. *I am a young mother with three children who are younger than five years of age. They are my greatest joy and I love being a mother. Lately, though, I'm really overwhelmed. My husband works long hours and attends evening school. I do the housekeeping, work part-time, pay the bills, take care of business, and raise the children. They are smart, nice, talented kids, but they are all strong-willed children as well. I feel like I'm pulled in so many directions, and no matter what I do, it's never enough. From the minute I wake up until late at night, I never get more than a minute to myself. The bottom line is that I've been losing my temper a lot lately. Then I'm even more upset because I feel so guilty.*

A. Here's what's wrong with the picture you describe: you are working not part-time or even full-time, but overtime! No one flies around wearing a supermom cape, but it sounds as though that is what you are trying to do. The person you are not taking care of is *you*—and everyone suffers because of it. It is easy to get so busy with all of life's have-tos that your own needs get shoved not only to the back burner but completely off the stove. The best thing you can give to your family is a calm, rested you.

Consider getting a high school student to help with the housework. Be creative if money is short; perhaps you can barter something. Trade babysitting hours with someone else so you can go for a walk, take a yoga class, or get in a swim and sauna at the local Y once or twice a week. Your family will notice the difference, and of course, so will you.

Being a parent is a great deal like pouring water from a pitcher: you can only pour out so many glasses without refilling the pitcher. All too often, parents and other caregivers suddenly realize they've poured themselves dry for their children—the pitcher is empty. Effective, loving parenting takes a lot of time

and energy. You can't do your best when you're tired, cranky, stressed out, and overwhelmed.

How do you refill your pitcher? Taking care of yourself—filling up your pitcher before it runs dry—can take any form. If you find yourself daydreaming in a quiet moment about all the things you'd like to do, that may be a clue that you should consider some ways to take care of yourself.

Caring for Yourself

It is important to take care of yourself as well as you take care of your child. Consider the following and try to integrate these practices into your daily life.

BUDGET TIME WISELY

Most parents find that they must adjust their priorities as their child grows. It can be extremely helpful—and quite a revelation—to keep track for a few days of exactly how you spend your time. Some activities, such as work, school, or tasks directly related to raising your children, can't be changed much. But most parents spend much of their time on activities that are not truly among their top priorities.

For instance, if you're often up during the night with a young child, make an effort to nap when your child naps. It is tempting to fly around the house doing all that "should" get done, but cleaning the bathroom and dusting the furniture will wait for you; you'll be happier and more effective if you get enough sleep.

Rula did not have the luxury of free time. Between her evening classes at the community college and her daytime work at an espresso stand, she managed to spend only a couple of hours each evening sharing dinner with three-year-old Abdu and getting him ready for bed before his grandmother arrived to watch him. Their short periods together too often were eaten up by hassles, which left Rula feeling impatient and short-tempered. She recognized that she needed a way to nurture herself if she was going to succeed at any of the roles she was trying to fill.

Rula thought about the forty-five minutes she spent crawling along in rush-hour traffic after dropping Abdu off at his childcare each day. She decided to try riding the bus instead and to use this time for herself. She would read a novel, listen to music or a podcast, or even close her eyes to practice meditation and slow breathing. This small change made a big difference to Rula. She felt refreshed, and the calming effect of these changes lasted throughout her day. She even found she enjoyed her time with Abdu more since she was less overwhelmed and could look forward to their time together with additional energy.

Time is precious and all too short when you share your life with young children; be sure you're spending the time you do have as wisely as you can.

MAKE LISTS

In a quiet moment, list all the things you'd like to do (or wish you could get around to). Then, when your child is napping or with a caregiver, spend those precious hours working your way down your list. But don't list chores and duties; instead, include on your list activities that nurture you, like curling up with a good book, soaking in the tub, or having a cozy chat with a friend. Taking time to write down your needs may make you more likely to honor them.

MAKE TIME FOR IMPORTANT RELATIONSHIPS

It's amazing how therapeutic a simple cup of tea with a good friend can be, and sometimes a vigorous game of racquetball can restore a positive perspective on life. You and your partner may trade time watching the children so each of you has time for friends, or you may choose to spend special time together with other couples whose company you enjoy. A date night out together should be on your list as well. Meeting friends at the park can give parents and children time to rest and relax together (especially if you turn off electronic devices and focus on your experience). Keeping your world wide enough to include people outside your family can help you retain your health and balance.

DO THE THINGS YOU ENJOY—REGULARLY

It is important that you find time for the things that make you feel alive and happy, whether it's riding your bicycle, playing softball, singing with a choir, tinkering with machinery, working in the garden, or designing a quilt. Hobbies and exercise are important for your mental and emotional health—and you'll be a far more patient and effective parent if you're investing time and energy in your own well-being. Join a book, hobby, or sports group with *regularly scheduled meetings* to dedicate time to the things that energize you and bring you personal satisfaction. Even twenty minutes a day for something you love is a good beginning.

Groups and More Groups: Avoiding Overscheduling

Most parents do all they can to provide a rich and stimulating environment for their young children. After all, they're learning and developing important skills during these early years. Many young children find themselves enrolled in a surprising number of classes and groups, often before the age of five. There are gymnastics, ballet, soccer leagues, and swim lessons. There are preschools and play groups. There are music and educational classes. Parents often discover that they are living in their vehicles, rushing their children from one activity to another.

While these activities can be enjoyable and stimulating for a young child, it is wise to limit the number you sign up for. Researchers have noted that time for families to relax and just "hang out" together has become scarce. Parents are irritable and tired; children have little or no time to exercise their creativity, learn to entertain themselves, or simply play.

Remember, your child needs connection and time with you far more than she needs the stimulation of these outside activities. Time to cuddle, crawl around on the floor together, or stroll outdoors is far more valuable than even the most popular group.

Learning to Recognize—and Manage—Stress

 Clenched teeth and fists, tight muscles, headaches, a sudden desire to burst into tears or lock yourself in the bathroom—these are the symptoms of parental stress and overload, and it's important to pay attention to them. Most parents—especially first-time parents— occasionally feel overwhelmed and exhausted and even angry or resentful. Because parents want so much to be good parents, they may find it difficult to discuss these troubling thoughts and feelings with others.

Mariam loved being a mom, even though it was sometimes hard to juggle parenthood with her job selling real estate. Five-year-old Lexey was bright, loving, and curious, and Mariam always looked forward to picking Lexey up from her caregiver and heading for home. Normally, the evening routine went smoothly and mother and daughter enjoyed being together. Tonight, however, Mariam was irritable and overwhelmed; her biggest deal of the year looked like it might fall through at any moment, and she really needed to spend some time going over the paperwork.

Unfortunately, Lexey was recovering from the flu and was still cranky and tired. Mariam tried to take shortcuts through their evening routine: she served a frozen meal, did the dishes herself, and rushed Lexey through her bath and evening playtime. Lexey grew quieter as the evening went on, sensing her mother's distraction and annoyance. Finally, when Mariam read only one story instead of the usual two at bedtime, Lexey snapped.

With her arms crossed on her chest and her chin out defiantly, Lexey stomped her foot. "You're rude, Mom," she said angrily. "You just want to sit at your old computer."

Stung by the accuracy of her daughter's words, Mariam lost her temper. "I'm tired, Lexey. I've had a difficult day and I work hard to provide for you. Just get into bed and let me work, okay?"

Lexey's face crumpled; angry tears sprang to her eyes. "I hate you!" she shouted.

Mariam felt the blood rush to her face and she drew back her hand. There was a moment of complete silence as mother and daughter glared at each other. Suddenly Mariam realized how close she'd come to slapping her daughter's face, and she took a step backward in shock.

"Oh, Lexey," she said. "Oh, honey, I'm so sorry. It's not your fault—I'm grumpy and tired." Mariam got down on her knees and held out her arms. "Can you forgive me?"

Lexey could. Mother and daughter had a long cuddle in the armchair, and Mariam read a second story. By the time she turned the lights out, peace and connection had been restored and all was well. It took Mariam a while longer, however, to deal with the unexpectedly strong feelings the encounter had created in her.

There's a difference between a feeling and an action. It's not unusual for parents of young children to be frustrated, overwhelmed, and exhausted, and most parents feel terribly guilty when they feel anger or resentment toward their children. The feelings are normal—but you need to be careful what you do with them.

If you find yourself wanting to snap or lash out at your children, accept those feelings as your cue to do something to care for yourself. Make sure your children are safely occupied, and then take a few minutes for a positive time-out (it works wonders for parents too). Better yet, arrange for some time to do something to nurture yourself. Exhaustion and frustration can lead even the best parents to say and do things they later regret; it's far better to invest the time it takes to help yourself feel better.

EMERGENCY RELIEF

In the event you feel completely unable to cope with stress, do not hesitate to seek help. Most communities offer a crisis line for immediate phone assistance. Some hospitals provide similar services; a few moments speaking to an understanding, reassuring adult may make a world of difference.

If you ever feel your child might be at risk, check to see if respite care is available in your community. It is not wrong or shameful to need help, and it shows true wisdom to ask for it.

Reach Out and Touch Someone

Beth looked back at the front window, where her friend Caroline, her three-year-old son Gregory, and his playmates were waving goodbye. As she slipped behind the wheel of the minivan, Beth looked at the two good friends who shared the backseat.

"Boy, am I ready for this," she said.

Anne and Joleen laughed. "Us too!" Joleen said. "And you'd better enjoy yourself—next week, the kids are all at your place."

Beth, Anne, Joleen, and Caroline had been sharing their "moms' day out" for about six months, and none could imagine how they'd survived without it. Each Saturday morning they took turns, with one of the four of them caring for the group's six children. Lunches were packed, activities were planned—and the three moms who had the day off had four blissful hours to shop, play tennis, take a walk, or just share conversation and a cup of coffee. All had felt a bit guilty at first, but they quickly learned to wave goodbye and drive away, knowing their children were well cared for—and would be happy to have a calm, cheerful mother pick them up. Because the women were careful always to return at the designated time, no one felt taken advantage of.

Support comes packaged in different ways. Whatever works for you and wherever you find it, accept it with gratitude. Parenting is too big a job to tackle alone. Children and their families need a community of support. The face that community wears may be that of a familiar relative, a parenting class, good friends, or even words floating through cyberspace. The important thing is that it is there. Use it—for everyone's sake.

QUESTIONS TO PONDER

1. Who or what constitutes your support system? How might you expand your current support system?

2. If you are in a relationship, how can you make time to nurture that relationship? If you are not in a relationship, how can you make time to connect with other adults or maintain friendships? Try out one of your ideas this week.

3. What do you do to refill your pitcher? Make a list of things that help you feel energized and refreshed. Look at your list and choose one thing you would most like to do. What preparations do you need to make for this to happen? How will you find the time? Make a commitment to do one thing this week to nurture yourself.

4. Looking for more support? A Positive Discipline class or workshop might help. Go to www.positivediscipline.com and/or www.positivediscipline.org.

CONCLUSION

The preschool years are often overwhelming for parents. Young children have an amazing capacity to take center stage in a family's life, often leaving the adults around them breathless with laughter—or exhaustion. Each day seems to bring a new discovery and, sometimes, a new crisis. It may seem as though the kitchen counter will never be cleared, the laundry will never be done, these years will never end.

But they do. Your job as a parent or teacher is to make yourself unnecessary. From the first moments of a child's life, you will steadily guide her toward independence—loving and supporting her when she falters, keeping constant faith that she will grow and bloom. You hover nearby as inconspicuously as you can, holding your breath when she stumbles, rejoicing when she continues on her way.

Yes, the preschool years are busy ones for parents and teachers. These years of testing and exploring can sorely try your patience, and you may catch yourself longing for the day when your child is older and needs you less. But if you are wise, you will take time to enjoy and savor these years.

Far sooner than you think, you will look across the room and stare in amazement at the stranger you see. Gone will be the preschooler with the chronically runny nose; in his place will be a grown child, ready for school and new friendships, ready to move further and further from the circle of your arms.

Your child will face life with whatever love, wisdom, and confidence you've had the courage to give him. There will surely be struggles, bumps and bruises, and tears; yet if you've done your job well, your child will know that mistakes are opportunities to learn and that life is an adventure to be enjoyed.

There is a beautiful fable about two little girls who discovered the value of struggle and perseverance. They found two cocoons hanging from a branch, and as they watched in awe, two tiny butterflies emerged. The little creatures were so damp and fragile that it seemed impossible they could survive, let alone fly. The girls watched as the butterflies labored to open their wings. One girl, fearing that the butterflies would not survive, reached for one and gently spread its delicate wings. The second girl offered the other butterfly a twig to cling to; then she carried it to the window ledge, where the sun could warm it. Both butterflies continued to toil valiantly. The one on the ledge eventually opened its wings, paused for a moment in the sun's gentle warmth, then flew gracefully away. But the butterfly whose wings had been pried open never found the strength to fly and perished without ever taking wing.

It can be painful to watch your young ones struggle, to know that you cannot always save them from trouble and pain no matter how vigilant you are. But wise parents know that, like the butterfly, children gather strength and wisdom from their struggles. It takes a great deal of courage—and a great deal of love—to refrain from lecturing and rescuing and to allow your child, with your encouragement, teaching, and love, to taste life for herself and learn its lessons.

You can't fight your child's battles. And even the most loving parent cannot guarantee that his child will never know pain. But there is a great deal you *can* do.

You can offer your child trust, dignity, and respect. You can have faith in her, and in her ability to learn and grow. You can take the time to teach: about ideas, about people, about the skills she will need to thrive in a challenging world. You can nurture her talents and interests, and encourage each small step she takes. You can help her discover the gifts of capability, competence, and responsibility.

Best of all, you can love and enjoy him, laugh and play with him. You can create memories he—and you—will cherish all your lives. You can steal into his room at night and feel again and again that overwhelming tenderness as you gaze on your child's sleeping face. You can draw on that love and tenderness to give you the wisdom and courage it takes to do what you must as a parent.

This book is all about learning from mistakes and celebrating successes. As authors and as parents, we hope you have found it useful. But the ultimate answers will always be found in your own wisdom and spirit; you will parent (and teach) best when you do so from your heart. Take a moment now and then to savor this special time of childhood despite the inevitable hassles and frustrations; enjoy your child as much as you possibly can. These are precious, important years, and you can only live them once.

ACKNOWLEDGMENTS

We are often asked, "Where do you get your stories?" They come from parents and teachers in our classes and workshops, preschools, and counseling practices. Many of the names and details have been changed to protect the privacy of the families who shared them with us; some are composites of several families. Positive Discipline is now in more than sixty countries; the books and materials have been translated into many languages. We have found that parents and children everywhere experience many of the same challenges as they grow together.

We owe our biggest thanks to our children and our grandchildren, who have provided us with personal family "laboratories" and who have put up with our many mistakes. As you have seen, we believe that mistakes are indeed wonderful opportunities to learn, and we have learned a lot over the years.

We appreciate the many wonderful people who are so eager to give children the love and guidance they need. We also appreciate our colleagues and friends who continue to work tirelessly to create more respectful families, schools, and communities. Some of the information in this book has been contributed and enhanced by other Adlerian professionals. We are grateful for them and the work they do.

The birth order information in this book was enhanced by the wise counsel we received from Jane Griffith, a past president of the North American Society of Adlerian Psychology and Professor Emerita of the Adler School of Professional Psychology in Chicago.

We want to thank a few people who helped us make this revision even better: Dr. Kathleen L. Wolf, research scientist at the College of the Environment, University of Washington, and WS Forest Service Urban Forestry studies key collaborator; Claire Helen Warden, founder of Auchlone Nature Kindergarten in Crief, Scotland, International Association of Nature Pedagogy consultant, and author of *Nurture Through Nature* (www.childrenandnature.org); and Kirsten Haugen, Nature Explore international educator (https://natureexplore.org) and World Forum Foundation for Early Care and Education consultant.

We have had excellent editorial help. We gratefully acknowledge Michele Eniclerico at Penguin Random House, our project editor for this revision. We also want to thank Paula Gray for her wonderful illustrations, which add so much to this—and our other—books.

A special thanks to the Learning Tree Montessori Childcare for much of the background material for the chapter on finding quality childcare and many of the examples in the chapters on class meetings and mistaken goals of misbehavior.

We will always be grateful to Alfred Adler and Rudolf Dreikurs, the originators of the philosophy upon which Positive Discipline is based, and to the Positive Discipline Association, which makes the teaching and sharing of these principles possible for the thousands of educators and trainers around the world.

Although our own children are grown now and busy living their own independent lives, we continue to love spending every moment we can with them and with the next generation, our grandchildren. May this book make the world a healthier and happier place for them, their peers, and the children they will one day parent.

NOTES

Chapter 2

1. Jane Nelsen, Cheryl Erwin, and Carol Delzer, *Positive Discipline for Single Parents*, rev. and updated 2nd ed. (New York: Three Rivers Press, 1999).
2. Jane Nelsen and Cheryl Erwin, *Positive Discipline for Your Stepfamily*, available as an ebook at www.positivediscipline.com.
3. Jane Nelsen, Riki Intner, and Lynn Lott, *Positive Discipline for Parenting in Recovery*, available as an ebook at www.positivediscipline.com.

Chapter 3

1. E. H. Erikson, *Childhood and Society*, 2nd ed. (New York: WW Norton, 1963).
2. Jane Nelsen, Cheryl Erwin, and Roslyn Duffy, *Positive Discipline: the First Three Years,* 3rd ed. (New York: Harmony Books, 2015).

Chapter 4

1. Peter Gray, "Early Academic Training Produces Long-Term Harm," *Psychology Today*, May 5, 2015, www.psychologytoday.com/blog/freedom-learn/201505/early-academic-training-produces-long-term-harm.
2. Jane Healy, *Endangered Minds: Why Children Don't Think and What We Can Do About It* (New York: Simon and Schuster, 1999).
3. Daniel J. Siegel and Tina Payne Bryson, *The Whole-Brain Child* (New York: Delacorte Press, 2011), 10.
4. American Academy of Pediatrics Policy Statement, *Pediatrics* 131, no. 1 (January 2013).

Chapter 5

1. For more information on helping children cope with death or divorce, see Jane Nelsen, Cheryl Erwin, and Carol Delzer, *Positive Discipline for Single Parents*, rev. and updated 2nd ed. (New York: Three Rivers Press, 1999); Jane Nelsen and Lynn Lott, *Positive Discipline A–Z* (New York: Three Rivers Press, 2006); and Roslyn Ann Duffy, "A Time to Cry: The Grieving Process," in *Top Ten Preschool Parenting Problems* (Redmond, WA: Exchange Press, 2008).

2. "Experiments with Altruism in Children and Chimps," YouTube, posted by johnnyk427, November 14, 2010, https://www.youtube.com/watch?v=Z -eU5xZW7cU.

Chapter 6

1. Jane Nelsen and Bill Schorr, *Jared's Cool-Out Space* (Lehi, UT: Positive Discipline, 2013).

2. For more information about time-out, see Jane Nelsen, *Positive Time Out and 50 Ways to Avoid Power Struggles in Homes and Classrooms* (New York: Three Rivers Press, 1999); and Roslyn Ann Duffy, "Time Out Do's and Don'ts," in *Top Ten Preschool Parenting Problems* (Redmond, WA: Exchange Press, 2007).

3. Feeling Faces charts are available at www.positivediscipline.com.

4. From Jane Nelsen and Adrian Garsia, *Positive Discipline Parenting Tool Cards*, illustrated by Paula Gray, available at www.positivediscipline.com.

Chapter 8

1. Erik H. Erikson, *Childhood and Society* (New York: Norton, 1963).

2. Jane Nelsen, *Positive Discipline* (New York: Ballantine Books, 2006).

Chapter 9

1. Stella Chess and Alexander Thomas, *Goodness of Fit* (New York: Brunner/ Mazel, 1999).

2. For more information on divorce and single parenting, see Jane Nelsen, Cheryl Erwin, and Carol Delzer, *Positive Discipline for Single Parents*, rev. and updated 2nd ed. (New York: Harmony Books, 1999); and Roslyn Ann Duffy, "Separation and Divorce: Different Houses—One Child," in *Top Ten Preschool Parenting Problems* (Redmond, WA: Exchange Press, 2008).

3. Carol Stock Kranowitz, *The Out-of-Sync Child*, rev. ed. (New York: Perigee, 2006).

Chapter 10

1. Rudolf Dreikurs, *Children, the Challenge* (New York: Plume Books, 1991).

2. Kristin Anderson Moore, Rosemary Chalk, Juliet Scarpa, and Sharon Vandiver,

"Family Strengths: Often Overlooked, but Real," Child Trends Research Brief, August 2002.

Chapter 11

1. Lynn Lott and Riki Intner, *Chores Without Wars* (Lanham, MD: Taylor Trade Publishing, 2005).

Chapter 12

1. For more information, see Jane Nelsen and Cheryl Erwin, *Positive Discipline for Childcare Providers* (New York: Harmony Books, 2010); and Jane Nelsen, Cheryl Erwin, and Steven Foster, *Positive Discipline for Early Childhood Educators: Positive Discipline Skills and Concepts for Those Who Love and Work with Young Children* (2018), available at www .positivediscipline.com.

Chapter 13

1. Kristin Anderson Moore, Rosemary Chalk, Juliet Scarpa, and Sharon Vandiver, "Family Strengths: Often Overlooked, but Real," Child Trends Research Brief, August 2002.

Chapter 14

1. Institute of Medicine, *Food Marketing to Children and Youth: Threat or Opportunity?* (Washington, DC: National Academies Press, 2006).
2. "Program Proves More Recess Improves Academic Performance and Behavior," SHAPE America, 2017, https://50million.shapeamerica.org/2017/11/program -proves-more-recess-improves-academic-performance-and-behavior.

Chapter 16

1. Jane Nelsen and Cheryl Erwin, *Positive Discipline for Childcare Providers: A Practical and Effective Plan for Every Preschool and Daycare Program* (New York: Harmony Books, 2010); Jane Nelsen, Cheryl Erwin, and Roslyn Ann Duffy, *Positive Discipline: The First Three Years*, 3rd ed. (New York: Harmony Books, 2015); Jane Nelsen, Cheryl Erwin, and Steven Foster, *Positive Discipline for Early Childhood Educators: Positive Discipline Skills and Concepts for Those Who Love and Work with Young Children* (2018), available at www .positivediscipline.com.
2. For more on the separation/connection process, see Roslyn Ann Duffy, "Love, Longing, L'Inserimento," in *Top Ten Preschool Parenting Problems* (Redmond, WA: Exchange Press, 2008).

Chapter 17

1. For more information on teaching class meeting skills to young children, see Jane Nelsen, Cheryl Erwin, and Steven Foster, *Positive Discipline for Early Childhood Educators: Positive Discipline Skills and Concepts for Those Who Love and Work with Young Children* (2018), available at www .positivediscipline.com.
2. For more information on family meetings, see Jane Nelsen, *Positive Discipline*, rev. ed. (New York: Ballantine Books, 2011); and Roslyn Ann Duffy, *Top Ten Preschool Parenting Problems* (Redmond, WA: Exchange Press, 2007).

Chapter 18

1. Autism Speaks, www.autismspeaks.org.
2. For more information on raising children with special needs, see Jane Nelsen, Steven Foster, and Arlene Raphael, *Positive Discipline for Children with Special Needs: Raising and Teaching All Children to Become Resilient, Responsible, and Respectful* (New York: Harmony Books, 2011).

Chapter 19

1. Eric Westervelt, "Q&A: Blocks, Play, Screen Time and the Infant Mind," NPR, February 12, 2015, www.npr.org/sections/ed/2015/02/12/385264747/q-a-blocks -play-screen-time-and-the-infant-mind.
2. National Association for the Education of Young Children and the Fred Rogers Center for Early Learning and Children's Media at Saint Vincent College, "Technology and Interactive Media as Tools in Early Childhood Programs Serving Children from Birth Through Age 8," January 2012, www.naeyc .org/sites/default/files/globally-shared/downloads/PDFs/resources/topics/PS_ technology_WEB.pdf.
3. Victoria L. Dunckley, "Gray Matters: Too Much Screen Time Damages the Brain," *Psychology Today*, February 27, 2014, www.psychologytoday.com/us/ blog/mental-wealth/201402/gray-matters-too-much-screen-time-damages-the -brain.
4. Technology and Information for All, www.tinfa.org.
5. American Academy of Pediatrics, "Policy Statement: Media and Young Minds," *Pediatrics* 138, no. 5 (November 2016).
6. U.S. Department of Education, "Early Learning and Educational Technology Policy Brief," October 2016.
7. National Association for the Education of Young Children, www.naeyc.org.
8. Common Sense, www.commonsense.org; Common Sense Media, www .commonsensemedia.org.
9. American Academy of Pediatrics, "How to Make a Family Media Use Plan," last

updated October 21, 2016, www.healthychildren.org/English/family-life/Media/Pages/How-to-Make-a-Family-Media-Use-Plan.aspx.

Chapter 20

1. Nathanael Johnson, *Unseen City: The Majesty of Pigeons, the Discreet Charm of Snails and Other Wonders of the Urban Wilderness* (New York: Rodale Books, 2016), xii.
2. Ibid.

Chapter 21

1. For more information about classes, trainings, and workshops, visit www.positivediscipline.org.

JANE NELSEN, Ed.D, coauthor of the bestselling Positive Discipline series, is a licensed marriage, family, and child therapist and an internationally known speaker. She's celebrating fifty years of marriage to her husband, Barry, and is the mother of seven, with twenty-two grandchildren and thirteen (and counting) great-grandchildren. Her books have sold more than two million copies.

CHERYL ERWIN, M.A., has been a licensed marriage and family therapist and parenting coach in Reno, Nevada, for more than twenty-five years. She is the author or coauthor of several books and manuals on parenting and family life, and she is a popular international speaker and trainer. Cheryl is married, has an adult son who still likes her, a wonderful daughter-in-law, and the two most remarkable grandchildren on the planet.

ROSLYN ANN DUFFY founded and codirected the Learning Tree Montessori Childcare, and she has written adult and children's texts, including *Top Ten Preschool Parenting Problems* as well as the internationally circulated column "From a Parent's Perspective." She lectures and trains in numerous cultures, is a parent to four and a besotted grandma to three, and lives and practices counseling in Seattle, Washington.

ALSO IN THE POSITIVE DISCIPLINE SERIES